INSIDE LINCOLN'S CABINET

THE CIVIL WAR DIARIES OF

Salmon P. Chase

SALMON P. CHASE

INSIDE LINCOLN'S CABINET

THE CIVIL WAR DIARIES OF

Salmon P. Chase

EDITED BY

DAVID DONALD

ASSOCIATE PROFESSOR OF HISTORY,
COLUMBIA UNIVERSITY

★ ★
★

LONGMANS, GREEN AND CO.

NEW YORK LONDON TORONTO

1954

LONGMANS, GREEN AND CO., INC.
55 FIFTH AVENUE, NEW YORK 3

LONGMANS, GREEN AND CO. LTD.
6 & 7 CLIFFORD STREET, LONDON W 1

LONGMANS, GREEN AND CO.
215 VICTORIA STREET, TORONTO 1

INSIDE LINCOLN'S CABINET:
THE CIVIL WAR DIARIES OF SALMON P. CHASE

PUBLISHED SIMULTANEOUSLY IN THE DOMINION OF CANADA BY
LONGMANS, GREEN AND CO., TORONTO

FIRST EDITION .

LIBRARY OF CONGRESS CATALOG CARD NUMBER 54–7475

Printed in the United States of America

Preface

SOME of the best American diaries record the turbulent years of the Civil War. The voluminous journals of Gideon Welles, the terse records of Edward Bates, the witty jottings of John Hay, the dull entries of Orville Hickman Browning, the Pepysian diaries of George Templeton Strong, and the intemperate ravings of Adam Gurowski are all in print, and they provide eyewitness accounts of the Lincoln administration whose authenticity and importance are equalled by no other historical source.

Of the important Northern Civil War diaries, one has been unduly neglected—the journals of Salmon Portland Chase, Lincoln's Secretary of the Treasury. Because of a dispute between literary executors, the diaries became scattered shortly after Chase's death. Some passages were published in the long, rambling *Account of the Private Life and Public Services of Salmon Portland Chase* (1874), by Robert B. Warden, and others appeared in Jacob W. Schuckers's *Life and Public Services of Salmon Portland Chase* (1874). Both books give skimpy, inaccurate, and unannotated entries wrenched from the journals. A portion of Chase's diaries appeared, virtually without editorial comment, in the *Annual Report of the American Historical Association for 1902.* It, like Warden and Schuckers, has long been out of print.

For a good many years I have hoped to edit Chase's Civil War diaries, believing that the importance both of the man and of his position warranted publication. I have tried to present the diaries just as Chase wrote them. Beyond standardizing the dates which head each entry, I have not tampered with the text except, in the interest of clarity, by substituting the word "and" for the too-frequent ampersands. The diaries contain a number of errors, made either by Chase himself or by the copyist who transcribed the diaries presented in the first five chapters, but I have not thought it necessary to clutter the pages with *sic's*. I have left names and places as Chase wrote them and have given the correct spellings in my notes. Annotating a diary in which so many characters appear, many in a quite fugitive fashion, has presented problems. In some cases I have not been able to trace down persons whom Chase mentions. Major characters have been discussed in the general introduction or in the opening paragraphs of each chapter, and most minor figures are identified in brief notes when first mentioned in the diaries. Rather than include an elaborate system of cross-reference notes, I have not annotated subsequent references to persons previously identified but have left that task for the index.

The Chase manuscripts are divided between the Historical Society of Pennsylvania and the Library of Congress, and without the assistance of those two great institutions the present volume could not have been undertaken. Except where otherwise indicated in the notes, Chapters I through VI are based on manuscripts in the Library of Congress, and Chapters VII and VIII on diaries in the Historical Society of Pennsylvania.

I am happy to say that Mr. Edwin Chase Hoyt has graciously given me permission to publish these records of his grandfather. The Columbia University Library and the New York Public Library have extended to me count-less courtesies. To the officials of the Bowdoin College Library, I am deeply indebted for their generous hospi-tality to a summer visitor. And without the encourage-ment of Mr. John L. B. Williams, of Longmans, Green & Company, I should never have ventured to undertake this project.

The index for this book has been prepared by Mrs. Helen H. Metz, of Elmwood, Illinois, and I am deeply indebted to her for undertaking this tedious but important assignment.

D. D.

For

My Mother and Father

Contents

Introduction

"I HAD . . . the honour of shaking hands with old Abe,"
a visiting Englishman wrote from Washington in 1863.
"In appearance he is much better than I expected. . . .
He has [a] particularly pleasant smile, a very jolly laugh,
and altogether looks like a benevolent and hearty old
gentleman." Most other Federal officials made unfavorable impressions upon young Leslie Stephen, but among
the mediocrities, one man stood out. "The most remarkable of the other members of the Administration," Stephen judged, "was Chase, a very fine, powerful-looking
man." [1]

Salmon Portland Chase, Lincoln's Secretary of the
Treasury, "looked as you would wish a statesman to
look." [2] Wearing his "blue broadcloth dress-coat with gilt
buttons, a white waistcoat, and black trousers," [3] Chase
was a figure to admire in any assembly. "Tall, broad-
shouldered, and proudly erect, his features strong and
regular and his forehead broad, high and clear, he was a
picture of intelligence, strength, courage, and dignity." [4]
The Secretary's reputation comported with his appear-

[1] See pages 273 to 330 for notes.

ance. He had none of the talents of a great popular leader. His "stately and occasionally pompous ways" [5] permitted no familiarities from any man, for he had vowed early in his career never to seek popular acclaim "by mingling with the populace, by base flattering of its passions, by drinking with it." [6] Nor was he an orator. When Rutherford B. Hayes first heard Chase speak, he reported the performance "unimpassioned and spiritless." "He appeared embarrassed and awkward," Hayes noted, "*lisped* slightly. Not by any means so good a speaker as I expected to find him." [7]

Despite these handicaps, Chase became one of the major political figures of his age. Like so many other outstanding nineteenth-century Americans—Clay, Webster, Calhoun, Douglas, Sumner, Blaine—he failed to become President, but he achieved an unusual record of distinguished service in all three branches of the Federal government. During his six years in the Senate, to which he was elected as a Free Soil Democrat in 1849, Chase rapidly emerged as the ablest antislavery leader in Congress. While Seward maneuvered and Sumner orated, Chase organized the antislavery Congressmen and directed their course in the day-by-day debates. In 1854, outraged by Stephen A. Douglas's Kansas-Nebraska Bill, which reopened the troubled issue of slavery in the Federal territories, Chase was principal author of the "Appeal to the Independent Democrats," which blasted this "gross violation of a sacred pledge . . . as part and parcel of an atrocious plot to exclude from a vast unoccupied region immigrants from the Old World and free laborers from our own States, and convert it into a dreary region of despotism, inherited by masters and slaves." [8] When he entered the Senate, Chase had been invited to neither party caucus, for he was said to be "outside of a healthy organization"; when he left, he was a recognized founder and leader of the Republican party.

Chase always felt that his peculiar ,talents were more truly executive than legislative, and his services as two-term governor of Ohio (1856–1860) tended to confirm his self-appraisal. He fostered bills to promote education, helped reorganize his state's financial system, cleaned out corruption in state offices, and sponsored an improved militia system. He regarded as equally important his ability to draw support from antislavery Democrats, antislavery Whigs, and nativistic Know-nothings—precisely the ingredients needed for a national Republican victory. "I will not deny," he confided to a friend shortly after his first election in 1855, "that it *seems* to me that I have as much . . . if not more of the right kind of strength [as presidential candidate] than any of the other gentlemen named. The elements required for a Presidential election have been harmonized in my election in Ohio." When the Republican National Convention of 1856 ignored his obvious availability and instead nominated the politically unknown Western adventurer, John Charles Frémont, Chase grumbled that the Republicans had "committed an act of positive injustice . . . in failing to take as their nominees men who truly personified the great real issue before the country." [9] The pattern thus established was to be repeated every four years for the next two decades, for Chase was cast in the reluctant role of presidential wallflower, always willing, never wanted. On the national scene, therefore, his executive abilities were tested only by his three-year term as Secretary of the Treasury.

In the third branch of the government Chase was to achieve greater distinction, for in 1864 he was appointed Chief Justice of the United States, the "one position in the Government," he had declared, "which I really w'd like to have, if it were possible to have it without any sacrifice of principle or public interest." [10] Under Roger B. Taney, Chase's predecessor, the Supreme Court had sunk to its lowest point in public esteem. During Chase's nine years of judicial service the Court weathered the tempestuous Reconstruction period, gradually reclaimed its powers, weakened by wartime actions of President and Congress, and, at the time of Chase's death in 1873, was ready again to assume its major, and sometimes even dominant, role in the national government.

Chase's public services were unquestionably important, but whether they were equally admirable is a matter upon which neither contemporaries nor later historians have agreed. Almost his every act has been a matter of heated controversy. His admirers thought him the greatest man of his age. ". . . I regard you as the best and ablest statesman in the nation," one correspondent wrote in December, 1860, urging Chase to enter Lincoln's cabinet, "and just that man, if he cannot be President, should be next in power and influence in the present crisis." [11] To many he seemed the only able and upright man in the Republican national administration. "The good things done at Washington people are disposed to place to your credit," Rutherford B. Hayes assured the Secretary. "The errors are charged to others." [12] Chase's administration of the Treasury Department was characterized by Hugh McCulloch, a successor in that responsible position, as "clearheaded, self-possessed, self-confident, patriotic, hopeful, bold." [13] After two years of Lincoln, Horace Greeley could still confidently write Chase: "I know no man in our country who is in my view better qualified for President than yourself. . . ." [14]

But for every word of praise there was an equal amount of criticism. From his daily observation of the Secretary of the Treasury, Gideon Welles drew a devastating character portrait: "Chase has a good deal of intellect, knows the path where duty points, and in his calmer moments, resolves to pursue it. But . . . He has inordinate ambition, intense selfishness for official distinction and power to do for the country, and considerable vanity. These traits impair his moral courage; they make him a sycophant with the truly great, and sometimes arrogant towards the humble. . . . That he is irresolute and wavering, his instinctive sagacity prompting him rightly, but his selfish and vain ambition turning him to error, is unquestionably true." [15] His Treasury administration was subjected to Congressional investigation, and the London *Times* blasted his financial policies as being both unwise and ineffectual: "If Themistocles was a proficient in the art of making a small state into a large one, Mr. Chase is at least equally entitled to claim the credit of making a great state into a little one." [16] And Abraham Lincoln, while admitting Chase's indubitable virtues, thought the Secretary "a little insane" on the subject of the presidency. [17]

Chase himself realized that he was a subject of controversy, and though he thought the censures unjustified, he was able to understand how divergent views might be taken of his course. He urged those who wrote about him "to stick to that which can never contradict itself—the truth." "Yet," he at once realized, "even the truth as to our feelings and impressions and even convictions may change so much as to give the impressions at one time the appearance of contradiction to statements made at another. . . . A very curiously contrasted character of me might be very easily made out from the writings and sayings of the same man at different times." [18]

II

Chase's Civil War diaries provide a partial key to the riddle of his personality. Their very limitations reveal a good deal about the Secretary of the Treasury. Here is no picture of life in wartime Washington, with its throngs of soldiers, its bemedalled diplomats, its extravagant entertainments, its festering hells for gaming, drink, and prostitution. The Secretary was a busy and a self-centered man; he was not writing social history but was making a record "not designed for publication, but simply in memoriam." [19] His diaries show none of the pyrotechnical wit exhibited in the journals of John Hay, Lincoln's private secretary. The Treasury Secretary had no sense of humor, and he thought the war no laughing matter. The caustic character analyses which make the diaries of Gideon Welles such a delight to read are seldom paralleled in Chase's war diaries. Nor did Chase leave a record of his private life. This three-time widower was still a handsome and attractive man, whose masterful ways and courtly manners attracted women, but his diary shows how far he was from being serious about romance. Though several of his platonic admirers are mentioned in his journal, the only one with whom Chase carried on an even half-earnest flirtation was Mrs. Carlotta Sewall Eastman ("Mrs. E." in the diaries), an attractive widow of Beverly, Massachusetts. Nor do Chase's journals reveal much about his family—the beautiful and glamorous Kate, whose marriage to Senator William Sprague of Rhode Island was the sensation of the 1863 social season; or the younger and more domestic Janet ("Nettie"), who was so close to her father's heart. As a young man, Chase had kept an intimate personal journal, recording with almost painful freedom his hates, his loves, and his hopes, but now he tended to confine his entries to factual reporting.

The defects of the Chase diaries are in a sense their strength. His record is lucid and objective. His informants sometimes spoke in error and often in malice; but Chase accurately reported just what they told him. It might, perhaps, be more amusing to have Chase's impressions of John Pope, but a great deal more accurate—and certainly a far more devastating—picture of that boastful general emerges from the diary's unadorned record of his braggadocio. And while Chase's occasional diary comments upon Lincoln are revealing, historians can feel fortunate that, on such momentous occasions as the signing of the Emancipation Proclamation, the Secretary transcribed the President's statements without editorial comment.

Chase revealed himself in his Civil War diaries almost as impersonally as he portrayed others. Though his devout Christianity had in no sense weakened, the long religious reflections which gave a confessional quality to his early diaries had largely disappeared; and the minute medical details of his daily life which filled his later journals did not yet occupy his mind. The total effect is one of a curious objectivity, and it is Chase himself who makes the worst showing among his cast of characters.

On some crucial matters, unfortunately, the diaries are silent. One would give much, for instance, to have Chase's own record of the secession crisis, but he seems to have kept no journal between Lincoln's election and December, 1861. If such a record did exist, it doubtless would reveal Chase's genuine reluctance to enter Lincoln's cabinet. Probably there was some residual resentment that the successful candidate had been Lincoln and not Chase. Perhaps Chase was a bit hurt when the President-Elect called him to Springfield and asked whether he would be able "to accept the appointment of Secretary of the Treasury, without, however, being exactly prepared to make . . . that offer." [20] But the insistence of his friends reinforced his profound sense of duty, and Chase resigned the Senate seat to which he had just been reëlected. "I accept the post which you have tendered me," he wrote Lincoln on March 6, 1861. "My distrust of my own judgment in this decision, and of my ability to perform adequately the duties about to devolve on me, is very great; but trusting to your indulgence and humbly invoking Divine favor and guidance, I will give my best endeavors to your service and our country's." [21]

Of his new chief Chase did not know very much, but what he did know was good. *"He is a man to be depended on,"* Chase decided after his Springfield talks with Lincoln. "He may, as all men may, make mistakes; but the cause will be want of sufficient information, not unsoundness of judgment or of devotion to principle." [22] It was clear that the new Chief Executive was going to need information, judgment, and principle, for he faced the most serious crisis in the nation's history. Before March 4th, seven Southern states had seceded from the Union, and while the Buchanan administration idly lamented the impending ruin, Federal forts throughout the Deep South, with the exceptions of Pickens at Pensacola and Sumter in Charleston Harbor, fell into Confederate hands. As leading politicians and generals turned in their resignations and headed South, the border states teetered between union and secession, and the national capital itself seemed likely to fall into Confederate hands.

Chase was confused and unhappy in the secession crisis. He supported the Union and denied the right of secession. "We of the West," he had said long before, "are in the habit of looking upon the Union as we look upon the arch of heaven, without a thought that it can ever decay or fall." [23] But he dreaded the prospect of civil war. If the border states could be kept in the Union, he thought, "it would be better to allow the seven States which had formed the so-called Confederate Government to try the experiment of a separate existence, rather than incur the evils of a bloody war and a vast debt." [24] As an antislavery man, he knew that secession would greatly weaken the South's peculiar institution, for there was no likelihood that fugitives who escaped across an international boundary could be recaptured. And Chase convinced himself that even the seven seceding states, "after an unsatisfactory experiment of separation," would return, chastened, to the national shelter and "the great cause of freedom and constitutional government [would be] peacefully vindicated." [25]

Far more than secession Chase feared weakness in the North. "To me it seems of importance that no compromise be now made—and no concession involving any surrender of principle," he wrote Republican leaders in Congress;

"but that the people of the Slave States and all the States be plainly told that the Republicans have no proposition to make at present. . . ." [26] To the delegates from the border states assembled at the abortive Peace Conference of February, 1861, Chase gave a warning against rushing "headlong into that unfathomable gulf . . . this unutterable woe of civil war," [27] but he had a slogan rather than a program for peace. "Our only safety," he urged Lincoln, "lies in the adoption and maintenance of the simple watchword—Inauguration first—Adjustment afterwards." [28]

But as the new administration entered upon its duties, it became clear that catchwords could not cure a crisis. Lincoln learned that the troops at Fort Sumter, unless reinforced, would have to surrender by the middle of April. To his untried cabinet the new President posed the question: Should Fort Sumter be supplied, even at the risk of war? Chase's answer exhibited the confusion of his position; he straddled. He was for reinforcement—but "If the attempt will so inflame civil war as to involve an immediate necessity for the enlistment of armies and the expenditure of millions I cannot advise it. . . ." [29] But on March 29th, ten days later, when the President again sought his cabinet advisers' views, hopes for peaceful secession, thoughts of conciliation, wishes for compromise had vanished, and Chase urged: ". . . Fort Sumter should, in my judgment, be reinforced. If War is to be the result I perceive no reason why it may not be best begun in consequence of military resistance to the efforts of the administration to sustain troops of the Union. . . ." [30] On April 12th, when the first Confederate shell exploded above the walls of Sumter, the last doubt was removed. "The attack on Fort Sumter," Chase declared later, "left nothing practicable except the assertion of the rightful supremacy of the National Government over all parts of the Union." [31]

III

Neither his estimate of the emergency nor his opinion of his colleagues could permit Chase to confine himself to the dull duties of the Treasury Department. Of Lincoln he as yet knew little, but the President had exhibited few evidences of transcendent statesmanship. A good deal of the time it seemed that he was under the thumb of the Secretary of State, William H. Seward. Chase never got along well with the able but shifty New Yorker. To the inflexible and austere Secretary of the Treasury, Seward's geniality seemed ingratiation, his laughter at the President's jokes, sycophancy, and his shrewd advice, eager self-promotion. "I have never been able to establish much sympathy between us," Chase complained of Seward. "He is too much of a politician for me." [32]

The other members of the original cabinet Chase found less important but hardly more admirable. Simon Cameron of Pennsylvania came into the War Department under an imputation of corruption, and he lived up to the worst expectations. Edward Bates of Missouri, the Attorney-General, seemed to Chase too conservative, and Montgomery Blair, the Postmaster-General, a lightweight. Caleb B. Smith of Indiana had been made Secretary of the Interior despite Chase's warning that "his railroad and other transactions . . . would impair the credit and endanger the success of [the] administration." [33] Of Gideon Welles, the Secretary of the Navy, who was so busily caricaturing Chase for posterity, the Treasury head took little notice, but, like most other observers, he viewed Welles as well intentioned, slow, and incompetent.

With one obvious exception, Chase tended to agree with the Missouri Unionist who swore: "I never since I was born imagined that such a lot of poltroons and apes could be gathered together from the four corners of the Globe as Old Abe had succeeded in bringing together in his Cabinet. . . ." [34] Chase knew he was able, and he thought his colleagues incompetent; it was his duty, therefore, to organize the Northern war effort. He began to issue orders, accept recruits, consult on strategy, and plan battles. When they received no answer from Cameron's inefficient office, generals and governors telegraphed Chase. "I will go to the War Department at once," he would reply, "and do all I can to urge the department to action." [35] And he got results.

Cameron seemed perfectly willing for Chase, in effect, to capture the War Department, and Lincoln welcomed Chase's aid. "The President and Secretary of War," the Ohioan related later, "committed to me for a time the principal charge of what related to Kentucky and Tennessee, and I was very active also in promoting the measures deemed necessary for the safety of Missouri. . . . While he was Secretary of War, General Cameron conferred much with me. I never undertook to do any thing in his department, except when asked to give my help, and I gave it willingly." [36]

Chase's voice was influential in determining military appointments. The selection of Irvin McDowell as first commander of the Army of the Potomac was partly brought about by the Secretary of the Treasury, and though the Union troops were badly defeated at First Bull

Run (July 21, 1861), the Secretary continued to have confidence in the general who appears so frequently in his diaries. "McDowell has been unfortunate," he explained to a critic; "but he is a loyal, brave, truthful, capable officer." [37] W. T. Sherman, David Hunter, John Pope, William Nelson, L. H. Rousseau, and James A. Garfield were other officers who profited by Chase's support.

To his friends Chase was faithful, but his hostility was inveterate toward those he thought untrue. The promotion of George Brinton McClellan to succeed McDowell was enthusiastically supported by the Treasury Secretary, who had watched with sympathetic interest the general's highly publicized victories, using Ohio troops, in western Virginia. When McClellan then replaced the aged Winfield Scott as general-in-chief, Chase rejoiced: ". . . Let us thank God and take courage." [38] The dashing "Little Mac" at first highly impressed Chase by his military bearing, his untiring concern for his troops, his passion for drills and inspections. Though progress seemed slow, McClellan's excuses were plausible, and the general seemed to understand Chase's warning that "The army and the Treasury must stand or fall together." In November McClellan assured the Secretary that decisive action would be taken before February 1st, and Chase used the promise to promote the sale of government bonds in New York.

But months went by and there was no action. McClellan fell ill, and nobody knew what his plans were. When he recovered, the army still lay idle. In February the President himself ordered an advance—but nothing happened. Finally, when McClellan did decide to move, he chose to attack Richmond from the east, by way of the Peninsula between the York and James rivers. A thin Confederate line at Yorktown frightened the general into a month's delay for siege operations, and by the time he pushed beyond, he had lost all opportunity for surprise. Chase was doubly disappointed—dissatisfied with the general's slow progress and angry that he had been deceived into making false pledges of success to the New York bankers. "McClellan is a dear luxury," he grumbled, "fifty days—fifty miles—fifty millions of dollars—easy arithmetic, but not satisfactory." [39]

Lincoln, too, was worried at the slow progress, and it is significant that he invited the Secretary of the Treasury to accompany him on a trip of inspection to Fort Monroe, behind McClellan's lines. There, within a week, Chase and the President supervised the capture of Norfolk, and Chase returned to Washington more than ever convinced that strategy was mostly a matter of courage and common sense. McClellan, he now decided, must go, for to continue the "Little Napoleon" in command could only result in "the waste of national resources, the protraction of the war, the destruction of our armies, and the imperiling of the Union." [40]

But when he demanded McClellan's removal, Chase learned that his own relations to the war had curiously changed since 1861. There had been a quiet revolution in the War Department. Because Secretary Cameron had so willingly tolerated his interference, Chase had been slow to join in the denunciation of his corruption, but by September, 1861, even he had come to "see and deplore" the defective organization of Cameron's administration. [41] It became necessary to arrange for the honorable retirement of Cameron, who was made minister to Russia, and, as Chase's diary clearly shows, the Treasury Secretary

thought himself instrumental in the plan which installed
Edwin M. Stanton in Cameron's place. Gideon Welles, on
the other hand, attributed the reorganization to Seward:
". . . The Secretary of the Treasury was the victim, not
to say the dupe of a prearranged scheme. . . . In this
whole transaction . . . Mr. Seward did not appear, although it was all his own work—Mr. Chase who seems to
have been, and undoubtedly himself believed he was the
means of effecting these changes . . . had really nothing
to do with them but to act a part which was adroitly contrived for him to execute." "In aptness and skill," the
acerb Navy Secretary concluded, "Mr. Chase was never a
match for Mr. Seward." [42]

Whether initiator or instrument, Chase found that the
brusque new Secretary of War intended to run his own
department. Though he found Stanton personally one of
the most agreeable of his colleagues, and though his presence was always welcome at the War Department, Chase
learned that the professionals had taken over. He was now
informed of military decisions after they had been made—
sometimes through the newspapers. His advice was seldom
sought and rarely followed. Where formerly he had been
the center of inside knowledge about the war, he had now
to report to his correspondents: ". . . I know too little
to have any confident opinion about any military matter."
"What right, indeed, has a secretary of the treasury, whose
business it is to provide money for the people to spend, to
have any wishes at all about the results of the expenditure?" he inquired ironically. [43]

Ignored by the makers of strategy, Chase lacked the information which would permit him to understand the
plans and the difficulties of the Union commanders, and

he became, therefore, the more sharply critical of their failure to bring victory. The disgruntled and the ambitious, the would-be heroes and the has-been generals captured his ear and filled his mind with complaints and projects which Chase, without much success, attempted to peddle to his cabinet colleagues. "Oh!" he lamented, "for a great general, honest and faithful, and inspired by our cause, at the head of the war." [44]

IV

After 1862, Chase was almost as remote from the making of political decisions as he was removed from the planning of strategy. In the early stages of the war he had been consulted on all important decisions, and if he did not always agree with the President's actions, he at least understood his problems. During these months Chase was eminently moderate. He warned his fellow-Republicans, never before in power as a party, against the dangers of doctrinaire inflexibility. "It is so natural for Republicans to be in the opposition to the administration," he observed, "that they do not as yet realize the duties of defending its measures as a matter of duty, relying on the President and his Cabinet to be true to their principles even when their policy must of necessity remain for a time undisclosed." [45]

But soon it appeared that the policy was undisclosed even to the Secretary of the Treasury. In fact, nobody seemed to know what was going on. Cabinet meetings were, as Gideon Welles recorded, "infrequent, irregular, and without system." Seward was often absent, though there was naturally "a reluctance to discuss and bring to a decision any great question without him," but he managed, Welles thought, to spend "a considerable portion of every day with the President, patronizing and instructing him, hearing and telling anecdotes, relating interesting details of occurrences in the Senate, and inculcating his political party notions." When Stanton came, it was only "to whisper to the President, or take the dispatches or the papers from his pocket and go into a corner with the President." [46]

Chase's efforts to introduce some administrative system among the President's advisers were unsuccessful, and soon he, like Bates and Welles, was wondering whether he should bother to attend the "Cabinet (so-called)." "We . . . are called members of the Cabinet," he reported indignantly to Senator John Sherman, "but are in reality only separate heads of departments, meeting now and then for talk on whatever happens to come uppermost, not for grave consultation on matters concerning the salvation of the country. . . . No regular and systematic reports of what is done are made, I believe, even to the President: certainly not to the so-called Cabinet." [47]

Measures which Chase might well have supported had he known their causes and their objectives appeared to him blind and wavering. Stanton and Lincoln adopted military policies which seemed to have no consequences except the useless expenditure of more millions which the Treasury Secretary was supposed unquestioningly to supply. "I," Chase protested, "though charged with the responsibility of providing for the enormous expenses entailed upon the country, have no control over—no voice even in deciding on—the measures by which the necessity for them is created." [48] As the war dragged on, with victory apparently as far away as ever, Chase's financial responsibilities daily became heavier, and his exasperation approached wit. "It seems as if there were no limit to expense," he lamented in May, 1864. "Contrary to all rules, the spigot in Uncle Abe's barrel is made twice as big as the bung-hole. He may have been a good flat-boatman and rail-splitter, but he certainly never learned the true science of coopering." [49]

Chase's remoteness from the seat of power led him to espouse crack-brained military projects—the flighty Ormsby M. Mitchel's proposal to march down the Mississippi River, making an army of untrained Negroes as he went; or an amphibious assault against Charleston, which Chase thought of leading himself. In civilian affairs, similarly, he came to advocate political measures of equally dubious statesmanship. Extremists and fanatics who attacked the administration's slowness to free the Southern slaves learned they would receive a ready hearing at the Treasury Department.

These antislavery views were naturally congenial to Chase, who had spent some of the most strenuous years of his life battling slavery. Sacrificing political and professional prospects in Southern-dominated Cincinnati, Chase had defended the liberty of fugitives who escaped across the Ohio, and in a series of famous cases he became nationally known as the "attorney-general for runaway slaves." Slavery he knew to be "a curse, a reproach, a blight, an evil, a wrong, a sin," [50] and opposition to it had been the lodestar of his political career. He had gone from Whig to Liberty to Free Soil to Democratic to Republican party with what professional politicians considered a chameleon-like display of opportunism, but Chase insisted that his every move had been motivated by his wish most effectively to curb slavery. "He never betrayed a party, never

abandoned a party in the ordinary sense," one of his supporters explained his course. "A party that could not be
useful had necessarily no hold upon him." [51] The "true
policy of practical, do something antislavery men" he had
always insisted was to "unite . . . for . . . practical
measures." "I care nothing for names," he assured Charles
Sumner in 1847. "All that I ask for is a platform and an
issue, not buried out of sight, but palpable and para-
mount." [52]

Despite his well-known antislavery views, Chase did
not enter the cabinet with any drastic plans for eliminat-
ing the Southern institution. "The question of Slavery
should not be permitted to influence my action one way
or the other," he assured his Southern friends.[53] The Republican victory seemed to assure "the denationalization
of slavery and the consequent inauguration of an era of
constitutional enfranchisement," [54] and Chase was not
going to hurry history. "I never was an abolitionist of that
school which taught there could never be a human duty
superior to that of the instant and unconditional abolition
of slavery," he wrote as late as 1863. "He who sees the
tower in the quarry and the oak in the acorn, requires no
imposed task from his creatures. But, for more than half
my life, I have been an abolitionist of that other school
which believed slaveholding wrong, and that all responsible for the wrong should do what was possible for them,
in their respective spheres, for its redress." [55]

In the first months of the war, when he was still being
consulted on matters of national policy, Chase persisted
in his moderate views. To enthusiasts who demanded the
immediate emancipation of all slaves, he pointed out the
folly of rash action. When ultra-abolitionists attacked Lin-

coln's proposals for gradual, compensated emancipation as criminal conspiracy with a monstrous evil, Chase strongly defended the President. "Until long after Sumter I clung to my old ideas of non-interference with slavery within the state limits," he explained later. "That the United States Government under the war powers might destroy slavery I never doubted. I only doubted the expediency of the exercise." [56] He did not always agree with his colleagues, even in these early days, but, he said, when "I have not been able to make my friends in the administration see as I have seen, . . . I certainly don't claim that all the wisdom is mine and none theirs." [57]

But as the war dragged along and expenditures climbed precipitously, Chase, increasingly out of touch with military and political realities, became more receptive to appeals for extreme action. Rumors that generals—McClellan, Halleck, Buell, in particular—were proslavery received credence, and other commanders learned that the sure way to win the Secretary's confidence was to urge the arming of Negro troops. In May, 1862, David Hunter ordered the enfranchisement of the slaves along the South-eastern coast, and Chase at once wrote to the President that it was "of the highest importance, whether our relations at home or abroad be considered, that this order be not revoked." [58] When Lincoln, after a close study of the political and constitutional implications of Hunter's act, ordered the general overruled, Chase was disappointed but not altogether surprised. "In my judgment," he wrote, "the military Order of Hunter should have been sustained. The President, who is as sound in head as he is excellent in heart, thought otherwise, and I, as in duty bound submit my judgment to his." [59]

The submission was certainly a perfunctory one, for Hunter had hardly been rebuked before Chase was advising other generals to attempt similar indiscretions in military politics. To the unsavory Benjamin F. Butler, Federal commander at New Orleans, Chase wrote freely:

. . . If some prudential considerations did not forbid, I should at once, if I were in your place, respectfully notify the slaveholders of Louisiana that henceforth they must be content to pay their laborers wages. . . .

It may be said that the order would be annulled. I think not. It is plain enough now that the annulling of Hunter's order was a mistake. It will not be repeated. . . .

And who better to begin the work than my friend Gen. Butler? [60]

As the President gradually moved toward emancipation, Chase was still not satisfied. The Emancipation Proclamation, issued on September 22, 1862, he welcomed, but he was unhappy that it excepted important counties in Virginia and Louisiana from its operation and that it was not to take effect until the first day of 1863. "You must anticipate a little," he prodded Butler, "the operation of the Proclamation in New Orleans and Louisiana." [61] Presently emancipation alone was not enough. "The American blacks must be called into this conflict," he argued in April, 1863, "not as cattle, not now, even, as contrabands, but as men." When moderates hesitated to arm the freedmen, Chase retorted: "Is this a time to split hairs of logic?" [62] And, looking beyond the war, Chase began agitation for Negro suffrage as the best security for the colored men's newly found freedom.

V

The less Chase was consulted on broad matters of governmental policy, the more extreme his views became; and as he assumed the attitude of embattled virtue, it became impossible to consult him. When the President did call on his Treasury head for advice, he was likely to receive stately moral discourses, coupled with chidings against weakness and transgressions. "I have urged my ideas on the President and my associates," Chase now wrote, a bit proudly, "till I begin to feel that they are irksome to the first, and to one or two, at least, of the second." [63]

As a good administrator himself, Chase made it clear that the failures, the weaknesses, and the imbecilities of the executive branch rested not upon himself and his cabinet colleagues, but upon the President alone. "You are wrong in blaming Stanton as you do," he instructed an Ohio correspondent in 1863. "Nor should you forget that a war managed by a President, a Commanding-General, and a Secretary, cannot, especially when the great differences of temperament, wishes, and intellectual characteristics of these three are taken into the account, reasonably be expected to be conducted in the best possible manner. This condition can only be remedied by the President, and, as yet, he fears the remedy most." [64]

It was probably inevitable that Chase should thus emerge into outright opposition to Lincoln. The two seemed to have been constructed to become antagonists. Assured in his own uprightness and convinced of his own ability, Chase could have little sympathy for Lincoln's humility. Chase was formal and unbending in manner;

Lincoln, informal to a degree of gaucheness and flexible to the point of opportunism. Lincoln's story-telling seemed to his humorless Treasury Secretary both a waste of time and a degradation of his high office. An incurable optimist, Chase was always embarking on grandiose projects and was forever disappointed when they failed. Lincoln, with his tragic sense, could be content with small victories. A man of first principles, Chase always knew what the right road was and tried to take it, and he became infuriated with Lincoln's "idiotic notion" that the best policy was to have no policy at all.[65]

Along with all these difficulties of personality and policy, it should not be forgotten that Lincoln and Chase did work together as a team for three critical years. Though Chase had doubts about the President's force and foresight, he never questioned his honesty and his good intentions. "If to his kindliness of spirit and good sense," Chase said of Lincoln at a time when their relations were almost ruptured, "he joined a strong will and energetic action, there would be little left to wish for in him." [66] That Chase never really understood Lincoln his diaries make abundantly evident, but sometimes the puzzled Secretary seemed aware of his own failing. A shipboard acquaintance remarked to him that President Lincoln must be very wise to steer so moderate a course; had he been more radical, he would have alienated the conservatives, and had he been more conservative, he would have lost the radicals. And Chase wondered: "Will this be the judgment of history?" [67]

Lincoln had a more profound understanding of his Secretary's character. Recognizing his deficiencies, he admired and trusted Chase's handling of the heavy burdens imposed by his Treasury office. "You understand these things," he would say, approving Chase's financial recommendations. "I do not." [68] The President showed the true extent of his respect for the Secretary when, despite personal and political differences, he appointed him Chief Justice. "Chase," Lincoln used to say, "is about one and a half times bigger than any other man that I ever knew." [69]

Not even Chase's open seeking of the presidency destroyed Lincoln's high esteem for him. In fact, the President viewed Chase's campaign as "a devilish good joke," another aspect of that universal and "voracious desire for office, . . . from which," the President added whimsically, "I am not free myself." [70]

Chase's attempt to win the Republican presidential nomination in 1864 has been one of the most sharply criticized moves in his political career. For his later fame he doubtless would have been better advised had he, like Seward, made himself unavailable, but it is important to understand how Chase and many of his fellow-Republicans could think otherwise. In 1863–64 it seemed plain that the Lincoln administration was a failure. The Confederacy appeared as strong as ever, and vast expenditures of money and blood had brought the North no nearer victory. Men of his own party were openly damning the President as a "Simple Susan," a "baboon," a man who was "doing twice as much today to break the Union as [Jefferson] Davis." [71] "This vascillation [*sic*] and indecision of the President," announced a Republican-sponsored pamphlet titled *The Next Presidential Election*, "has been the real cause why our well-appointed armies have not succeeded in the destruction of the rebellion. . . . The cant about 'Honest Old Abe' was at first amusing, it then became ridiculous, but now it is absolutely criminal." [72]

If Lincoln was to be replaced, it was natural that party leaders should think of Chase as his successor. And it was equally reasonable that Chase should so consider himself. He yearned for the presidency; it was in his blood. Not selfish ambition, as he saw it, but an earnest desire to serve the people drove him on. Of his domineering uncle, Bishop Philander Chase, the Secretary wrote an unconscious description of himself: "Certainly, he lived to Govern; but he liked to govern for the good of others, not his own." [73]

To later historians it has seemed that Chase was constantly scheming to promote himself, that he intrigued with enemies of the Lincoln administration, and that he used his high office to build a potent patronage régime devoted to his own advancement. As his diaries show, there is a good deal of truth to all these charges, but perhaps one should try also to understand Chase's point of view. He knew he was able, and he thought he would make a good Chief Executive. "Perhaps I am over-confident," he concluded in October, 1863; "but I really feel as if, with God's blessing, I *could* administer the Government of this country so as to secure . . . our institutions: and create a party, fundamentally and thoroughly democratic, which would guarantee a succession of successful administrations." [74]

At the same time he would never consciously use his position to promote his own legitimate aspirations. "I should despise myself," he protested in all sincerity, "if I felt capable of appointing or removing a man for the sake of the Presidency." [75] But with Chase self-delusion was almost a talent, for his diaries show that he did appoint those who favored his ambitions. To reconcile his theory and his practice one must put himself into the Secretary's position—and then what better test of a subordinate's intelligence or loyalty could there be than an appreciation of the outstanding merits of his chief?

Chase always insisted that he would not, and could not, lift a hand to advance his presidential prospects. "So far as the Presidency is concerned, I must leave that wholly to the people," he announced. "Whatever disposition they make of it, I shall be content." [76] Still, if he forbade the consideration of his name, he would not be permitting a true popular choice, and he felt impelled to declare that he was available. ". . . I have not the slightest wish to press any claims upon the consideration of friends or the public," he assured a Wisconsin friend. "There is certainly a purpose, however, to use my name, and I do not feel bound to object to it." [77]

The story of the collapse of the Chase presidential boom in 1864 and of his subsequent resignation from the Treasury is chronicled in his diaries. His critics called his withdrawal from the race "a mere sham, and very ungraceful at that," [78] and they said his tardy support for Lincoln in the campaign was motivated by his desire to become Chief Justice. Chase indignantly denied such reports. "The truth is," he later recalled, "that the bringing forward of my name for the Presidency was not sought by me; and when it was brought forward and I felt the embarrassments created by it for me in my service as head of the Treasury I availed myself of the first honorable opportunity to ask that no further consideration might be given to my name; and though much urged afterwards to allow it to be used steadfastly refused." [79]

But then the Chief Justice wrote, in another connection, "I dare not vouch for the entire authenticity even of what I seem to remember best." [80] His contemporary diary record, now printed for the first time, reveals the nature and extent of Chase's presidential interests in the summer of 1864, after he had officially withdrawn from the contest and had resigned his Treasury post.

VI

For all his military, antislavery, and political interests, Chase gave most of his time to the Treasury Department. During the first months of the Lincoln administration, his industry was a matter of marvel, and it was said "that he was seen only in going to and coming from the place of his official labors." [81] The Treasury certainly needed his attention, for it was in a chaotic state. In 1861 there were only 383 clerks in the great Treasury Building on Fifteenth Street, which stood next door to the White House and frowned down Pennsylvania Avenue toward the Capitol, and they were supposed to handle the entire financial business of the Federal government. As Chase entered office, some of his subordinates resigned to join the Confederacy, some lingered disloyally at Washington, and still more daily awaited the spoilsman's ax.

From his office, with its gray velvet carpet, its oiled black walnut furniture upholstered with blue cloth, its carved window-cornices, each holding in the center the gilded scales of justice above the key of the Treasury, Chase ruled a patronage empire. There were six auditors of the treasury, each with a staff, assigned to receive and

adjust accounts of the different executive departments;
two comptrollers' offices, to prescribe the manner of keeping and rendering of government accounts; the Commissioner of Customs, in charge of all the tariff revenues; the
Treasurer of the United States, to guard the moneys of
the Federal government; the Solicitor, to superintend all
civil suits commenced by the United States; and, in addition, such miscellaneous offices as the Light-House Board,
the United States Coast Survey, and the Superintendent
of Marine Hospitals.

Under Chase this bureaucracy was to grow mightily.
War taxes caused the creation of the Internal Revenue
Division, and the establishment of the national banking
system necessitated a new Comptroller of the Currency.
Additional clerks had to be hired to superintend the issuing of government bonds, of treasury notes, of "fractional"
paper currency (of less than one-dollar denominations).
All these employees had to be watched and checked, both
for honesty and for loyalty. Always there were problems.
When Chase permitted the hiring of some women clerks—
reluctantly, for he himself, while an admirer of feminine
beauty, brusquely refused to do business with women—
rumors soon spread that the Treasury Extension sheltered
"a kind of Government house of ill fame, where pretty
women toiled until morning over ale and oyster sup-
pers." [82] By the time Chase left office in 1864, the number of clerks in his department had increased to two
thousand, and, in addition, there were numerous, lucrative, and politically influential appointments of assistant
treasurers, customs-house officials, and internal revenue
men throughout the nation.

In accepting his post, Chase wrote to Lincoln that his

"foremost wish was . . . to prove . . . a faithful friend to yourself and a faithful servant of the people." [83] He soon learned that the two objectives were mutually exclusive, for there was no necessary correlation between Republicanism and ability. Throngs of job-seekers—"unpractical authors, sore-throated, pulpitless clergymen, briefless lawyers, broken down merchants, poor widows, orphaned daughters" [84]—descended upon the Secretary, and all claimed to have helped elect Lincoln.

Chase tried to defend his department's independence against these swarms of patronage-hungry Republicans. For the highly responsible position of Assistant Treasurer at New York, for instance, he asked to retain John J. Cisco, a Democrat appointed by Pierce and continued in office by Buchanan. Secretary Seward wanted to install one of his henchmen in this lucrative office, which annually handled more than a million dollars, and Chase was obliged to protest to the President: "Don't let Cisco go out now. If you do I fear very bad results. Mr. Seward *ought not* to ask you to overrule my deliberate judgment as to what is best for the Dept. and your administration. . . ." [85]

Republican Congressmen were no more successful than cabinet members in influencing Chase. The Secretary flatly refused to acquiesce in their demands to control treasury appointments. "When neither the President nor the Secretary . . . has knowledge of a person clearly fitted for any office within the District of a Member of Congress," he admitted, "it is certainly expedient that the member should be consulted; but he can have no right to any controlling voice. To recognize such a right would be to make the officers of the Government dependants of the Members and no Department and least of all the Treasury

Department could be successfully administered on that theory." [86]

Rebuffed, the Congressmen would ask the President to overrule Chase. Generally he refused, for, as Senator Morgan of New York complained, "the President rather appoint Chase's friends *than to say no*." [87] But on a few important occasions Lincoln did have to intervene, and Chase resisted fiercely what he regarded as an infringement of his necessary administrative freedom. With each crisis his tone toward the President became increasingly stiff, and in May, 1863, when Lincoln, without consultation, removed a customs official of Chase's choice, the Secretary wrote a long protest:

It has been and is my ardent desire to serve you by faithful service to the country in the responsible post to which you have called me; but I cannot hope to succeed in doing so, if the selection of persons, to fill important subordinate places in the Department, is to be made, not only without my concurrence, but without my knowledge.

I can ask, of course, nothing more than conference. The right of appointment belongs to you; and if, after fair consideration of my views in any case, your judgment . . . differs from mine, it is my duty to acquiesce . . . ; unless, indeed, the case be one of such a character, as to justify my withdrawal from my post. . . .

The blank Commission which you direct me to send to you is enclosed. . . . It is enclosed, however, with my most respectful protest against the precedent; and with the assurance that . . . I will, unhesitatingly, relieve you from all embarrassment . . . by tendering you my resignation.

Lincoln filed the paper with the endorsement, "First offer of resignation." [88]

There were to be several other such occasions, when, rather than force the issue, Lincoln yielded. "He prefers," recorded John Hay, who saw the problem only from the President's viewpoint, "letting Chase have his own way in these sneaking tricks than getting into a snarl with him by refusing him what he asks." But at last, in June, 1864, even Lincoln's patience wore thin. As the diaries reveal, the Secretary again offered his resignation, and now that Chase had been obliged to withdraw from the presidential contest and now that his own renomination was assured, the President felt free to accept it. Their relations had reached the point where either President or Secretary must resign, said Lincoln, and "Mr. Chase elected to do so." [89]

Often interpreted as mere political petulance, Chase's repeated battles over appointments were really efforts to maintain his department's efficiency. To his own subordinates he gave both freedom and responsibility. When Hugh McCulloch was appointed Comptroller of the Currency, Chase told him: "Manage . . . the Bureau in your own way; when you need clerks, and as you need them, send their names to me and they will be appointed." [90] The Secretary, in turn, expected Lincoln to extend to him the same trust.

There is no doubt that, administratively speaking, Chase's position was correct; if he was to bear the enormous responsibilities of his office, he must have able and loyal subordinates. But Chase was ignoring the fact that in the American government patronage is one of the major incentives to party loyalty. The President had to coöperate with Congressmen in appointments if he expected their support for crucial wartime legislation. And Chase's unctuous words about integrity and ability also neglected to take account of his own notoriously poor judgment of men. For all his good intentions, Chase was, as his diaries so plainly show, highly susceptible to flattery, and those who lavishly praised the Secretary's achievements and favored his elevation to the presidency seemed to him to be showing evidence of competent judgment and disinterested loyalty.

Under the guise of personal friendship and political support, a good many of the incompetent and corrupt won their way into Chase's department. Perhaps the most seriously tainted division of the Treasury was the group of agents assigned to regulate trade with the Southern states. A system of licenses and permits was set up, and soon it became an open invitation to corruption. Chase's diaries show him alarmed about the extent of the evil but unable to check it. "It is impossible for me to look after all the acts of all the agents of the department," he protested; "but whenever informed of any delinquency, I institute proper investigation, and, if the delinquency is found actually to exist, take proper measures. . . ." [91] His political enemies, however, claimed that the Secretary was blind to the malfeasance of those who favored his own political prospects, and Francis P. Blair, Jr., openly charged that a "more profligate administration of the Treasury Department never existed under any Government." [92]

To counterbalance such charges, it should be pointed out that nobody questioned Chase's personal integrity and that the Treasury Department was on the whole efficient and honest. Chase's major appointees were men of considerable stature: George Harrington, the industrious Assistant Secretary of the Treasury, who ruined his health in his country's service; Elisha Whittlesey, the veteran

Treasury aide whom Chase promoted to the post of First Comptroller; Lucius B. Chittenden, the Register, who had to sign each bond issued by the United States government; George S. Boutwell, who set up the Bureau of Internal Revenue; and Hugh McCulloch, whose great abilities made the national banking system a working reality. The Treasury administration was far from perfect, but, after an elaborate survey of the patronage in the two Lincoln administrations, Harry J. Carman and Reinhard H. Luthin have concluded: "The most competent appointments of subordinates made by any member of Lincoln's original Cabinet seem to have been made by Chase." [93]

VII

The real test of Chase's administrative ability is, of course, his handling of Civil War finances. Extravagantly lauded by many contemporaries, Chase's policies have generally been condemned by most later economists. His annual reports, declared Sidney Ratner, reveal "no adequate grasp of the serious financial situation." [94] In his elaborate *History of the Greenbacks*, Wesley C. Mitchell blamed Chase's ignorance and inexperience for the decision to issue legal-tender notes, which "increased the debt incurred during the war by a sum running into the hundreds of millions." [95] More recently Don C. Barrett concluded that Chase did not bring to his office "those larger considerations of a finance minister which would lead to a proper anticipation of future needs and to a comprehensive and well-digested scheme of finance." [96] Even more harsh was Albert S. Bolles's standard financial history of the United States: "Unskilled in finance, unwilling to learn, and, when going astray, persisting in his course, Mr. Chase's failure was inevitable." [97]

However sound economically, these verdicts are essentially unhistorical. They do not take into consideration the problems which Chase faced. The Secretary of the Treasury did not inherit a going concern. The United States was on the edge of bankruptcy. Profligacy and maladministration in the Buchanan administration had combined with the panic of 1857 to convert a Treasury surplus into a deficit, but no constructive steps were taken to increase income. The pro-Southern tariff of 1857 reduced the one major source of Federal revenue, for the United States had not had any excise taxes since 1817. So deep was the distrust of Buchanan's counselors that loans could be floated only at exorbitant rates of interest, and even then there were few purchasers. To meet the crisis Chase's agile predecessors had toyed with expedients. Some proposed that the loyal state governments offer to guarantee the notes of the Federal Treasury; others, that notes be issued against the unsold Federal domain. No one had either the courage or the authority to demand a regular system of taxation and an economical administration. Chase was confronted, therefore, with a virtually empty Treasury, with a mounting pile of requisitions to be paid, with an inherited American reluctance to pay taxes, and with a popular faith that some financial panacea could cure the Treasury's problems.[98]

The new Secretary was not a man of economic erudition, nor did the crisis permit a deliberate formulation of his fiscal policies. From the start Chase's financial plans were marked by a high degree of improvisation. It is easy to see, in retrospect, that many of his views were wrong and many of his actions badly timed. In his first report, made to Congress in July, 1861, he adopted the popular but shortsighted policy of urging that three-fourths of the coming year's expenditures be financed by borrowing; the remaining sum he hoped to raise through a slight increase in the tariff, whose returns he greatly overestimated, through a direct tax, from which there was small hope of collecting the sums levied against the Southern states, and through a low income tax, which was not even to take effect for ten months. In December, despite much urging, the Secretary still failed to demand a workable system of taxation, and his report to Congress in that month has been given a major responsibility in forcing the banks to suspend specie payments.

In the Secretary's defense it must be said that he, like most other Northerners, thought the war would be ended within a year. Newspapers were screaming, "On to Richmond!" and generals were blithely promising early victories. Had Chase urged preparation for a war that was ultimately to cost the nation twenty billion dollars,[99] he would have been esteemed as "crazy" as was General W. T. Sherman for wanting an army of two hundred thousand men in 1861. And, had the Secretary then convinced the President, Cabinet, and Congress of the correctness of his estimates, so pessimistic a forecast would certainly have had a demoralizing effect upon "the people at a time when the sudden outbreak of flagitious rebellion had deranged their business, and temporarily diminished their incomes." [100]

Farsighted the Secretary's plans cannot be considered, nor, indeed, efficient, but it must be remembered that he was operating with untested assistants to meet unascertained demands from uncertain resources. The difficulties he faced were in good part inherited, and the gradual restoration of Federal credit in 1861 was due in no small part to the Secretary's reputation for efficiency and integrity.

If Chase's policies did not bear the marks of deliberate planning, they nevertheless reflected the Secretary's fundamental economic preconceptions, and critics have sometimes attributed to ignorance actions which were the logical result of Chase's economic and political premises. It seems hardly just to blame the man for failing to do what he tried to avoid. The fact was that the first Republican Secretary of the Treasury was a Democrat. He had not always been so. That a Chase, raised in a family of sturdy New Hampshire Federalists and educated in the polished Whiggery of William Wirt's household should have become a Jacksonian in economic policy is one of the most inexplicable things about this man who regarded himself as "an enigma." [101]

— He had not always held loco-foco ideas. As a youth in Washington Chase had sneered at the "People's president," Andrew Jackson, and had mourned the retirement of John Quincy Adams. "He had performed his duty and was content with that consciousness," Chase confided in his diary report of his hero's defeat. "The misled people could take from him his office but they could not deprive him of that. . . . For me," the young conservative continued, "I would prefer to fall with the fallen than rise with the rising." [102] Even after he had settled in Cincinnati, Chase's strongly conservative views were openly expressed. To Alexis de Tocqueville Chase had confided his analysis of popular government: "We have carried 'Democracy' to its last limits. The right of voting is universal. Thence result . . . some very bad elections. . . . I am convinced that no distinguished men in the Union but believe a very wide suffrage harmful." [103]

But as he grew older, Chase came to repudiate his Whig views and to adopt every one of the Jacksonian positions he had reviled. ". . . I do not at all concur in Whig views of public policy," he wrote in 1846. "I do not believe in a high tariff, in a Bank of the United States, or a system of corporate banking." [104] On the tariff his free-trade views became so well known that as a potential presidential candidate in 1859 he had to assure protectionist friends that he would "take practical views of this Tariff question as every other, avoiding ultraism in every direction." [105] In the best Jacksonian tradition he deplored the evils of paper money. "The best practicable currency in my judgment," he asserted in his inaugural as governor of Ohio, "would be a currency of coin, admitting the use of large notes only for the convenience of commerce." [106] These and other "maxims of true Democracy," thought Chase, "are identical with those of true Christianity, in relation to the rights and duties of men as citizens." [107]

Chase left the Democratic party, it is true, but he left it reluctantly and only because he felt Democrats were not living up to their own principles. "No Democrat who has any real living faith in the great cardinal doctrine of the Democracy, that all men have equal rights," he contended, "can doubt that slave-holding is grossly inconsistent with Democratic principles." [108] Because the pro-Southern leaders of the Democratic party were losing sight of this basic issue, Chase was willing to join others, from any party, in an effort to check their mad course, but he always made it clear that he stood "upon democratic antislavery ground." "If . . . we could have a real democracy, applying democratic principles to slavery as well as every other question," he wrote rather wistfully, "I should, of course, prefer that organization to every other." [109]

Chase brought to his office, therefore, all the Jacksonian clichés—fear of monopoly, distrust of bankers, preference for revenue tariffs, advocacy of hard money. Never were a man's principles to be more sorely tested by practice.

Since the war was largely financed through borrowing, it was Chase's loan policy which most clearly revealed his Jacksonian antecedents. Bankers thought that the Secretary, after instituting an adequate tax system, should sell government securities on the market, both in Europe and in America, for what they would bring. Chase replied that it did not comport with the dignity of the Federal government to trade and dicker in Wall Street and State Street and Chestnut Street; anyway, to sell government bonds far below par would lower national morale. The bankers wanted long-term loans, bearing a high rate of interest. Chase, holding the Jeffersonian belief that the "idea of perpetual debt is not of American nativity, and should not be naturalized," [110] favored short-term issues of indeterminate period (e.g., bonds redeemable by the Treasury after five but before twenty years—popularly called "5–20's"), and he fought for a low rate of interest on Federal securities. The bankers thought that they should be the principal agents for handling the national loans, but Chase wished to secure a broad popular subscription to government stocks.

None of these issues were so clearly drawn at the beginning of the war, but the critical months of 1861 confirmed

Chase's belief that bankers had their own interests at heart, rather than the country's. In his first bond issues he "acquiesced with reluctance" in the banks' wishes,[111] and to keep the government afloat he sold twenty-year bonds, many below par. In August it was necessary to float another loan, for $50,000,000, but the bankers were reluctant, complaining that Chase was "too stringent in his ideas about the rates of interest; and on some other points illiberal, and not sufficiently considerate of their interests." Chase expressed his hope that the banks would support the government. "If not," he threatened, "I will go back to Washington, and issue notes for circulation; for it is certain that the war must go on until the rebellion is put down, if we have to put out paper until it takes a thousand dollars to buy a breakfast." [112] The bankers yielded.

A second loan of $50,000,000 was taken by the banks in October, but when a third installment of equal amount was proposed for December, the capitalists pointed to their dwindling specie reserves and asked that Chase "allow the proceeds of the loan to remain on deposit until paid out to the creditors of the government." [113] Chase, as a good Jacksonian, had an instinctive distrust of bank notes, and he insisted that the loan be paid in specie into the vaults of the subtreasury. Much against their will, the banks complied. The withdrawal of so large a sum, combined with the Secretary's failure to recommend stringent taxation in his December report and the threatened war with Great Britain over the *Trent* affair, proved too much of a strain. On December 30, 1861, the banks began to suspend specie payment.

Capitalists thought the crisis was caused by Chase's blundering, but the Secretary was merely confirmed in his distrust of bankers. He determined to seek aid elsewhere. From the beginning he had had in mind a wide popular subscription to Federal bond issues, believing that "Every holder of a note or bond, from a five cent fractional note to a five thousand dollar bond, has a direct interest in the security of national institutions and in the stability of the national administration." [114] But the subscription agents tried by the Treasury in 1861 proved costly and ineffectual, and it was not until late 1862, when the enterprising Jay Cooke was appointed "General Subscription Agent of the Government Loan," that mass purchases began. Door-to-door solicitation, high-pressure propaganda campaigns, and elaborate newspaper publicity employed by Cooke made the 5–20 issue an extraordinary success. In his December, 1863, report Chase was able to point to sales totalling $400,000,000. "The history of the world," he declared proudly, "may be searched in vain for a parallel case of popular financial support to a national government." [115]

The other half of the Secretary's positive financial program was the establishment of a national banking system. One might think such a project odd in a Jacksonian, with financial prejudices inherited from the fight against that "Monster," the Second Bank of the United States. But Chase had no intention of creating a new banking monopoly; he intended instead to restore control over the currency to the national government, where it constitutionally belonged. The system of state banks, issuing unregulated quantities of paper, Chase thought a menace to national prosperity. "They were established under the laws of twenty-nine different States; they were granted different privileges, subjected to different restrictions, and their circulation was based on a great variety of securities, of different qualities and quantities. . . . There were State banks with branches, independent banks, free banks, banks organized under a general law, and banks with special charters." [116] The inability of these state banks to meet the Treasury's needs in 1861–62 confirmed the Secretary's "profound sense of the present necessity of a national currency to the successful prosecution of the war against rebellion, and of its utility at all times in protecting labor, cheapening exchanges, facilitating travel, and increasing the safety of all business transactions." [117]

He proposed, therefore, the creation of a national banking system, not a restoration of Nicholas Biddle's "Monster," but an extension of the free-banking system established by New York in 1838. Banking associations should purchase a required minimum of government bonds (and in this fashion larger sales of government stocks could be assured) ; upon depositing these with the Treasurer of the United States, they should then receive United States Treasury notes to the amount of 90 per cent of the deposited bonds. These notes Chase hoped would replace the several thousand irregular, depreciating, and often counterfeit varieties of state bank notes and would form a true national currency. Moreover, the national banks thus established, under the supervision of a Federal Comptroller of the Currency, would be sounder and more dependable, both to the public and to the government.

First made public in his December, 1861, report, Chase's banking proposals met with hostility. Though "intelligent businessmen" favored the idea, a Massachusetts economist wrote the Secretary: "It is . . . regarded with great suspicion by the Banks, especially the smaller and

weaker ones, whose business is not, and never was legitimate Banking but the manufacture and issue of inconvert-
ible paper money." [118] It was not till 1863, against strenuous opposition, that Chase was able to push the national
banking act through Congress, and even then the measure
was so inadequately drawn that the system developed
slowly. Not until it was reorganized in 1864 and a tax
upon state bank notes was imposed in the following year
did the national banking system become the principal
financial structure of the Union. It lasted, without serious
modifications, until the creation of the Federal Reserve
System in 1913, and Chase always regarded it as one of
his major achievements. "As to the National Banks," he
wrote proudly after the war, "I do not regard them as
perfect institutions, nor their managers as anything extraordinary in the way of saintship. But I believe them well
adapted to the commercial wants of the country. . . . I
dare say the system can be improved; but it is not every
tinker who can improve it." [119]

But, regardless of its ultimate adequacy (and it must be
remembered that the system as finally established heavily
benefited the creditor classes and regions of the country [120]), the national banking system was a long-range
solution for a problem which demanded an immediate
answer. Early in 1862 Federal finances were at their
most critical stage. Taxation could not bring in revenue
for another year; a national banking system was a project
for the future; and popular loans seemed to have failed.
Chase blamed the bankers; the bankers accused the Secretary. The only answer to the emergency seemed to be the
issue of fiat money—non-interest-bearing paper, with no
other backing than the government's promise to pay.

Chase came to this conclusion slowly and reluctantly, for as a Jacksonian hard-money man he had for years feared "the risk of a depreciated, depreciating, and finally worthless paper money; the immeasurable evils of dishonored public faith and national bankruptcy." [121] But the crisis demanded some action; the Congressional committees on finance pressed for Chase's assent to legal-tender issues; and the Secretary yielded. "There was no help for it," he later remarked. "It was a political necessity if nothing else, but it was a war necessity also." [122] After the war, as Chief Justice, Chase was to rule the legal-tender act unconstitutional (Hepburn v. Griswold).

By objective standards, there was probably no necessity for the issuance of greenbacks, and they added enormously to the cost of the war. Moreover, the first issue led to another, and then to another, until by the end of the war some $450,000,000 of the legal tenders were authorized. Chase had, a hostile commentator observed, "forced himself into the trap, and was continually weaving the web tighter, thus making release more and more difficult. A sadder example of financial helplessness has been rarely seen." [123]

Chase's own view was decidedly different. The greenbacks had been issued because the banking system was inadequate and because Congress had not imposed adequate taxes; they kept the government going until Chase's positive financial program could be put to work. Such a measure, doubtless, in an ideal world would never have been adopted; but in an ideal world political pressure and economic necessity are not ruling considerations.

The Secretary's problems were not over, even after the issuing of greenbacks, the creation of an internal revenue system, and the adoption of a national banking act. By 1864 he was facing another crisis. With a fall election coming up, Congress failed to adopt Chase's now rigorous proposals for taxation to meet the mounting war costs. Political pressure did not permit the Secretary again to use Jay Cooke as subscription agent for the new government loan, and when Chase turned once more to the bankers, they, in effect, went on strike. Chase's attempt to reduce interest rates from 6 per cent (which the 5–20's had borne) to 5 per cent (which his new 10–40 loan would carry) they regarded as political grandstanding, and bond sales almost ceased.

In this fresh economic crisis it seemed to Chase that the President gave him but indifferent support. The emergency coincided with Chase's final effort to maintain the administrative independence of his department, and to the overworked Secretary, Lincoln appeared to begrudge him the choice of his own agents to carry out the imperfect laws unwillingly conceded by Congress. In view of his own slowness to urge taxation and his resolute efforts to prevent presidential "meddling" in his department's policies, Chase's feeling was hardly fair; but it was certainly natural. The oppressive isolation of his position seemed too great. To safeguard his political future, his administrative staff, and his financial policies, he had to secure positive presidential backing, and, as he had often done before, he submitted his resignation. This time, much to his surprise, it was accepted.

Chase's reactions were mixed. "It was a real relief to have my resignation accepted," he wrote a friend, "and yet I should not have retired because of any desire for relief. I felt able with God's favor to carry the load and did not doubt, if I could have the cordial support of Mr. Lincoln in the administration of my department, of complete success. But that I could not have." [124] On reflection, though, along with some regret for leaving his "great work half over," Chase had only pride for his achievements. He had made, he thought, "few mistakes. . . . Indeed, on looking back over the whole ground, with an earnest desire to detect error . . . , I am not able to see where, if I had to do my work all over again, I could in any matter do materially otherwise than I have." [125]

Not even Chase's most enthusiastic admirer could concur in such self-laudation, yet the Secretary's achievements, in the face of incredible difficulties, had been remarkable. "As Secretary of the Treasury," concluded the *Nation,* "he found a field the magnitude of which no imagination had previously measured. Financially speaking, some of his projects were costly and unsound, but admirably adapted to our ignorances, prejudices, and ways. . . . Indeed, his action appears titanic when we contrast it with the feebleness which in 1814 brought the Treasury to absolute bankruptcy. . . ." [126] And perhaps American problems in financing later wars should further increase our admiration for the great Civil War Secretary of the Treasury.

1

A Winter of Crises

[DECEMBER 9, 1861–MAY 1, 1862]

CHASE seems to have kept no diary during either the secession winter of 1860–61 or during his first nine months in the Treasury Department. Events moved so rapidly that the harassed Secretary probably had little time for journalizing. As the diary begins in December, 1861, the panic caused by Union defeat at First Bull Run had subsided, but major crises impended.

The Treasury faced its worst winter. In August Chase had made arrangements with the associated bankers of New York, Boston, and Philadelphia for a loan, which finally totaled $150,000,00, paid in three installments. Agreeing to furnish coin to the government at once, the banks were to be repaid by the sale to the public, through subscription agents and through the banks themselves, of three-year Treasury notes bearing 7.30 per cent interest. From the beginning the bankers complained that the Secretary's insistence upon hard money was draining their specie reserves. They had little confidence in the national banking system which Chase urged in his first annual report to Congress (December, 1861), and his failure to recommend heavy taxation increased their distrust of his policies. In late December the banks suspended specie payments, and further loans seemed impossible. After almost daily consultation with financial leaders, Chase thought he had reached a satisfactory understanding with them in January, 1862, but when the banks rejected his proposals, there seemed no alternative to issuing legal-tender Treasury notes (greenbacks).

Other department heads also had their problems during this winter of disappointments. In November Captain Charles Wilkes of the United States Navy seized two Confederate envoys, James Murray Mason and John Slidell, from a British ship, the *Trent*, and Secretary of State Seward found himself facing a diplomatic break with Great Britain unless the prisoners were released. In the cabinet discussion, Chase added his voice for the surrender of the diplomats. Of a very different sort was the crisis in the War Department, where the obvious incompetence of Secretary Simon Cameron made his replacement a necessity. In January, 1862, Chase, along with Seward, helped engineer the appointment of the domineering but efficient Edwin M. Stanton.

The war itself progressed with painful slowness. The capture of Beaufort (Port Royal), South Carolina, in November, 1861, General Ulysses S. Grant's successes at Fort Henry and Fort Donelson in February, and Farragut's winning of New Orleans in April were cheering but hardly decisive victories. The Army of the Potomac, magnificently reorganized by General George B. McClellan, lay idle all winter around Washington. In mid-winter McClellan fell ill of typhoid, and nobody knew his plans. When he recovered, there was still little progress. After much urging he moved his army toward Manassas in March—to find the feared Confederate fortifications there defended by logs painted to resemble cannon. His Peninsular campaign, commenced in late April, never had Chase's confidence, and even after McClellan reached Fort Monroe, it seemed that he dallied and waited in eternal preparation. Meanwhile, in the Shenandoah Valley, ominous movements of Stonewall Jackson's troops threatened weakened Washington.

∽ ∽ ∽

Dec. 9, 1861, Monday. Had conversation with Messrs. Stevens and Vail [1] about reimbursement. They contended that the Banks were entitled to be reimbursed, in coin, for all Two Years' Bonds and 60 Day Notes received in payment of Subscriptions, whether paid by the Banks themselves on account of deposits, or by individuals for Bonds. I denied the right of the Banks to reimbursement for Bonds paid by them, but promised to take the other into consideration.

Mr. Cisco telegraphed that the Banks had paid the first instalment of the 7 per cent Loan.

Gov. Fish,[2] Mr. Case [3] and many others called in the evening.

The Annual Report went to Congress today.

Dec. 10, Tuesday. Mr. Haight,[4] M. C. from N. Y., called and stated results of Bank Meeting yesterday. Mr. Gallatin [5] only opposed payment of first instalment; objecting that the Secretary had recommended a tax on Bank circulation, and so had broken his agreement.

A number of gentlemen called at the office on applications for office and otherwise.

At 12, went to President's to Cabinet Meeting. A

deputation from New York, consisting of Judge Davies, Mr. O'Gorman and Mr. Savage,[6] represented the importance of an exchange of prisoners, with special reference to the case of Col. Corcoran.[7] After their withdrawal some conversation took place on this subject. Mr. Blair favored exchanges generally. Mr. Bates objected to the recognition of the Confederates as belligerents by regular exchanges. Mr. Seward thought best to take the matter under consideration and defer a conclusion; urging that it would be bad policy to abandon the position taken as to privateers, which he thought had been effectual in protecting our commerce from general depredation. My own view was that we had already acknowledged the rebels as belligerents by the institution of the blockade, but not as National belligerents; that we were therefore at liberty to adopt what course we pleased in respect to privateers; that Mr. Seward's view was correct at the time the policy was proclaimed; that now, with a stronger and better built Navy to protect our commerce, we could well afford to allow privateering, provided they could get ships and men, precisely as we allowed War on land; and that I would not object to sending Smith,[8] who had been convicted of piracy at Philadelphia, to Fortress Monroe, and let Gen. Wool [9] exchange him for Corcoran. I thought it would be a very good bargain. In fact, the system of exchanges did not seem to me to be attended by the difficulties which embarrassed other gentlemen; but I thought the whole thing could be done without recognition of the rebels as National belligerents, by allowing the exchanges to take place between Gen. Wool and Gen. Huger.[10] Nothing was decided, but the matter is still reserved for further consideration.

It was proposed to invite Gen. McClellan to a meeting of the Cabinet tomorrow, to learn his plans. Objection made by Mr. Blair, and the President took it into consideration.

Gen. Hunter's application for authority to muster a Brigade of Indians was considered, in connection with a proposition of Gen McClellan to invade Western Texas from the North and from the Gulf simultaneously. I expressed my approval of the latter, and my disapproval of the former for want of power, the President having already exhausted the authority, given him by Congress, to raise men. This view was generally concurred in and the subject dropped.

I directed the attention of the President to complaints made against Gen. Smith [11] at Paducah, and was glad to learn that Gen. McClellan had already directed him to be superseded.

Some conversation took place in respect to organizing courts at Beaufort; and it was agreed that I should see certain Southern gentlemen and then confer with Judge Bates as to what should be done.

Sent copies of Report to Messrs. Ketchum, Williams, Gallatin and Coe,[12] with letters expressing the hope of their concurrence in its views.

Dec. 11, Wednesday. A multitude of callers at the office this morning, among them Wade [13] of the Senate and Ashley [14] of the House, Chairmen of the Territorial Committees in their respective houses. To both of them I gave my views in brief as to the relations of the insurrectionary States to the Union; that no State nor any portion of the people could withdraw from the Union or absolve themselves from allegiance to it; [15] but that when the attempt was made, and the State government was placed in hostility to the Federal Government, the State organization was forfeited and it lapsed into the condition of a Territory with which we could do what we pleased; that we could form a Provisional Government, as was done in Western Virginia, or, when we occupied any portion of a rebellious State, such as Beaufort, we could organize territorial Courts and, as soon as it became necessary, a Territorial Government; that those States could not properly be considered as States in the Union but must be readmitted from time to time as Congress should provide. Messrs Wade and Ashley expressed their concurrence.

Senator Johnson [16] of Tennessee called, and gave an account of the military operations in Kentucky during the summer, of which he was a witness. He said there was nothing to prevent a march into Tennessee and the possession of Knoxville immediately after the Battle at Camp Wild Cat; but that Gen Sherman was so intimidated by Buckner's alleged strength and purposes that he was much of the time incapacitated for command.[17]

Mr. Speed [18] of Louisville called my attention to restrictions placed by our Special Agent upon shipments of provisions to Louisville. I told him that Louisville, being a loyal city, stood upon the same footing as Washington, and that Mr. Mellen [19] should be instructed accordingly.

Mr. Hooper,[20] M.C. from Boston, expressed a cordial approval of my report.

Genl. Meigs and Judge Advocate Lee [21] called at my request, the former more especially with reference to the collection and disposition of Cotton at Port Royal. He promised to place bagging, bale-rope etc for 1000 Bales at the disposal of the Agent of the Treasury Department there. I proposed to transfer the whole business to him; but we did not determine whether the transfer should be made. With Maj. Lee and also with Gen Meigs, I had some conversation about government for seceded States. Maj. Lee seemed to favor Military Commissions for the trial of questions not cognizable by Courts Martial. He promised to send an Order of Gen Scott,[22] issued in Mexico, which might serve as a precedent.

Wrote to Messrs Aspinwall, Sprague and Minturn,[23] giving them the substance of what Gen Meigs had said about the Cotton business, and telling them that, should I retain the management, I should be glad to avail myself of their counsel and support.

Dec. 12, Thursday. Judge Key [24] called this morning and read draft of Bill for the emancipation of slaves in the District of Columbia.

Col. Sullivan [25] of Ohio called, being here on business connected with the B. & O. R.R., and represented his interviews with Genl McClellan as highly satisfactory. Among other things he stated that when Gen. Kelley advanced upon Romney, the rebels supposed he designed to attack Winchester—that they called upon Johnston for help—that he at first refused to send any, and finally only sent a Regiment of raw recruits, who had recently gone to Manassas from Winchester; thus showing that, important as Winchester was, no troops could be spared from Manassas.[26]

Genl. McClellan called at 12 M. and remained about an hour and a half.

The Secretary was absent in New York from Dec. 18 to Dec. 21st.   H. G. P[lantz].[27]

Dec. 25, Wednesday. The 'Trent' Affair. Remarks of Secretary Chase at the Cabinet Meeting.

In my judgment, the case stands precisely thus: In taking the rebel Envoys and their Secretaries from the 'Trent,' without invoking or proposing to invoke the sanction of any judicial tribunal, Capt. Wilkes clearly violated the Law of Nations, and in that very principle which the United States have ever most zealously maintained. Great Britain, therefore, has a right to ask from us a disavowal of the act, and the restoration of the persons to the condition in which they were taken; and, if this right be insisted on, it is our duty, however disagreeable, to do what is thus asked.

On the other hand, the circumstances under which the act of Capt. Wilkes was done, not only repel the imputation of aggressive or unfriendly intent, but entitle him to commendation for the motives by which his conduct was governed and reduce the seizure and removal from the 'Trent' of the Rebel Commissioners, to a mere technical violation of the neutral rights of England. Mason and Slidell were Commissioners bearing despatches from the rebel government to Europe, and their character and charge were known to the commander of the 'Trent.' At the time of the seizure, therefore, the 'Trent' was knowingly employed, in violation of English Law, of the Royal Proclamation, and of her duty to the United States as a friendly nation. Conscious of the fact, the commander refused, when requested, to exhibit his passenger List. The capture was, of course, warranted, and Capt. Wilkes, in making it, performed only his plain duty to his Government. He had a right to break up the voyage and send the steamer as prize into a port for trial and condemnation.

But the steamer was employed in the conveyance of mails and passengers; and Capt. Wilkes was desirous to avoid the public injury of delaying the transmission of the former and the private hardship likely to result from interrupting the voyage of the latter.

Governed mainly by these motives, he obeyed what seemed to him the dictates of humanity and friendly consideration for a friendly nation, by removing the contraband persons from the 'Trent' with the least possible inconvenience to all concerned, and suffering the vessel with her other passengers and mails to proceed to her destination. In doing this, he surrendered a prize which might have tempted cupidity, without a thought that, by the self-same act, he was depriving himself of the only means of justifying the capture, either of persons or vessels, through a judicial decision.

Certainly it was not too much to expect of a friendly nation, and especially of a nation of the same blood, religion and characteristic civilization as our own, that, in consideration of the great rights, she would overlook the little wrong; nor can I now persuade myself that, were all the circumstances known to the English Government, as to ours, the surrender of the rebel Commissioners would be insisted on.

The technical right is undoubtedly with England. As rebels or as traitors to our Government, the pretended Commissioners would have been safe on a neutral ship. It was only in their character as Envoys that they were subject to arrest as contraband. As contraband, they could not rightfully be taken from the ship until after the judicial condemnation of the ship itself, for receiving and carrying them. However excused or even justified by motives, the act of removing them as prisoners from the 'Trent,' without resort to any judicial cognizance was in itself indefensible. We cannot deny this without denying our history. Were the circumstances reversed, our Government would, I think, accept the explanation, and let England keep her Rebels; and I cannot divest myself of the belief that, were the case fairly understood, the British Government would do likewise.

But we cannot afford delays. While the matter hangs in uncertainty, the public mind will remain disquieted, our commerce will suffer serious harm, our action against the rebels must be greatly hindered, and the restoration of our prosperity, largely identified with that of all nations, must be delayed. Better, then, to make now the sacrifice of feeling involved in the surrender of these rebels, than even avoid it by the delays which explanations must occasion. I give my adhesion, therefore, to the conclusion to which the Secretary of State has arrived.

It is gall and wormwood to me. Rather than consent to the liberation of these men, I would sacrifice everything I possess. But I am consoled by the reflection that while nothing but severest retribution is due to them, the surrender, under existing circumstances, is but simply doing right; simply proving faithful to our own ideas and traditions under strong temptations to violate them; simply giving to England and to the world the most signal proof that the American Nation will not, under any circumstances, for the sake of inflicting just punishment on Rebels, commit even a technical wrong against neutrals.

Jan. 1, 1862, Wednesday. Went to President's at 11, with my two daughters and Miss Walker.[28] Prodigious crowd around the gates. Afterwards received at our own house. Mrs Genl McDowell, Mrs. Bridge and Miss Walker assisted Kate. All the Diplomatic Corps except Stoeckel,[29] and many officers of the Army, called. When Lord Lyons [30] came in, I saluted him with 'Pax esto Perpetua'; and he expressed the hope that his conduct had always been that of a Peacemaker.

Jan. 2, Thursday. Resumed ordinary duties at Department, Mr. Harrington still absent.

In the evening Kate had big Turkey, and Mr Sumner [31] and Genl. McDowell dined with us.

Jan. 3–4, Friday and Saturday. Routine.

Jan. 5, Sunday. Attended church at The Trinity in the morning.

In the evening received a despatch from Mr. Garrett,[32] President of the B. & O. R.R., stating that the enemy had advanced to Hancock and were shelling the town—that the Union troops had fallen back to the Maryland side— that the enemy was in possession of a considerable portion of the newly prepared Road. Sent the despatch by Col. Barstow [33] to Genl McClellan—Wrote to Lander who had been ordered to the command at Romney.

Senator Chandler [34] came in converse about Gen McDowell being put in command of the Army of the Potomac and of military affairs generally; and evinced an excellent spirit.

Jan. 6, Monday. Received a note from McClellan's Aid, saying that the General had read the despatch sent him last night, and would take immediate measures to protect the Road; that re-inforcements would be immediately sent to Hancock; and that Genl. Banks [35] had been ordered to support Lander.

In fulfillment of engagement with the President of the American Bank Note Company, went to Ulke's,[36] who took a number of Photographs.

Cabinet Meeting held at night to confer with the Joint Committee of the two Houses of Congress on the Conduct of the War.[37] The members of the Committee, especially Messrs. Chandler Wade, Johnson, Odell and Covode, were very earnest in urging the vigorous prosecution of the War, and in recommending the appointment of Genl. Mc-Dowell as Major-General, to command the Army of the Potomac.

A great deal of discussion took place. I expressed my own views, saying that, in my judgment, Genl. McClellan was the best man for the place he held known to me— that, I believed, if his sickness had not prevented he would by this time have satisfied everybody in the country of his efficiency and capacity—that I thought, however, that he tasked himself too severely—that no physical or mental vigor could sustain the strains he imposed on himself, often on the saddle nearly all day and transacting business at his rooms nearly all night—that, in my judgment, he ought to confer freely with his ablest and most experienced Generals, deriving from them the benefits which their counsels, whether accepted or rejected, would certainly impart, and communicating to them full intelligence of his own plans of action, so that, in the event of sickness or accident to himself, the movements of the army need not necessarily be interrupted or delayed. I added that, in my own opinion, no one person could discharge fitly the special duties of Commander of the Army of the Potomac, and the general duties of Commanding General of the Armies of the United States; and that Genl. McClellan, in under-

taking to discharge both, had undertaken what he could
not perform.

Much else was said by various gentlemen, and the discussion was concluded by the announcement by the President that he would call on Genl. McClellan, and ascertain
his views in respect to the division of the commands.

Jan. 8, Wednesday—Special Loan Committee from
New-York here.

Gave the usual dinner to Committees of Finance of the
two Houses. Present, Messrs. Fessenden, Simmons, Sherman, Howe and Pearce, of the Senate, and Messrs. Ste-
phens [Stevens], Morrill, Spaulding, Corning, Horton,
Stratton, Hooper and Maynard, of the House. Messrs.
Bright and McDougall, of the Senate, and Mr. Phelps, of
the House, were absent.[38] Mr. Jay Cooke, of Philadelphia,
was also present.

After dinner, Messrs Coe, Russell and Vermilye [39] came
in. Messrs C. & V. were very desirous that I should cancel
so much of the loan as remained unpaid; for which I
promised consideration but declined giving any definite
answer.

Jan. 9, Thursday. Mr. Russell came to breakfast. After
breakfast we discussed somewhat his Financial Suggestions. He proposes a Board of Exchequer, to be appointed
by the President and Senate, to whom Bonds of the U.S.
shall be issued, and by whom 80 per cent of the amount
shall be returned in circulating Notes; that similar Bonds
shall be issued by the Board and 75 per cent of the
amount issued to any depositor and redeemed by the U.S.
if necessary; that Associations for Banking purposes shall
be authorized, to whom 90 per cent of Bonds deposited
may be issued, with provisions for reserves of specie, etc.

Called at Ulke's coming to Department. At Dept. attended to the usual business and made appointment with Committees from Philadelphia and New-York to come to my house at Eight this evening.

Went to the Capitol and heard Mr. Sumner's speech, which was, in the main, admirable in manner and matter. Told him I thought he had better omit the word '*penitent,*' applied to England in connection with her implied recantation of ancient pretensions by her demand for Mason and Slidell; and that it would have been well to omit the argument against the right to capture and bring in the ship for having Commissioners or Despatches on board, inasmuch as that argument contradicted the position taken by Mr. Seward on the same question.[40] Most of the foreign Ministers were present, and full galleries.

Returning to the Department, received a visit from General McDowell, who showed me his map, and the relative position of our own and the enemy's forces near Washington.

Kate and Mr. Cooke came in, saying that Nettie was ill, but doing well, at Philadelphia. Kate determined to go by this evening's train with Mr. Cooke, and promised to telegraph me to-night.

Jan. 10, Friday. Bank Committees here.

Jan. 11, Saturday. Many callers at Department—among them Genl. McDowell and Col. Key. Genl McD. enquired about McClellan's plans and I told him what I knew of them, in strict confidence. Col. Key was about to have an interview with Genl. McClellan, and wanted to know what I would recommend. I replied that McC. should (1st.) Relieve himself of the imputation of nepotism and favoritism in the selection of his staff; (2d.) That he should not allow the President to wait on him, but should honor the office by sending one of his aids regularly to the President; and (3d.) That he should call into his counsels the most experienced and able men in the army, and should insist on the appointment of McDowell as Major-General at once.

Had conversation with Edwin M. Stanton, about Lander, McClellan &c. Requested Col. Sullivan to see War Department about B. & O. R.R.

Finance Committees and Bank Committees met at office at 3 P.M.

Jan. 12, Sunday.[41] At church in the morning. Good, plain sermon. Wished much to join in communion, but felt myself too subject to temptation to sin. After church went to see Cameron by appointment; but being obliged to meet the President, etc., at one, could only excuse myself. At President's found Generals McDowell, Franklin,[42] and Meigs, and Seward and Blair. Meigs decided against dividing forces, and in favor of battle in front. President said McClellan's health was much improved, and thought it best to adjourn till to-morrow, and have all then present attend with McC. at three. Home, and talk and reading. Dinner. Cameron came in. Advised loan in Holland, and recommended Brooks, Lewis, and another whom I have forgotten. Then turned to Department matters, and we talked of his going to Russia and Stanton as successor, and he proposed I should again see the President. I first proposed seeing Seward, to which he assented. He declared himself determined to maintain himself at the head of his Department if he remained, and to resist hereafter all interference. I told him I would in that event stand by him faithfully. He and I drove to Willard's, where I left him, and went myself to Seward's. I told him at once what was in my mind—that I thought the President and Cameron were both willing that C. should go to Russia. He seemed to receive the matter as new, except so far as suggested by me last night. Wanted to know who would succeed Cameron. I said Holt [43] and Stanton had been named; that I feared Holt might embarrass us on the slavery question, and might not prove quite equal to the emergency; that Stanton was a good lawyer and full of energy; but I could not, of course, judge him as an executive officer as well as he (S.) could, for he knew him when he was in Buchanan's Cabinet. Seward replied that he saw much of him then; that he was of great force—full of expedients, and thoroughly loyal. Finally he agreed to the whole thing, and promised to go with me to talk with the President about it to-morrow. Just at this point Cameron came in with a letter from the President proposing his nomination to Russia in the morning! He was quite offended, supposing the letter intended as a dismissal, and, therefore, discourteous.[44] We both assured him it could not be so. Finally he concluded to retain the letter till morning, and then go and see the President. Seward was expecting General Butler,[45] and Cameron said he ought to be sent off immediately. I said, 'Well, let's leave Seward to order him off at once.' C. laughed, and we went off together, I taking him to his house. Before parting, I told him what had passed between me and Seward concerning Stanton, with which he was gratified. I advised him to go to the President in the morning, express his thanks for the consideration with which his wishes, made known through me as well as by himself orally, had been treated, and tell him frankly how desirable it was to him that his successor

should be a Pennsylvanian, and should be Stanton. I said
I thought that his wish, supported as it could be by Seward
and myself, would certainly be gratified, and told him that
the President had already mentioned Stanton in a way
which indicated that no objection on his part would be
made. I said also that, if he wished, I would see Seward,
and would go to the President after he had left him, and
urge the point. He asked why not come in when he should
be there, and I assented to this. We parted, and I came
home. A day which may have—and seemingly must have
—great bearing on affairs. Oh, that my heart and life were
so pure and right before God that I might not hurt our
great cause! I fear Mr. Seward may think Cameron's
coming into his house pre-arranged, and that I was not
dealing frankly. I feel satisfied, however, that I have acted
right, and with just deference to all concerned, and have
in no respect deviated from the truth.

Jan. 13, Monday. To-day Genl. Cameron resigned his
place as Secretary of War, and E. M. Stanton, of Penna.,
was appointed in his stead. Many called, among them
both Messrs Cameron and Stanton.

Jan. 14, Tuesday. The day was occupied wholly in conferences with members of the Bank Committees and
Boards of Trade of the three cities who are here consulting on Financial matters, and with Senators and others
who called in regard to the change in the Cabinet.

Mr. Fessenden [46] of the Senate, and Mr. Stanton, were
together with the Secretary, for more than an hour.

Mr [Gilbert] Rodman, Chief Clerk of the Department,
died suddenly this morning, and at 2 o'clock, I attended
the funeral services. His remains were taken to Philadelphia.

Jan. 15, Wednesday. The consultations with Bankers and Members of the Boards of Trade from New-York, Boston and Philadelphia were terminated to-day, and the result was reduced to writing, as follows:

1st. The general views of the Secretary of the Treasury are assented to.

2d. The Banks will receive and pay out the U.S. Demand Notes [47] freely, and sustain, in all proper ways, their credit.

3d. The Secretary will, within the next two weeks, in addition to the current daily payment of a Million and a half of Dollars in U.S. notes, pay the further sum of at least Twenty Millions of Dollars in 7.30 Three Years Bonds to such public creditors as desire to receive them, and thus relieve the existing pressure upon the community.

4th. The issue of U.S. Demand Notes not to be extended beyond the Fifty Millions now authorized; but it is desired that Congress will extend the provisions of the existing Loan Acts, so as to enable the Secretary to issue in exchange for U.S. Notes or in payment to creditors, Notes payable in one year, bearing 3.65 per cent interest, and convertible into 7.30 Three Years Bonds, or to borrow under the existing provisions to the amount of Two Hundred and Fifty or Three Hundred Millions of Dollars.

5th. It is thought desirable that Congress should adopt a general Law relating to the Currency and Banking Associations, embracing the general provisions recommended by the Secretary in his Report.

6th. It is believed that this action and legislation will render the making of U.S. Demand Notes a legal tender, or their increase beyond the Fifty Millions now authorized, unnecessary.

The gentlemen assenting to these propositions were, from New-York, Messrs Coe,

> Boston, Mr. Walley,[48]
>
> Philadelphia [No name is given.]

About an hour after this understanding was arrived at (each gentleman agreeing to urge the plan embodied in it upon the adoption of the Banks of his city, and expressing his belief that it would be cordially sustained) a sub-Committee from the House Committee of Ways and Means, consisting of Messrs Spaulding, Hooper and Horton, called at the Department. Mr. Hooper expressed his decided opinion that the U.S. Notes must necessarily be made legal tender. Messrs Spaulding and Horton expressed no opinion and it was agreed that the Secretary should confer with Mr Stevens, Chairman of the Committee, this evening.

Jan. 16, Thursday. The Bankers left for home to-day, news having first reached Washington of the rise in the value of stocks in New-York, consequent upon the receipt there, by Telegraph, of the result of the Financial Conferences of the past few days.

Jan. 17, Friday. Wrote to Mr. Stevens expressing the hope that the arrangement adopted on Wednesday would meet his approval and be sanctioned by the banks.

Jan. 20, Monday. Mr. Stanton took formal possession of the War Department to-day. Paid respects to the outgoing and incoming Secretaries.

Mr. Walley telegraphed that Boston Banks would not assent to proposed arrangement, and advised the immediate making of U.S. Notes legal tender.

Jan. 22, Wednesday. A Committee from the Chamber of Commerce of Cincinnati waited on me this morning, to urge the location of the proposed new armory at Cincinnati. They also represented the earnest feeling of the People of Cincinnati and the West in favor of greater energy and decision in the conduct of the war, and alluded to the state of politics in Ohio. Told them that Cincinnati, 'never very kind, was always very dear to me,' and that I had already presented her claims for the armory and should continue to do so. As to the conduct of the war, I gave them every assurance, and especially expressed confidence in Mr. Stanton, as a man who would be master of his Department, and yield to no one save the President. On Politics, I said that the Democratic Party must be reconstructed as a party of Freedom.

Messrs Cisco, Barney [49] and Andrews [50] came from New-York to confer about Government property there. Mayor Opdyke [51] accompanied them, but returned to-day. He favors a Legal-tender law.

Mar. 6, Thursday. To-day the President sent a Message to Congress, recommending coöperation by Federal Government with States in abolition of Slavery within their limits.

The following is a draft of a Message on this subject, prepared and submitted to the President during the last week of December.[52]

Message.

In my Annual Message communicated to Congress at the commencement of the present session, I took occasion to say:

'The Union must be preserved and hence all indispensable means must be employed. We should not be in haste to determine that radical and extreme measures, which may reach the loyal as well as the disloyal, are indispensable.'

Reflecting since, with great solicitude, upon the condition of the country, and sharing, in full proportion, the desire which pervades the whole community for a speedy suppression of the rebellion, I have reached the conclusion that it is my duty to submit to the consideration of Congress some suggestions which seem to me to deserve their most serious attention.

It is known to all that the most potent falsehood by which the fomentors of discontent and promoters of insurrection inflamed the minds of citizens of the slaveholding States, and prepared them for rebellion under the guise of secession, was the assertion that the party by which I was chosen President of the United States designed to interfere, through the agency of the Federal Government, with the institution of slavery in the States where it existed. It is equally well known to all who have taken any pains to inform themselves, that such interference was never designed or sanctioned by that party; but was, on the contrary, in all its declarations, whether by National or State Conventions, distinctly and emphatically disavowed and repudiated. No well-informed person can now reasonably doubt that, under an Administration conducted upon the principles set forth in those declarations, the Institution of Slavery, existing under State Constitutions and Laws, would have been as absolutely safe from Federal interference, as it has been under any Administration since the establishment of the Union.

It is true that the majority of the people, by whose suffrages the existing Administration was called to the concerns of government, cherishing on this subject the sentiments of Washington and Jefferson, of Franklin and Adams, opposed the extension of Slavery beyond State limits, and proposed to afford it no Governmental support within the sphere of exclusive National jurisdiction. But it is equally true that they regarded Slavery within State limits, as beyond that sphere and meant to perform fully, in reference to Slaves held under State laws, as well as in reference to every other matter of duty to every citizen of every State every Constitutional obligation.

The rebellion, therefore, except so far as its chiefs and some of their more deluded followers were concerned, was inspired and is sustained by a delusion. Were the people of the rebellious districts even now to reject the consuls [sic] of their misleaders; reorganize loyal State governments; and again send Senators and Representatives to Congress; they would find themselves at peace, with no institution changed, and with their just influence in the National Councils unabridged and unimpaired. With peace so restored, prosperity and happiness would return.

A pacific conquest of this delusion having been made impossible by the bombardment of Sumter, it became necessary to preserve the Union by War; and the question now most imperatively demanding attention and solution is, by what means can this War be best abridged without sacrificing its object.

Without now adverting to the military measures demanded for the suppression of rebellion, it seems fit to direct your attention to one of another nature. I have already observed that the rebellion, so far as the people of the Slave States participate in it, is prompted by a delusion—by the groundless fear of interference with State concerns and especially in the matter of Slavery, by Federal authority. The real motives with its chiefs and the initiated are, first, resentment at defeat of their schemes for the subjection of the Federal Administration to the permanent supremacy of slaveholders as a separate ruling class; and, secondly, ambition to found a government, either consolidated or federal, Republican or Monarchical, of which Slavery shall be the central idea, and which they themselves may administer and control.

To dispel the illusion of the masses, and to deprive the leaders of the hope of success in their cherished schemes, will go far towards extinguishing the rebellion, by withdrawing its aliment.

I suggest, therefore, for the consideration of Congress, the expediency of offering by Joint Resolution, to the acceptance of the several States within whose limits Slavery exists under sanction of loyal State governments, a compensation, not exceeding a certain sum for each person held as a slave according to the last Census, to be paid to the States and distributed to individuals in proportions ascertained by their own legislation, in case the people thereof, through their own Conventions or Legislatures, shall see fit to accept such compensation and make provision for emancipation.

Such a proposition on the part of Congress, submitted frankly to the free acceptance or rejection of the loyal States, would be a distinct and emphatic repudiation of all pretence of Federal authority to interfere with slavery within State limits, by referring the whole subject to the States and people immediately interested; it would afford clear evidence of fraternal sentiments, by manifested readiness to assume as a common burden the cost of a benefit shared by all, but by none more largely than by the enfranchising States; and it would, so far as accepted by the loyal Slaveholding States, strengthen the bonds of Union between themselves and their brethren, while it would, in the same degree, destroy the hope of bringing these loyal States into their scheme of extending Slaveholding empire yet cherished by the leaders of the rebellion; compel them to see for what wretched husks of sovreignty [*sic*] they have prodigally wasted their rich inheritance of safety, honor, prosperity and power under the Federal Constitution; and arouse, in the minds of the misled masses, irresistible desires to return to the Union from which, in an evil hour, under coercion or delusion, they have attempted to withdraw.

March 10, Monday. This morning Judge (Col.) Key came into the office, dressed for the march towards Manassas, which the Army of the Potomac is making. He bade me goodbye most cordially—thanking me repeatedly for my kindness, by which, he said, I had won his faithful and life-long friendship; there was no man in the country for whom he had so high a respect and regard—no man whose advancement he so much desired, nor whom he so wished to serve.

March 13, Thursday. Revd. Dr. Fuller,[53] of Baltimore, called, and asked advice as to the course he should pursue in regard to his plantations and slaves at Port Royal. He wished to know what were his rights in respect to them.

Told him that, as a loyal man, he was Proprietor of the *land*. How about the negroes? he asked. They were free, I replied. He thought his right to them was the same as his right to the land. Told him opinions would differ on that point, but that, for one, I should never consent to the involuntary reduction to Slavery of one of the negroes who had been in the service of the Government. Told him further what I thought of the character of the rebellion and its results, etc.

He said he was willing to acquiesce in the experiments of the Government, but expressed grave doubts of the success of the undertaking at Port Royal. Quoted Machiavelli's saying 'Next to making freemen slaves, it is most difficult to makes [*sic*] slaves freemen.'

March 14, Friday. To-day the vote was taken in the Senate on the confirmation of General McDowell as Major-General of Volunteers. Senator Wade sent me the vote, which was as follows:

For confirmation. . . . —22.
Against confirmation. . . . —13.
Absent or Not Voting. . . . —14.

March 17, Monday. W. D. Bickham,[54] of the Cincinnati Commercial, called having just returned from Manassas.

He reports that the stories of Wooden Guns and absence of fortifications are fully sustained by the facts, that the rebels must have been evacuating for weeks; that they left neither a cannon nor a good gun behind them—that we left more property to be wasted and destroyed in our own camps when we made the movement, than we found at Manassas. He says that what was left shows that the rebels have lived well—having molasses, sugar, rice, corn-meal in abundance. They did not leave more than $20,000 worth of property behind them—consisting of clothing, and useless guns and some swords.

April 11, Friday. The House of Representatives, after a long and exciting Session passed the Senate Bill, abolishing Slavery in the District of Columbia, without amendment.

The vote in the Senate was—Yeas: 29
　　　　　　　　　　　　　　Nays: 14
The vote in the House was—Yeas— 92
　　　　　　　　　　　　　　Nays— 38

April 16, Wednesday. The President signed the Emancipation Bill this morning.

May 1, Thursday. This has not been an eventful day, though it has brought information of great events.

Genl. Saxton [55] came to breakfast, and the Rev. Mr. French,[56] just arrived from Port Royal, happened in. We talked over Port Royal matters, inter alia. Mr. F. don't like many things—thinks the Unitarians don't get hold of the work in the right way. The negroes are mostly Baptists, and like emotional religion better than rational, so called. They '[word omitted by copyist] to Jesus,' and cannot understand a religion that is not founded on His Divinity. Many marriages have been 'confirmed' among them. He had laid much stress on the duty of regular marriages between those who have been living together without that sanction. On some plantations, the masters had allowed and encouraged marriages by ministers—on others, little was cared about it. A good deal of cotton had been planted, and more corn. The work of cultivation was going on as well as could be expected. Mr. F. thought Mr. Snydam [57] would make a good Collector. I talked to Gen. S. about the work before him. He said the Secretary of War had authorized him to procure one or two thousand red flannel suits for the blacks, with a view to organization. No arms to be supplied as yet.

Gov Dennison,[58] with Col Milliken [59] and Messrs Donaldson [60] and Butler of Columbus, called. Gov. D. commended Col. M. to me.

To Department and usual morning business—applications for office from Senators, Representatives and others. Promised nothing to nobody. Wilmot [61] most urgent for McKean,[62] but Dunn quite so for his nephew. Col. Milliken came in and related case—read his letters—wrongfully dismissed—my old friend T. C. H. Smith [63] mixed up in it. Endorsed strongly his statement to Secretary of War. R. J. Walker and F. P. Stanton came in with argument in Porter Case,[64] which I took and promised to examine. Saxton and French came in—had seen Secretary of War, and S. had received Instructions—read them and found them nearly same as had been written, omitting reference to my Instructions to Agents of Treasury Department. Went over to War Department about 5 P.M.—Stanton gone to dinner—read despatches. Banks thinks his work done in Shenandoah Valley and wishes to advance. McDowell reports force in front, on authority of deserters from Yorktown—impressed men who had got away and were trying to reach their homes—4 Regiments and some cavalry and artillery under Smith (Gus.)[64] say 3000—abt. 3000 more under [word omitted by copyist]—Jackson coming to join them with, say, 5 to 10,000—Whole force not over, I judge, from 12 to 16,000 and mostly raw and badly armed. Smith's force in large part detailed from Yorktown, where I do not believe the rebels now have 60,000 men—not equal to 40,000 good troops. Strange that McClellan dallies and waits in eternal preparation. Strange that the President does not give McDowell all the disposable force in the region and send him on to

Richmond. Telegram from McD. copies extracts from Richmond papers, giving correspondence between Mayor of N.O. and Com. Farragut. Mayor's letter insolent.[66] Also gives account of fall of Ft. Macon, where rebels were permitted to retire with honors of war,[67] wh. I think wrong.

Home abt. 6 to dinner. Judge Lane [68] dined with me. Knew McClellan when Superintendent of Central R.R. was good Supt. but had no occasion for display of abilities needed now. Knew John Wilson [69] well—unscrupulous in action agt. persons he disliked—sanguine—not always judicious—but capable where work and energy and not much breadth and solidity required.

(Mr Lathrop came in at Dept.—told him he had been appt. Coll. at N.O. and wd. have Instruction as soon as confirmed. Chandler came in and introduced him to Mr L. Asked him to have confn. and Bill extending powers to prevent aid to rebels passed—wh. he promised)

2

General Chase

[MAY 7–JUNE 26, 1862]

NEITHER Lincoln nor Chase enthusiastically approved
McClellan's plan to attack Richmond from the Peninsula.
Intent on his own campaign, the general seemed to ignore
the defenses of Washington, and at the last moment the
worried President held back McDowell's corps of the
Army of the Potomac to protect the capital. Lincoln's
faith in McClellan's strategy was further weakened when
he learned how the Confederate ironclad, the *Virginia*
(formerly the *Merrimac*), on March 8th had decimated
the Federal fleet at Hampton Roads. Though checked by
the timely appearance of the armored Union vessel, the
Monitor, the *Merrimac* still lurked in Norfolk Harbor,
protected by the batteries of Sewell's Point, and she might
emerge at any time to cut Federal communications. Mc-
Clellan's month-long delay before Yorktown and his clam-
orous appeals for reinforcements did little to reassure the
President.

Desiring "to ascertain by personal observation whether
some further vigilance and vigor might not be infused into
the operations of the army and navy," Lincoln decided to
visit Fort Monroe, where the veteran General John E.

Wool, an earnest critic of McClellan, commanded, and
the President invited Stanton and Chase to accompany
him. Chase kept no diary of the expedition, but his letters
to his younger daughter, Janet,[1] provide a day-by-day
record of what the Secretary called "a brilliant week's
campaign of the President."

❧ ❧ ❧

Revenue Steamer 'Miami'
Off Fortress Monroe, May 7, 1862.

My darling Nettie

I write to you from the cabin of the Steamer Miami,
just outside of two steam transports loaded with troops
embarked for a proposed attack on Norfolk.

We came here night-before-last, having left Washington on Monday evening. Our party consisted of the President, Secretary Stanton and General Viele,[2] who had just
returned from Port Royal where he had commanded a
Brigade charged with most important duties in the reduction of Fort Pulaski. Our staunch little Steamer bore us
rapidly and pleasantly down the River until we were some
10 or 15 miles below Alexandria, when the night which
had come on with a drizzling rain became so thick and
dark that the Pilot found himself unable to discern the
right course. We were, therefore, obliged to cast anchor
and wait for a clearer sky. By 3 of Tuesday morning we
were again on our way. We passed Aquia about day, and
found ourselves about noon tossing on the Chesapeake. It
would have amused you to see us take our luncheon. The
President gave it up almost as soon as he began, and declaring himself too uncomfortable to eat, stretched himself
at length on the locker. The rest of us persisted; but the

plates slipped this way and that—the glasses tumbled over and slid and rolled about—and the whole table seemed as topsy-turvy as if some Spiritualist were operating upon it. But we got thro, and then the Secretary of War followed the example of the President and General Viele and I went on deck and chatted.

Between 8 and 9 we reached our destination. Mr. Stanton at once sent a message to General Wool notifying our arrival and after a while the General and a number of his staff came on board. It was now near 10; but after a short conference it was determined that the President, Mr. Stanton, General Wool, and myself with General Viele should visit Commander Goldsborough [3] and talk with him about the condition of things and the things to be done. As it was not easy to get along side the Minnesota in the night on the Revenue Steamer, we took a tug and were soon within hail. As directed in response to our hail, we went to the port side. And there were the narrow steps up the lofty side, with the guiding ropes on either hand hardly visible in the darkness. It seemed to me *very* high and a little fearsome. But etiquette required the President to go first and he went. Etiquette required the Secretary of the Treasury to follow and I followed. We got up safely of course, and when up it did not seem so very much of a getting upstairs after all.

But I must not stop to describe the Minnesota though the noble ship is worth description; nor shall I tell you of the conference except that it related to military and naval movements in connection with the dreaded 'Merrimac.'

The next morning—yesterday—Wednesday—we of the Miami were up pretty early, for it isn't easy somehow to sleep late on ship-board. We were to breakfast at 9 with

General Wool and Mr. Stanton proposed we should visit
the Vanderbilt first. She was already for her encounter
with the Merrimac, enormously strengthened about the
bow with timbers so as to be little else for many feet (say
50) from the prow than a mass of solid timber plated outside with iron. We stood a moment on her wheel-house
and looked down through the immense diameter of her
wheels, the frame-work of which seemed slight and curiously interlaced; but was in fact of the strongest wrought
iron bars and adjusted carefully to the greatest strength.
The weight of one wheel was 100 tons and the diameter
thro which we looked 42 ft. From the Vanderbilt we sailed
round the Monitor and Stevens and then back to the
wharf; but I must omit in this letter the breakfast—the
visit to the Monitor and Stevens—to the Rip Raps—Commander Goldsborough's coming and discussion—the appearance of the Merrimac and disappearance—the Review
—the visit to ruined Hampton—the determination to direct Commander Goldsborough to send the Galena and 2
gunboats up the river—how it was determined to attempt
the reduction of the batteries at Sewalls Point next morning—how we went to the Rip Raps—how the fleet moved
to the attack—how the great guns of the Rip Raps joined
in the fray throwing shot and shell more than 3 miles—
how the Merrimac came down and out—how the Monitor
moved up and quietly waited for her—how the big wooden
ships got out of the way, that the Minnesota and Vanderbilt might have fair sweep at her and run her down—how
she wouldn't come where they could—how she finally retreated to where the Monitor alone could follow her—all
this and much more I must leave untold this morning, for
since I wrote the first half and more of this letter, a night

is past and the sun of the 8th of May has risen splendidly
over Ft Monroe.

Your affectionate Father,
S. P. C.

Head-quarters, Department of Virginia
Ft. Monroe, Va., May 8, 1862.

My darling Nettie

I was obliged to close my letter to you this morning
quite abruptly—with a mere synopsis of events. I will now
give you a little better idea of what took place yesterday.

Yesterday morning we came ashore early. Commander
Goldsborough came at the same time, on a summons from
the President and it was then that the attack on Sewalls
Point Batteries was determined on. After the orders had
been given, the President, Mr. Stanton, and myself went
over to the Rip Raps in a tug to observe its execution. It
was not a great while before the great ships were in motion. The Seminole took the lead, the San Jacinto and the
Dakota and finally the Susquehanna followed, whose Captain, Lardner,[4] was the commanding officer of the vessels
engaged. With these ships were the Monitor and little gun-
boat Stevens, which Commander Stevens presented to the
Treasury Department and which I christened the 'Stevens'
in honor of him.[5] By and by the Seminole reached her
position and a belch of smoke, followed in a few seconds
by a report like distant thunder, announced the beginning
of the cannonade. Then came the guns from the Rip Raps
where we were and soon the Monitor and the Stevens
joined. In a little while the small battery at the extreme
point was silenced, and the cannonade was directed on a
battery inside the point a half-mile or a mile nearer Nor-

folk. While this was going on, a smoke curled up over the woods on Sewell's Point 5 or 6 miles from its termination, and each man, almost, said to the other, 'There comes the Merrimac;' and sure enough it was the Merrimac. But before she made her appearance we had left the Rip Raps and had reached the landing on our way to Head-Quarters. Just as we were going ashore, the Monster came slowly about from behind the Point and all the big wooden vessels began to haul off. The Monitor and Stevens, however, held their ground. The Merrimac still came on slowly and in a little while there was a clear sheet of water between her and the Monitor. Then the great rebel terror paused—then turned back—and having finally attained what she considered a safe position, became stationary again. This was the end of the battle. Its results were on one side nobody and nothing hurt, with a certainty that the battery at the extreme Point was useless to the rebels and the battery on the inside much less strong and much less strongly manned than had been supposed. The results on the rebel side we can't tell but only know that their barracks were burnt by our shells. Another certainty is that the rebel Monster don't *want to* fight and *won't* fight if she can help it, except with more advantage than she is likely to have. Enough for one day.

Steamer Baltimore, May 11, 1862

My darling Nettie.

I believe I closed my last letter to you with an account of the bombardment. That was thought to have shown the inutility of an attempt to land at Sewall's Point while the Merrimac lay watching it; and it at once became a question, what should now be done? Three plans only seemed feasible; to send all the troops that could be spared around to Burnside and let him come on Norfolk from behind—that is, from the South;[6] to send them up James River to aid McClellan; or to seek another landing place out of reach of the Merrimac. In this state of things, I offered to take the Miami, if a tug of less draft and capable, therefore, of getting nearer shore could accompany me, and make an examination, in company with an officer, of the coast East of the Point. Col. Cram [7] offered to go and General Wool said he would accompany us. We started accordingly and being arrived opposite a point which I mark 'a' on the poor draft I send you,[8] sent a boat's crew on shore to find the depth of water. We had already approached within some 500 yds. in the Miami, and the tug had approached within perhaps 100, of the shore. The boats went very near the shore and then pulled off, somewhat to my surprise. But when they returned to the boat the mystery was explained. They had seen an enemy's picket and a soldier standing up and beckoning to his companions to lie close; and they had inferred the existence of an ambush and had pulled off to avoid being fired upon. When the officer of the boat and Colonel Cram came on board, they could still see the picket on horseback, and pointed his position out to me; but I, being near sighted, could not see. It was plain enough that there was no use in landing men to be fired upon and overcome by a superior force, and so the order was given to get under way to return to Ft. Monroe. We had, indeed, accomplished our main purpose, having found the water sufficiently deep to admit of landing without any serious difficulty. But just as we were going away, a white flag was seen waving over the sand-bank on shore, and the

General ordered it to be answered at once, which was
done by fastening a bed-sheet to the flag-line and running
it up. When this was done, several colored people appeared on shore—all women and children. Fearing the
flag and the appearance of the colored people might be a
cover intended to get our people within rifle-shot, I directed two boats to go ashore, with full crews well armed.
They went; and pretty soon I saw Col. Cram talking with
the people on shore, while some of the men were walking
about on the beach. Presently, one boat pulled off towards
the ship, and when she had come quite near, I observed
the colored people going up the sand bank and Colonel
Cram preparing to return with the other boat. It occurred
to me that the poor people might have desired to go to
Ft. Monroe and might have been refused. So I determined
to go ashore myself, and jumping into the returned boat,
was quickly on the beach. The Colonel reported his examination entirely satisfactory, and I found from the colored
people (one of whom, however, turned out to be a white
woman living near by) that none of them wanted to leave
and we all returned to the ship. These women were the
soldiers who had alarmed our folks.

We had made an important discovery—a good and convenient landing place, some 5 or 6 miles from Ft. Monroe,
capable of receiving any Number of troops and communicating with Norfolk by quite passable roads, with a distance by one route of 8 or 9 and by another of 12 or 13
miles.

When I got back to Ft. Monroe I found the President
had been listening to a Pilot and studying a chart and had
become impressed with a conviction that there was a
nearer landing and wished to go and see about it on the

spot. So we started again and soon reached the shore, taking with us a large boat and some 20 armed soldiers from the Rip Raps. The President and Mr. Stanton were on the tug and I on the Miami. The tug was, of course, nearest shore and as soon as she found the water too shoal for her to go farther safely the Rip Raps boat was manned and sent in. Meantime, I had the Miami got ready for action and directed the Captain to go ashore with both boats and all the men they could take fully armed. Before this could be done, however, the other boat had pulled off shore and several horsemen who appeared to be soldiers of the enemy were seen on the beach. I sent to the President to ask if we should fire on them, and he replied negatively. We had again found a good landing, which at the time I supposed to be between 2 and 3 miles nearer Ft. Monroe but which proved to be only ½ to ¾ of a mile nearer.

Returning to Ft. Monroe it was agreed that an advance should at once be made on Norfolk from one of these landings. General Wool preferred the one he had visited and it was selected. It was now night but the preparations proceeded with great activity. 4 Regiments were sent off and orders given for others to follow. Col. Cram went down to make a bridge of boats to the landing, and General Wool asked me to accompany him the next morning.

Next morning (yesterday) I was up early, and we got off as soon as possible. As soon as we reached the place, I took the tug which brought us down and went up the shore to where the Presidents boat had attempted to land the evening before. I found the distance to be only ¾ of a mile and returned to the Miami where I had left the General. He had gone ashore and I at once followed. On shore, I found General Viele with an orderly behind him. He asked if I would like a horse and I said Yes. He thereupon directed his Orderly to dismount and I mounted. I then proposed to ride up where the pickets had been seen the night before. He complied. We found a shed where the pickets had staid and fresh horse-tracks in many places, showing that the enemy had only withdrawn a few hours. Meantime Mr. Stanton had come down and on my return to General Wool asked me to go with the expedition, and I finally determined to do so. Accordingly I asked General Wool for a squad of dragoons and for permission to ride on with General Viele ahead of him. He granted both requests. After going about 5 miles General Viele and myself came up with the rear of the advance (which had preceded us 3 or 4 hours) and soon heard firing of artillery in front. We soon heard that the bridge which we expected to cross was burnt—that the enemy's artillery was posted on the other side—and that Generals Mansfield and Weber were returning. About ½ or ¾ of a mile from the burning bridge we met them, and of course turned back. Returning we met General Wool who determined to leave a guard on that route and take another to it. There was now a good deal of confusion, to remedy which and provide for contingencies, General Wool sent General Mansfield [9] to Newport News to bring forward his Brigade and brigaded the troops with him, assigning General Viele to command of one and General Weber [10] to command of the other. Things now went much better. The cavalry and Major Dodge [11] were in advance. General Wool and staff next and then a body of sharp-shooting skirmishers—then the main body of Viele's brigade—and then Weber's. We stopped everybody from whom we

could obtain information and [it] was not long before we
were informed that the intrenched camp, where we expected the rebels would fight if anywhere, had just been
evacuated and that the barracks were fired. This pleasant
intelligence was soon confirmed by the arrival of Dodge's
dragoons who told us that the cavalry were already within
it.

We kept on and were soon within the work—a very
strong one—defended by many heavy guns of which 21
still remained in position. The troops as they entered gave
cheer after cheer and were immediately formed into line
for the further march, now only two miles, to Norfolk.
General Wool now invited General Viele, General Weber,
and Major Dodge to ride with us in front and so we proceeded until we met a deputation of the city authorities,
who surrendered the city in form. General Wool and myself
entered one carriage with two of the deputation and General Viele another with the others, and so we drove into
town and to the City Hall, where the General completed
his arrangements for taking possession of the City. These
completed, and General Viele being left in charge as Military Governor, General Wool and myself set out on our
return to Ocean View, our landing place, in the carriage
which had brought us to the City Hall; which carriage,
by the way, was that used by the rebel General Huger and
he had, perhaps, been riding in it that very morning.

It was sundown when we left Norfolk—about 10 when
we reached Ocean View—and near to 12 when we
reached Ft. Monroe. The President had been greatly
alarmed for our safety by the report of General Mansfield
as he went by to Newport News; and you can imagine his
delight when we told him Norfolk was ours. Stanton soon

came up to his room and was equally delighted. He fairly
hugged General Wool.

For my part, I was very tired and glad to get to bed.

This morning, as the President had determined to leave
for Washington at 7, I rose at 6 and just before 7 came
into the parlor where Commander Goldsborough aston-
ished and gratified us that the rebels had set fire to the
Merrimac and had blown her up. It was determined that
before leaving, we would go up in the Baltimore, which
was to convey us to Washington, to the point where the
suicide had been performed and above the obstructions in
the channel if possible, so as to be sure of the access to
Norfolk by water which had been defended by the exploded ship. This was done; but the voyage was longer
than we anticipated, taking us up to the wharves of Norfolk, where, in the Elizabeth River, were already lying the
Monitor, the Stevens, the Susquehanna and one or two
other vessels. General Wool and Commander Goldsborough had come up with us on the Baltimore and as soon as
they were transferred to the Susquehanna, our prow was
turned down stream and touching for a moment at the
Fort we kept on our way towards Washington, where we
hope to be at Breakfast tomorrow.

So has ended a brilliant week's campaign of the President, for I think it quite certain that if he had not come
down, it would still have been in possession of the enemy
and the Merrimac as grim and defiant and as much a
terror as ever. The whole coast is now virtually ours. There
is no port which the Monitor and Stevens cannot enter and
take.

It was sad and pleasant to see the Union flag once more
waving over Norfolk and the shipping in the harbor and

to think of the destruction accomplished there a little more than a year ago.

I went to Norfolk last night by land with the army; this morning by water with the navy. My campaign too is over.

～ ～ ～

Chase returned from Fort Monroe reasonably satisfied with the progress of the armies. Not only had Norfolk been taken, but McClellan at last was on the move, and in the bloody battle of Seven Pines (Fair Oaks) on May 31– June 1, Confederate General Joseph E. Johnston was wounded and his army thrown back on the defenses of Richmond. Realizing the extent of McClellan's opportunity, Chase urged that all available men be rushed to his support.

But before the planned concentration could occur, Union forces were thrown on the defensive. While the new Confederate commander, Robert E. Lee, parried McClellan's blows against Richmond, Stonewall Jackson was operating in the Shenandoah Valley, threatening to attack Washington by way of Harpers Ferry. Union forces in the area were badly organized and under divided command. Jackson's precept, "To mystify, mislead and surprise," was completely successful. "By successive blows upon Shields, Milroy, Banks, and Frémont (in the battles of Kernstown, McDowell, Winchester, Cross Keys, and Port Republic) he had the Union authorities mystified as to his movements, caused Northern newspapers to shriek 'Washington is in danger,' and brought about the detachment of McDowell's corps from McClellan's army." [12] Lincoln's plan to trap Jackson's army in the Valley was unsuccessful, for the wily Confederate slipped between two Federal armies and raced to Richmond, where he joined Lee in the Seven Days battles (June 25–July 1), which forced McClellan back to Harrison's Landing on the James.

Though he kept no diary during these weeks, Chase dictated a "Narrative of Operations" on June 26, 1862, which revealed both his active role in the crisis and his high estimate of his own military ability.[13]

∽ ∽ ∽

On Sunday morning, May 11, the President, becoming uneasy on account of his long absence from Washington, determined to return forthwith. The explosion of the Merrimac, however, detained him long enough to go to the spot, ascertain the exact condition of things and return to Ft. Monroe, whence we proceeded immediately towards Washington. On our way up, I remarked on the probability that a small force, say 5000 men, embarked on transports and convoyed by gunboats, might contribute largely to the taking of Richmond, if sent immediately up James River. But nothing was determined on. After our return to Washington I frequently spoke of this matter and urged the sending of General Wool up James River with all his disposable force. It was thought General McClellan could be reinforced more effectually in another direction.

General McDowell was ordered to concentrate his whole corps, including Shields' division, at Fredericksburgh, with a view to march upon Richmond from that point. Shields' [14] division, which had been in the valley of the Shenandoah, was marched across the country and joined McDowell.

On Friday, May 23d., the President and Secretary of

War visited the army at Fredericksburg and returned to Washington on Saturday morning, highly gratified by the condition of the troops and anticipating an imposing and successful advance on the Monday following. On the afternoon of the same Saturday I was sent for to the War Department and found that intelligence had been received of the taking of Front Royal and the annihilation of Kenley's [sic] Regiment on the preceding day.[15] The enemy was reported to have pushed forward to Middletown and cut off the retreat of Banks, supposed to be at Strasburg. An order was immediately dispatched to General Frémont to advance to Harrisonburg, and do all in his power for the relief of Banks. An Order was also sent to General McDowell to detach 20,000—or one-half his force—sending them partly by land to Catlett's station and partly by water to Alexandria and Washington. To expedite these movements, I was directed to proceed immediately to Fredericksburg and confer personally with General Mc-Dowell. I left accordingly the same afternoon, and reached Fredericksburg about 1 o'clock A.M., Sunday. I found that General McDowell had given all the necessary orders for the movements directed by the President. The march began early the next morning, and successive divisions and regiments followed, until, during the course of the day, the whole 20,000 were on their march. I returned to Washington Sunday night accompanied by General Shields, and found the President, with the Secretary of War, Secretary of State, and several Senators and Representatives, at the War Department. By this time intelligence had been received that Banks had retreated early on Saturday morning from Strasburg, reaching Winchester the same night, and that his retreat had been continued through Sunday, and that a portion of his troops had already arrived at Williamsport. General Saxton had been ordered to Harper's-Ferry, and reinforcements had been and were still rapidly being pushed forward to that point.

On Monday, Shields' division arrived at Catlett's Station, and Geary's division,[16] which had been stationed along the line of the Manassas Gap Rail Road, had fallen back to Manassas. Ord's division [17] followed, partly by water and partly by land, and, with Shields, was concentrated within a day or two at Manassas. McDowell came from Fredericksburg at the instance of the President and took command in person, having ordered King's division [18] to advance towards Martinsburg as a supporting column. Shields pushed forward to Front Royal, which place he reached on Friday. McDowell followed, also reaching Front Royal on Saturday. The object of this movement was to cut off the retreat of Jackson through Front Royal.

Meantime Frémont, observing the spirit though not the letter of his Orders, had marched to Moorfield and thence to Wardensville a few miles distant from Strasburg—his directions being to occupy Strasburg and cut off the retreat of Jackson by that road. Unfortunately Frémont did not reach Strasburg until Jackson, defeated by Saxton on Friday in his attack upon Harper's-Ferry, and being apprised no doubt of the movements in his rear, had passed through Strasburg, on his retreat down the valley.

While this combined movement, intended to capture Jackson and his force, was in progress, General McClellan was constantly asking for reinforcements at Richmond. I had no confidence in his ability to handle a great army, but inasmuch as the President was unwilling to give the command to any other General I thought it of great importance that he should be reinforced as far as possible. To this end, in the course of the week, I urged on several occasions that one-half of McCall's division [19] be sent down to form a junction with McClellan's army, and that General Wool, with 10,000 of his force, be sent up from Ft. Monroe and Norfolk by James River, to effect, if possible, the capture of Fort Darling,[20] or at least to cooperate with McClellan, whose lines, I supposed, could be extended from Bottom's Bridge [21] to the James River. These reinforcements were not sent, partly, as I suppose, because the President was unwilling to weaken the advance at Fredericksburg, and partly because he was unwilling to order General Wool, who was at variance with McClellan, to a coöperation which might lead to collision between the Generals and so to unpleasant results.

I also urged that, inasmuch as McDowell's force had been drawn over into and near the Shenandoah Valley, his three divisions—Shields', Ord's and King's—should be massed and ordered forward to Charlottesville and Lynchburg. This movement had been proposed by General Shields, as a movement to be executed from Fredericksburg. General McDowell also had proposed the same. As much reluctance was manifested against undertaking this movement, as had been in respect to the reinforcement of McClellan.

On Friday, June 14, the President determined to send 20,000 men to McClellan. To effect this object, he directed the embarkation of the whole of McCall's division at Fredericksburg and annexed the Department of Virginia, which had been under General Wool, to the command of McClellan. Wool was transferred to Baltimore and Dix [22] to Ft. Monroe, to avoid the apprehended difficulties from placing the Department, while under the command of General Wool, also under the command of McClellan. Most of the drilled troops at Ft. Monroe—of whom there were about 14,000—were sent to McClellan and their places supplied mainly with new levies. Thus, long after I had proposed the reinforcement, the arrangement was made by which they were sent.

On the same day, upon the President expressing his gratification that the reinforcements had been sent to McClellan, I replied to him that his satisfaction would be much increased if he would order McDowell, with his three divisions, strengthened if necessary by portions of Banks and Fremont's commands, on the southward expedition to Charlottesville and Lynchburgh. I endeavored to impress upon him the idea that this movement would be of great importance to McClellan by creating a diversion in his favor and by cutting off the supplies which reached Richmond through Lynchburg, from East Tennessee. I was not successful in impressing the President with the correctness of my views. I suppose that his difficulty arose, partly from a desire to have McDowell in a position from which he could directly reinforce McClellan and partly from apprehension of disagreement between the Major Generals commanding the separate bodies which it might be necessary to combine in the Charlottesville Expedition. This, of course is mere conjecture. What is certain is, that the Expedition was not organized or attempted.

Subsequently (June 24) the President, having become convinced of the necessity of combining these three bodies under one command, created the Army of Virginia, [(]to consist of these three bodies) and placed it under the command of General Pope, who was junior in rank, though of the same grade, as Major Generals Frémont, Banks and McDowell, who were made subject to his orders.

I understood that the object of this consolidation was, to make the movement upon Charlottesville which I had been so anxious to see attempted.

3

The End of Pope

[JULY 21–DECEMBER 10, 1862]

THE FIRST of July saw Union forces in the East disorganized and demoralized. McClellan's Army of the Potomac huddled on the James River under the protection of Federal gunboats. Troops in central and western Virginia were worn ragged by their unsuccessful pursuit of Jackson. Lincoln thought it time for new leaders to take over, and he summoned generals from the West, where Union troops had been more successful. Chase did not know the new commanding general, but Henry Wager Halleck's reputation as "Old Brains" and his equally fictitious responsibility for Federal victories at Pea Ridge, Forts Henry and Donelson, and Corinth gave the Secretary new hope. Even more acceptable was John Pope, named to head the regrouped forces in central Virginia. The swaggering Pope was the last major military leader to confide in Chase, and the Secretary enthusiastically approved both his loudly trumpeted plans to take the offensive and his announced hostility toward slavery.

Pope pushed directly forward into Virginia, against Stonewall Jackson's forces, and the Federals at least held their own at Cedar Mountain (August 9). But when Lee, ignoring McClellan's dispirited army, slipped away from Richmond and joined Jackson, Pope was promptly thrown back toward Manassas. Fighting desperately, Pope appealed for aid. Chase thought McClellan deliberately retarded the departure of his army from the Peninsula and disobeyed his orders to rush reinforcements to Pope. The Union disaster at Second Bull Run (August 29–30) he blamed on McClellan and his clique, and not even Lee's invasion of Maryland could reconcile him to restoring the "Little Napoleon" to supreme command.

Not all Chase's attention could be given to military problems, even when the capital itself seemed threatened. Loans had to be floated and Treasury notes to be issued as usual. Under the new internal revenue act just adopted by Congress, the Secretary of the Treasury had to select assessors and collectors for each of the 186 internal revenue districts. Within nearly every state, rival Republican factions vied for this patronage, and Chase was supposed both to select honest and intelligent men and to effect a delicate balance of political forces.

Within the cabinet itself the political equilibrium was uneasy. The President was gradually shifting toward emancipation as a military necessity, but the reluctance of Montgomery Blair and Seward seemed to hold him back. Northern war governors and antislavery zealots in Congress demanded a cabinet reorganization. Chase's diary shows that, like many other Radical Republican leaders, he tended to hold the Secretary of State responsible both for the delay in emancipation and for the reinstatement of McClellan.

∾ ∾ ∾

July 21, 1862, Monday. Early this morning, Count Gurowski [1] called and told me that, yesterday, at a great
dinner at Mr. Tassara's [2]—the only Americans present
being Gov. Seward and Senator Carlisle [3]—Gov. Seward
remarked that he had lately begun to realize the value of
a CROMWELL, and to appreciate the *Coup d'etat* : and that
he wished we had had a Cromwell or a Coup d'etat for
our Congress. The Count said that the diplomats present
were very much disgusted, and that the language of Gov.
Seward injured the Administration much in the estima-
tion of all intelligent foreigners.

After the Count left, I received a notice to attend a
Cabinet meeting, at 10 o'clock. It has been so long since
any consultation has been held that it struck me as a
novelty.

I went at the appointed hour, and found that the President had been profoundly concerned at the present aspect
of affairs, and had determined to take some definitive
steps in respect to military action and slavery. He had
prepared several Orders, the first of which contemplated
authority to Commanders to subsist their troops in the
hostile territory—the second, authority to employ negroes
as laborers—the third requiring that both in the case of
property taken and of negroes employed, accounts should
be kept with such degrees of certainty as would enable
compensation to be made in proper cases—another provided for the colonization of negroes in some tropical
country.

A good deal of discussion took place upon these points.
The first Order was universally approved. The second was
approved entirely; and the third, by all except myself. I
doubted the expediency of attempting to keep accounts

for the benefit of the inhabitants of rebel States. The Colonization project was not much discussed.

The Secretary of War presented some letters from Genl. Hunter, in which he advised the Department that the withdrawal of a large proportion of his troops to reinforce Genl. McClellan, rendered it highly important that he should be immediately authorized to enlist all loyal persons without reference to complection. Messrs. Stanton, Seward and myself, expressed ourselves in favor of this plan, and no one expressed himself against it. (Mr. Blair was not present.) The President was not prepared to decide the question, but expressed himself as averse to arming negroes. The whole matter was postponed until tomorrow.

After the meeting of the Cabinet, Messrs. Speed,[4] Holloway and Casey [5]—the first, a distinguished lawyer of Louisville, a State Senator, and now Postmaster of the city; the second, a large slaveholder in South-western Kentucky; the third, M.C. from the South-western District—called at the Department. Messrs. Speed and Casey were decided in favor of the most decided measures in respect to Slavery and the employment of negroes in whatever capacity they were fitted for. Messrs. Speed and Casey assured me that Mr Holloway (though a large slaveholder) was in favor of every measure necessary for success and that he held no sacrifice too great to insure it. He would cheerfully give up slavery if it became necessary or important.

Mr. Casey, Mr. Horton [6] and Genl. Pope dined with me. Mr. Horton condemned severely the conduct of the campaign on the Peninsula and the misrepresentations made to the public in regard to it. Genl Pope expressed

himself freely and decidedly in favor of the most vigorous
measures in the prosecution of the war. He believed that,
in consequence of the rebellion, Slavery must perish, and
with him it was only a question of prudence as to the
means to be employed to weaken it. He was in favor of
using every instrument which could be brought to bear
against the enemy; and while he did not speak in favor of
a general arming of the slaves as soldiers, he advocated
their use as laborers, in the defence of fortifications and in
any way in which their services could be made useful without impairing the general tone of the service. He said he
was now waiting, by request of the President, the arrival
of Genl. Halleck; and he regarded it as necessary for the
safety and success of his operations that there should be a
change in the command of the Army of the Potomac. He
believed that Genl. McClellan's incompetency and indisposition to active movements were so great, that if, in his
operations, he should need assistance, he could not expect
it from him. He had urged upon the President the importance of superseding Genl. McClellan before the arrival of
Halleck, representing the delicacy of Halleck's future position, and the importance of having the field clear for him
when he assumed the general command. The President,
however, had only promised that he (Genl. Pope) should
be present at his interview with Genl Halleck, when he
would give the latter his opinion of McClellan.

July 22, Tuesday. This morning, I called on the President with a letter received some time since from Col. Key,
in which he stated that he had reason to believe that if
Genl. McClellan found he could not otherwise sustain himself in Virginia, he would declare the liberation of the
slaves; and that the President would not dare to interfere

with the Order. I urged upon the President the importance of an immediate change in the command of the
Army of the Potomac, representing the necessity of having
a General in that command who would cordially and
efficiently coöperate with the movements of Pope and
others; and urging a change before the arrival of Genl.
Halleck, in view of the extreme delicacy of his position in
this respect, Genl. McClellan being his senior Major-
General. I said that I did not regard Genl. McClellan as
loyal to the Administration, although I did not question
his general loyalty to the country.

I also urged Genl. McClellan's removal upon financial
grounds. I told him that, if such a change in the command
was made as would insure action to the army and give it
power in the ratio of its strength, and if such measures
were adopted in respect to slavery as would inspire the
country with confidence that no measure would be left
untried which promised a speedy and successful result, I
would insure that, within ten days, the Bonds of the U.S.—
except the 5-20s—would be so far above par that conver-
sions into the latter stock would take place rapidly and
furnish the necessary means for carrying on the Government.[7] If this was not done, it seemed to me impossible to
meet necessary expenses. Already there were $10,000,000
of unpaid Requisitions, and this amount must constantly
increase.

The President came to no conclusion, but said he would
confer with Gen. Halleck on all these matters. I left him,
promising to return to Cabinet, when the subject of the
Orders discussed yesterday would be resumed.

Went to Cabinet at the appointed hour. It was unanimously agreed that the Order in respect to Colonization

should be dropped; and the others were adopted unanimously, except that I wished North Carolina included among the States named in the first order.

The question of arming slaves was then brought up and I advocated it warmly. The President was unwilling to adopt this measure, but proposed to issue a Proclamation, on the basis of the Confiscation Bill, calling upon the States to return to their allegiance—warning the rebels the provisions of the Act would have full force at the expiration of sixty days—adding, on his own part, a declaration of his intention to renew, at the next session of Congress, his recommendation of compensation to States adopting the gradual abolishment of slavery—and proclaiming the emancipation of all slaves within States remaining in insurrection on the first of January, 1863.[8]

I said that I should give to such a measure my cordial support, but I should prefer that no new expression on the subject of compensation should be made, and I thought that the measure of Emancipation could be much better and more quietly accomplished by allowing Generals to organize and arm the slaves (thus avoiding depredation and massacre on the one hand, and support to the insurrection on the other) and by directing the Commanders of Departments to proclaim emancipation within their Districts as soon as practicable; but I regarded this as so much better than inaction on the subject, that I should give it my entire support.

The President determined to publish the first three Orders forthwith, and to leave the other for some further consideration. The impression left upon my mind by the whole discussion was, that while the President thought that the organization, equipment and arming of negroes, like other soldiers, would be productive of more evil than good, he was not unwilling that Commanders should, at their discretion, arm, for purely defensive purposes, slaves coming within their lines.

Mr. Stanton brought forward a proposition to draft 50,000 men.[9] Mr. Seward proposed that the number should be 100,000. The President directed that, whatever number were drafted, should be a part of the 300,000 already called for. No decision was reached, however.

July 25, Friday. No Cabinet to-day. Went to War Department in the morning, where I found the President and Stanton. We talked about the necessity of clearing the Mississippi, and Stanton again urged sending Mitchell.[10] The President said he would see him. Stanton sent for him at Willards [Hotel], and sent him to the President.

In the evening I called for Mitchell to ride, with H. Walbridge.[11] Asked him the result. He said the President had asked him with what force he could take Vicksburgh and clear the river, and, with the black population on its banks, hold it open below Memphis; and had bid him consider. He had replied that, with his own division and Curtis'[12] army, he could do it he thought, but he would consider and reply.

I told him now was the time to do great things.

July 26, Saturday. Sent order to close and encrape the Department, in respect to ex-President [Martin] Van Buren, just deceased.

The President came in, to talk about the controversy between the Postmaster General and 6th Auditor,[13] in regard to rooms. Agreed to see the Attorney General, for whom I afterwards sent. The Attorney General had not heard of Rabe's[14] removal, of which I spoke to him, and I directed

Mr. Harrington to telegraph Rabe that the removal had been made without my knowledge or that of the Attorney-General.

Genl Pope came in about 1 P.M., and went to Photographer's with me and Col. Welch.[15] He talked as if McClellan might be retained in command and retrieve himself by advancing on Richmond, which was now quite feasible there being but few troops on the North side of the James. I replied that no such advance would be made; or, if made and successful, would only restore undeserved confidence and prepare future calamities.

Mitchell called. He had seen the President, who had postponed his decision until he could consult Halleck. Mitchell had all his orders ready for rapid movement. Told him his only course was to wait and see.

Talked with Pope about Mitchell, who inclined to think him visionary. I asked him to get acquainted with him which he promised.

Wrote Mrs. E. in reply to letter received from her.

July 27, Sunday. A telegram from Genl. Morgan [16] this morning apprised me of his resignation, and of his wish that I would secure its prompt acceptance. I went, therefore, to the War Department, wishing to oblige him, and also to secure Garfield's [17] appointment in his place. Mr. Stanton was not in, but saw Watson.

Talked with Watson [18] about the state of things. He mentioned two conversations with McClellan in November of last year, in both of which Watson expressed the opinion that the rebels were in earnest—that peace, through any arrangement with them, was not to be hoped for—and that it would be necessary to prosecute the war, even to the point of subjugation, if we meant to maintain the territorial integrity of the country. McClellan differed. He thought we ought to avoid harshness and violence— that we should conduct the war so as to avoid offence as far as possible;—and said that if he thought as Watson did, he should feel obliged to lay down his arms.

It was during the same month that he told me of his plan for a rapid advance on Richmond, and gave me the assurance that he would take it by the middle of February; which induced me to assure the capitalists in New-York that they could rely on his activity, vigor and success.

From the War Department I went to the President's, to whom I spoke of the resignation of Morgan and of substituting Garfield, which seemed to please him. Spoke also of the financial importance of getting rid of McClellan; and expressed the hope that Halleck would approve his project of sending Mitchell to the Mississippi. On these points he said nothing. I then spoke of Jones,[19] the Sculptor, and of the fitness of giving him some Consulate in Italy, which he liked the idea of. He read me a statement (very good) which he was preparing in reply to a letter from [Thomas J. Durant] in New-Orleans, forwarded by Bullitt.[20]

After some other talk and reminding him of the importance of a talk between me and Halleck about finances as affected by the war (by the way, he told me he desired Halleck to come and see me last Saturday, but he did not come) I returned home. Was too late for church. Read various books—among others, Whitfield's [21] life. What a worker!

Spent evening with Katie and Nettie, and read H. W. Beecher's [22] last sermon in the Independent.

Not a caller all day. O si sic omnes dies!

Aug. 1, Friday. No events of much importance to-day.
—A cabinet meeting was held and a good deal of talk took
place, but no results.—Blair sent me his paper on Colonization to which he referred in our long talk of yesterday.—
A nice letter from my friend Mrs. Eastman.—Spent a few
moments at the War Department—telegram came that
the enemy has been shelling McClellan's position from
Point Coggin.[23]—Wrote to Genl. Pope and Genl. Butler,
touching, in both letters, the Slavery question.[24]—Called
on Genl. Halleck in the evening, and talked a good while
with him. Judged it prudent not to say much of the war
He spoke of Buell [25] as slow but safe; of Grant,[26] as a good
general and brave in battle, but careless of his command.
Of Thomas,[27] he spoke very highly.

Aug. 2, Saturday. At Department all day—went neither
to the President's nor the War Department.

Genl Shields called and talked over movement up the
Shenandoah. He told me that when he received peremptory orders to return, he had held communication with
Frémont and Jackson's capture was certain. I told him of
my urgency that McDowell should be ordered forward
with his entire command from Warrenton per [28] Front
Royal, to Charlottesville and Lynchburg; that the President was not ready to act; that McDowell himself was
apparently disinclined, preferring concentration at Manassas and then advance to Richmond. Plain enough now,
he said, that this was the true movement. He had himself
telegraphed McDowell that Jackson would be Patterson-
ized [29] by recall of troops from pursuit. The troops were,
nevertheless, recalled; and, by peremptory order from the
President himself, those of Shields were directed to return

to Manassas and those of Frémont to resume position as a corps of observation.

Here was a terrible mistake. It would have been easy to take Charlottesville and Lynchburgh—very easy; the capture of Jackson, though not at the time seen at Washington to be practicable, was, nevertheless, within easy possibility; his defeat and the dispersion of his force certain. Our troops were called off when they were just upon him. The course of the whole movement was changed, for no reason that I could see. Charlottesville and Lynchburgh were saved to the enemy, with their stores and the Rail Roads on which they are situated, forming the great East and West communication of the rebels. A wide door for Jackson to Richmond was opened—the very door through which, a little later, he passed; fell, in coöperation with the rebel army at Richmond, on McClellan's right, left unsupported as if to invite disaster; defeated it; and then, with the same army, pursued the Union main body to the James. Sad! sad! yet nobody seems to heed. Genl. Shields and I talked this all over, deploring the strange fatality which seemed to preside over the whole transaction. He dined with us; and, after dinner, rode out with brother Edward [30] and Nettie.

In the evening, several callers came in. Beebe,[31] from Ravenna, a faithful friend—John R. French [32]—Smith Homans [33]—Chas. Selden—and some others. Selden says that at Cincinnati, old Mr. Molitor [34] and Revd. Edw. Purcell [35] spoke very kindly of me.

Aug. 3, Sunday. Genl. Shields came to breakfast and to visit the Ohio men of his command in the Cliftburne Hospital. He told me he desired greatly to have a command of 5000 men, and be allowed to dash as he could, breaking the lines and communications of the enemy. My daughters went with him to the Hospital.

Soon after they left, I received a summons to a Cabinet Meeting. The President spoke of the Treaty said to have been formed between the Cherokees and Confederates, and suggested the expediency of organizing a force of whites and blacks, in separate Regiments, to invade and take possession of their country. Statistics of the Indians were sent for, from which it appeared that the whole fighting force of the Cherokees could hardly exceed 2500 men. Mr. Usher,[36] Assistant Secretary of the Interior was not in favor of the expedition. He thought it better to deal indulgently with deluded Indians, and make their deluders feel the weight of the Federal authority. Most, on the whole, seemed to concur with him.

Mr. Usher mentioned a report that the Louisville Democrat [37] had come out openly for disunion, saying that it was now manifest that the Government was in the hands of the Abolitionists. The President said, this was equivalent to a declaration of hostility by the entire Douglas Party of Kentucky, and manifested much uneasiness.

There was a good deal of conversation on the connection of the Slavery question with the rebellion. I expressed my conviction for the tenth or twentieth time, that the time for the suppression of the rebellion without interference with slavery had long passed; that it was possible, probably, at the outset, by striking the insurrectionists wherever found, strongly and decisively; but we had elected to act on the principles of a civil war, in which [38] the whole population of every seceding State was engaged against the Federal Government, instead of treating the

active secessionists as insurgents and exerting our utmost
energies for their arrest and punishment;—that the bitter-
nesses of the conflict had now substantially united the
white population of the rebel States against us;—that the
loyal whites remaining, if they would not prefer the Union
without Slavery, certainly would not prefer Slavery to the
Union; that the blacks were really the only loyal population worth counting and that, in the Gulf States at least,
their right to Freedom ought to be at once recognized,
while, in the Border States, the President's plan of Emancipation might be made the basis of the necessary measures
for their ultimate enfranchisement;—that the practical.
mode of effecting this seemed to me quite simple;—that
the President had already spoken of the importance of
making of the freed blacks on the Mississippi, below Tennessee, a safeguard to the navigation of the river;—that
Mitchell, with a few thousand soldiers, could take Vicksburgh;—assure the blacks freedom on condition of loyalty; organize the best of them in companies, regiments
&c., and provide, as far as practicable, for the cultivation
of the plantations by the rest;—that Butler should signify
to the slaveholders of Louisiana that they must recognize
the freedom of their workpeople by paying them wages;
—and that Hunter should do the same thing in South-
Carolina.

Mr. Seward expressed himself as in favor of any measures likely to accomplish the results I contemplated, which
could be carried into effect without Proclamations; and
the President said he was pretty well cured of objections
to any measure except want of adaptedness to put down
the rebellion; but did not seem satisfied that the time had
come for the adoption of such a plan as I proposed.

There was also a good deal of conversation concerning the merits of Generals. I objected pretty decidedly to the policy of selecting nearly all the highest officers from among men hostile to the Administration and continuing them in office after they had proved themselves incompetent, or at least not specially competent, and referred to the needless defeat of McClellan and the slowness of Buell. Seward asked what I would do. I replied, Remove the men who failed to accomplish results, and put abler and more active men in their places. He wished to know whom I would prefer to Buell. I answered that if I was President, or Secretary of War authorized to act by the President, I would confer with the General in Chief; require him to name to me the best officers he knew of; talk the matter over with him; get all the light I could; and then designate my man.

As much as anything, the clearing of the Mississippi by the capture of Vicksburgh was discussed. I reminded the President that after the evacuation of Corinth it would have been an easy matter to send down a few thousand men and complete our possession of the river; and of his own plan of putting Gen. Mitchell at the head of his own division and Curtis' army, and sending him to take Vicksburgh, almost adopted more than two weeks ago. Mr. Usher suggested that since Genl. Halleck had decided against this plan, on the ground that Mitchell's division could not be spared from Buell's command, and Curtis' army was needed to prevent a foray from Arkansas into Missouri, it might be well to raise a special force by volunteering for this one object, of taking Vicksburgh, opening the Mississippi and keeping it open. I heartily seconded this idea and it was a good deal talked over.

At length, the President determined to send for Genl. Halleck and have the matter discussed with him. The General came, and the matter was fully stated to him both by Gov Seward and myself. He did not absolutely reject the idea, but thought the object could be better accomplished by hastening the new levies; putting the new troops in the positions now occupied by the old regiments; and setting these last to the work of opening the Mississippi. He expressed the strongest convictions as to the importance of the work, and his desire to see it accomplished at the earliest possible period. At this moment, however, the necessary troops could not be spared for the purpose Taking into consideration the delay incident to raising a special force, equal, perhaps, to that demanded by Gen. Halleck's plan, and the other disadvantages it was thought best to drop the idea.

In connection with this subject, Genl Halleck spoke of the distribution of troops in the West. He said that Hardee [39] had broken up his camp south of Corinth, and transferred his army to Chattanooga, where he now had probably 40 or 50,000 men; that Price [40] had attempted to cross the river into Arkansas, but had as yet failed to accomplish his purpose; that a considerable force was, however, advancing northward into Missouri; and that he had sent a division and brigade, say 7000 men, to Curtis (making his whole force about 17,000) and instructed him to prevent the invasion of Missouri; that he had also detached from Grant about 15,000 men, say three divisions, to take positions at Decatur to support Buell if necessary; that Grant had still under his command about 43,000, of whom 7000 under Jackson [41] had been ordered to the [word omitted by copyist] to watch Price; that

Buell had 60,000, with which force he was approaching Chattanooga. These numbers give the whole force in the West, exclusive of troops occupying St. Louis and various Posts and Camps north of the Ohio;—Buell, 60,000 —Grant, including detachments, except Curtis', 58,000— Curtis 17,000—in all, 135,000 men, excellent troops. He stated McClellan's army at present and fit for duty at 88,000; absent on leave 33,000; absent without leave, 3,000; present but sick, 16,000—in all, say, 140,000. Another statement makes the number fit for duty 91,000, and the total 143,000.

The President read a communication from Genl. H. proposing that 200,000 militia should be drafted for 9 months, and that the 300,000 men to fill old and form new regiments should be obtained without delay; and to prevent the evil of hasty and improper appointments and promotions, that a Board of Officers should be organized, to which all proposed action of that sort should be referred. The General condemned, respectfully but as decidedly, the inconsideration which has hitherto marked the action of the Government in this respect, and stated one case where a Colonel had been tried and convicted of gross misconduct and was on the point of being dismissed, when he came on to Washington and returned with a Brigadier's Commission!

The General commanded my sincere respect by the great intelligence and manliness he displayed, and excited great hopes by his obvious purpose to allow no lagging and by his evident mastery of the business he has taken in hand. I cannot agree with him as to the expediency of retaining McClellan and Buell in their important commands; and I was sorry to hear him say, in reply to a question of the President, as to what use could be made of the black population of the borders of the Mississippi, 'I confess, I do not think much of the negro.'

Neither Mr. Stanton nor Mr. Blair were present at the meeting to-day.

When the Cabinet Council broke up, I proposed to Mr. Usher, who made a most favorable impression on me, to ride home in my carriage; but he was called back by the President, and I, finding my carriage had not come, rode home with Mr. Bates.

Aug. 6, Wednesday. Nothing much thought of to-day except the great War Meeting—which was immense.[42] None of the Cabinet there except myself and Mr. Bates. The President, after Mr. Chittenden had finished, said to me (the people clamoring for him) 'Well! Hadn't I better say a few words and get rid of myself?' Hardly waiting for an answer, he advanced at once to the stand. He was received with most uproarious enthusiasm. His frank, genial, generous face and direct simplicity of bearing, took all hearts. His speech is in all the prints, and evinces his usual originality and sagacity.

Prof. Read and his son, Capt. Read,[43] and Assistant-Secretary Usher dined with me. Mr. Bates and Dr. Schmidt [44] came from meeting with me and stopped at my house. After Mr. Bates went, I played chess with the Doctor, who was far my overmatch—he beating me with ease two or three times, while I only, by accident, beat him once

Aug. 7, Thursday. Very little accomplished as yet, though much, I hope, in the train of accomplishment. Engaged nearly all day on selections for recommendation of Collectors and Assessors. Prepared letter to President, con-

taining names &c. of candidates, with my recommendations, for Connecticut; made up in very small part on my
own personal Knowledge, but mainly on the representations and advice—sometimes agreeing and sometimes not
—of the Senators, Representatives, State officers and Secretary Welles.

In the evening, went to War Department, where I saw
Curtis' dispatch from Helena, urging the clearing out of
the Mississippi before attempting inland operations; and
McClellan's, announcing advance of the enemy on Mal-
vern Hill, and his purpose to order the retirement of
Hooker's Division; and those of various Governors announcing progress of volunteering and preparations for
drafting—on the whole, very encouraging and denoting
the greatest possible earnestness and determination among
the people.

Home. Taylor, Davis and Hopper (all Clerks) called.
—Wrote my friend E. and sent some pencil scribblings.—
Mr. Gest called, but not able to see him.

Aug. 8, Friday. Sent letter and scrap to my friend E.,
and sundry other letters to sundry people—particularly
Gen. Pope's recommendation of young Perkins, with my
heartiest endorsement, to Gov. Tod. Also sent Gen. Pope,
by Maj. Johnson, some photographs of himself and Col.
Welch, taken by the Treasury artist before he went to the
field.

Attended Cabinet Meeting. Autograph letter from
Queen Victoria announcing marriage of Princess Alice.[45]
—Seward gave account of Order prepared by Gen. Hal-
leck, Secretary Stanton and himself, forbidding changes of
domicil and granting of passports, until after the draft.—
Nothing proposed and nothing done of any moment.

Directed Connecticut Abstract and my letter of recommendation to be sent to President.

Aug. 15, Friday. p. and r. un peu de Marius.[46] Saw in *'Republican'* account of interview invited by President with colored people, and his talk to them on Colonization.[47] How much better would be a manly protest against prejudice against color!—and a wise effort to give freemen homes in America! A Military Order, emancipating at least the slaves of South-Carolina, Georgia and the Gulf States, would do more to terminate the war and ensure an early restoration of solid peace and prosperity than anything else that can be devised.

Commissioner Boutwell[48] breakfasted with me. After breakfast took up tax appointments in Indiana and Ohio, and arranged both substantially to my satisfaction, and, I hope, of all concerned.—President sent for me about the Connecticut appointments. Found there Collector Babcock,[49] State Senator Pratt (or Platt)[50] and Secy. Welles. Arranged the business. The State Senator got a Mr. Wright,[51] of Middlesex, with Mr. Welles' consent, vice Cowles.—Mr. Dix,[52] by general consent, was substituted for Hammond.[53]—Hollister[54] was agreed to in place of [Rufus L.] Matherson whom Burnham[55] recommended. —Howard[56] was retained at Hartford. The President said he felt much relieved. Returned to Department and instantly engaged on other Tax appointments.

No Cabinet to-day. Went to War Department. Stanton said Halleck had sent Burnside to James River, to act as second in command—or as adviser of McClellan, in reality to control him. He thought the experiment would fail, and wished I would go and see Halleck. Went. Asked about the mission of Burnside. Halleck said he could not disclose it as it was uncertain what it would really turn out to be. Asked him what was the hostile force at Richmond? He thought 75,000 to 80,000 men—Before Pope? About 60,-000—Whole army in Virginia? About 150,000. I thought it not possible, unless Western force was much reduced. He thought a levy en masse had been made, and that it was possible for the enemy to bring 600,000 to 700,000 into the field. I thought the whole number could not at this time exceed 300,000 to 350,000; of which at least 180,000 to 230,000 were in the West, South-West and South-East.—I enquired about East Tennessee and the Mississippi River, but got no satisfactory information on either point. He said, however, that 15,000 men had been sent from Decatur to reinforce Buell, and 15,000 from Grant to Decatur; and that Curtis was needed to prevent further inroads into Missouri. The whole interview was very unsatisfactory, though the General was very civil— Left with him Memoranda in behalf of Col. Carrington.[57]

The papers show that the rebels mean to execute their threat of treating Pope's officers and soldiers as felons, and not as prisoners of war.[58] This cannot be permitted without shameful disgrace. When will the Administration awake to its duty.

Rode out with Parsons.[59]—Judge Harris called at night when Boutwell and I were engaged on Tax appointments. Invited him to breakfast in the morning.

Aug. 16, Saturday. Nothing in public affairs of special note to-day. New regiments begin to arrive, but what reason to hope more from new levies than old? None, that I see, except Genl. Halleck;—if he fails, all fails. Pope telegraphs that his whole force is as near the Rapidan as the nature of the country will permit, and that he is pushing strong reconnoissances beyond.—Grant telegraphs that 15,000 men have gone to Decatur to replace 15,000 sent to reinforce Buell—that he is now weak and may be attacked, though there is no indication yet of more than feints towards Missouri.—Nothing from Burnside or McClellan.

Sent Katie $150 and Varnum,[60] rent, $375.

Mr. Harrington brought in the Postage Currency.[61] I directed that it should be received as furnished by the P. O. department—i.e. perforated instead of clipped, perforation being considered partial safeguard against counterfeiting.

Judge Roselius,[62] Dr. Cottman [63] and Mr. C. Bullitt, of New-Orleans, dined with me. Also, Messrs. Usher, Assistant Secretary of the Interior, Maj. [Thomas L.] Smith, First Auditor, [T. W.] Meline, Clerk in Treasury Department, Col. R. C. Parsons; Reverdy Johnson [64] and Col. Seaton.[65] Sumner came in after dinner. Retired when he went away.

Aug. 17, Sunday. At home all day, except when at church.

Aug. 18, Monday. Busy, except when interrupted by callers, with list of Collectors and Assessors. Saw Chandler and Gov. Blair [66] at President's, and closed Michigan appointments. President insisted on Stanley,[67] to save Trowbridge's [68] feelings, instead of Mills,[69] whom I recommended as best man; and Chandler and Blair concurred —none of us, however, knowing Stanley.

Thurlow Weed [70] dined with me. Parsons was at home, but had dined, and went away. After dinner, left Weed at Willard's, where I went to call on Colonels Corcoran and Wilcox,[71] returned yesterday from their long captivity in Richmond. They had gone to dine at the President's; and

I went to Mr. Cutts' [72] and spent an hour with Mr. C. and Mrs. D.[73]

Aug. 19, Tuesday. Col. Corcoran and Mr. Mellen breakfasted with me. Col. C. gave interesting particulars of rebeldom, and thinks their force larger than I have supposed. He says, however, that their rolling-stock and roads are in such bad order that no more than 300 can be moved at a time.

R. G. Corwin,[74] J. G. Gest and Rep. Steele [75] called—all about Collectorships. Went to Department, and sent Ohio appointments to the President.

Went to Cabinet. President uneasy about Pope. He sent to War Department for telegrams. There was one from Pope, at Culpepper [*sic*], retiring across Rappahannock, while the force of the enemy was beyond the Rapidan at Gordonsville; one from Burnside, at Falmouth, saying that the first division of the Army of the Potomac will reach Aquia this evening. Nothing more of immediate importance.—Troops coming in to-day—11,000 already arrived. Money wanted for Bounties.

Returning to Department, telegraphed Cisco to negotiate three or four millions at rate not more than one per cent below market. Stock telegram states sales to-day at $5\frac{3}{8}$ to $5\frac{1}{2}$.

Closed Indiana appointments. Signed letter transmitting Pennsylvania recommendations to President. Spent much time with Weed over New-York appointments. Ely [76] called, and I advised him to come tomorrow. Thomas Brown [77] called and gave interesting personal history.

Dined, at 7, with Messrs. Roselius, Cottman and Bullitt —only guests, Col. Seaton, Reverdy Johnson and myself.— Went to War Department. Met Stanton in the hall, and

took him in my carriage to his house. He was much dissatisfied with the President's lack of decision, especially as
to McClellan. Thinks Burnside too partial to McClellan
to be safe.

Home. Read a little.

Aug. 29, Friday. The Secretary of War called on me in
reference to Genl. McClellan. He has long believed, and
so have I, that Genl. McClellan ought not to be trusted
with the command of any army of the Union; and the
events of the last few days have greatly strengthened our
judgment.—We called on Judge Bates, who was not at
home.—Called on Genl. Halleck, and remonstrated
against Gen. McClellan commanding.—Secy. wrote and
presented to Genl. H. a call for a report touching McC's
disobedience of orders and consequent delay of support
to Army of Va. Genl. H. promised answer tomorrow
morning.

Aug. 30, Saturday. Judge Bates called, and we conversed in regard to Genl. McClellan—he concurring in
our judgment. Afterwards I went to the War Department
where Watson showed me a paper expressing it.[78] I suggested modifications. Afterwards saw Stanton. He approved the modifications, and we both signed the paper.
I then took it to Secy. Welles, who concurred in judgment
but thought the paper not exactly right and did not sign
it. Returned the paper to Stanton.

Promised report from Genl. Halleck was not made.

Aug. 31, Sunday. Much busied at Department to-day,
although it is Sunday; and spent much time with the
President, endeavoring to close appointments under Tax
Law.

David Dudley Field [79] called and said we had sustained

a serious defeat yesterday, and that the Secretary of War wished to see me. Went to the Department and found that Gen. Pope had, in fact, been defeated partially, and had fallen back to Centreville. Fitz John Porter [80] was not in the battle, nor was Franklin or Sumner,[81] with whose corps the result would have probably been very different. Little fighting to-day.—Clerks went out to battlefield as nurses, Mr. Harrington with them.

Sept. 1, Monday. This has been an anxious day. An Order appears declaring command of his corps in Burnside; of that portion of the Army of the Potomac not sent forward to Pope, in McClellan; of the Army of Virginia and all forces temporarily attached, in Pope; of the whole, in Halleck.[82] Reports from Pope's Army state that its losses are heavy, but in good spirits—confirm that neither Franklin nor Sumner arrived,—and that McClellan failed to send forward ammunition.

On suggestion of Judge Bates, the remonstrance against McClellan, which had been previously signed by Smith,[83] was modified; and, having been further slightly altered on my suggestion, was signed by Stanton, Bates and myself, and afterwards by Smith. Welles declined to sign it, on the grounds that it might seem unfriendly to the President—though this was the exact reverse of its intent. He said he agreed in opinion and was willing to express it, personally. This determined us to await the Cabinet Meeting tomorrow.

Meantime, McClellan came up on invitation of Halleck, and held personal conference with him and the President. Soon after, a rumor pervaded the town that McClellan was to resume his full command. Col. Key called at my house and told me that he supposed such was the fact.

Sept. 2, Tuesday. Cabinet met, but neither the President nor Secretary of War were present. Some conversation took place concerning Generals. Mr. F. W. Seward [84] (the Secretary of State being out of town) said nothing. All others agreed that we needed a change in Commander of the Army. Mr. Blair referred to the report [support?] he had constantly given McClellan, but confessed that he now thought he could not wisely be trusted with the chief command. Mr. Bates was very decided against his competency, and Mr. Smith equally so. Mr. Welles was of the same judgment, though less positive in expression.

After some time, while the talk was going on, the President came in, saying that not seeing much for a Cabinet Meeting to-day, he had been talking at the Department and Head Quarters about the War. The Secretary of War came in. In answer to some inquiry, the fact was stated, by the President or the Secretary, that McClellan had been placed in command of the forces to defend the Capital—or rather, to use the President's own words, he 'had set him to putting these troops into the fortifications about Washington,' believing that he could do that thing better than any other man. I remarked that this could be done equally well by the Engineer who constructed the Forts; and that putting Genl. McClellan in command for this purpose was equivalent to making him second in command of the entire army. The Secretary of War said that no one was now responsible for the defense of the Capital; —that the Order to McClellan was given by the President direct to McClellan, and that Genl. Halleck considered himself relieved from responsibility, although he acquiesced, and approved the Order;—that McClellan could now shield himself, should anything go wrong, under Hal-

leck, while Halleck could and would disclaim all responsibility for the Order given. The President thought Gen.
Halleck as much responsible as before, and repeated that
the whole scope of the Order was, simply to direct Mc-
Clellan to put the troops into the fortifications and command them for the defence of Washington. I remarked
that this seemed to me equivalent to making him Commander in Chief for the time being, and that I thought it
would prove very difficult to make any substitution hereafter, for active operations;—that I had no feeling whatever against Genl. McClellan;—that he came to the command with my most cordial approbation and support;—
that until I became satisfied that his delays would greatly
injure our cause, he possessed my full confidence;—that,
after I had felt myself compelled to withhold that confidence, I had (since the President, notwithstanding my
opinion that he should, refrained from putting another in
command) given him all possible support in every way,
raising means and urging reinforcements;—that his experience as a military commander had been little else
than a series of failures;—and that his omission to urge
troops forward to the battles of Friday and Saturday,
evinced a spirit which rendered him unworthy of trust,
and that I could not but feel that giving the command to
him was equivalent to giving Washington to the rebels.
This and more I said. Other members of the Cabinet expressed a general concurrence, but in no very energetic
terms. (Mr. Blair must be excepted, but he did not
dissent.)

The President said it distressed him exceedingly to find
himself differing on such a point from the Secretary of
War and Secretary of the Treasury; that he would gladly

resign his plan;[85] but he could not see who could do the work wanted as well as McClellan. I named Hooker, or Sumner, or Burnside—either of whom, I thought, would be better.

At length the conversation ended and the meeting broke up, leaving the matter as we found it.

A few Tax Appointments were lying on the table. I asked the President to sign them; which he did, saying he would sign them just as they were and ask no questions. I told him that they had all been prepared in accordance with his directions, and that it was necessary to complete the appointments. They were signed, and I returned to the Department.

Sept. 3, Wednesday. The getting the Army into the works, and making general arrangements, went on to-day. Gen. McClellan assumed the command and returned to his old Head Quarters, as if the disastrous expedition of near eight months had been only the absence of a few days, unmarked by special incident; and, with the same old Staff, except the French Princes, Mr Astor and Mr. Gantt,[86] he went out, as of old, to visit the fortifications and the troops.—Pope came over and talked with the President, who assured him of his entire satisfaction with his conduct; assured him that McClellan's command was only temporary; and gave him some reason to expect that another army of active operations would be organized at once, which he (Pope) would lead.

In my Department nothing especial occurred; but the expenses are becoming enormous.

Sept. 4, Thursday. McDowell came over to-day and gave me a circumstantial account of the recent battles—

attributing our ill success to the conduct of McClellan in not urging forward reinforcements, and especially to the conduct of Porter and his division on the day of the last battle. He stayed all night.

Sept. 5, Friday. The President, at Cabinet Meeting, read Pope's Report, which strongly inculpates McClellan, Porter, Franklin and Griffin;[87] and asked opinion as to its publication. All against it, on the score of policy under existing circumstances. President stated that Porter, Franklin and Griffin would be releived [*sic*] from command and brought before a Court of Inquiry; and also, I think, that the Order had been made.

The President had previously, at the Department, told me that the clamor against McDowell was so great that he could not lead his troops unless something was done to restore confidence;[88] and proposed to me to suggest to him the asking for a Court of Inquiry. I told him I had already done so, and would do so again. So, availing myself of a Messenger from Gen. Pope who came during the meeting, I sent a note to McDowell, asking him to come over. He accordingly came in the evening, and I suggested the matter to him. He thought it hard to make the demand when there were no charges. I told him I thought he could assume the charge made by the Michigan officer who, when dying, scrawled a letter saying he died a victim to Pope's imbecility and McDowell's treachery. He reflected, and then said he would make the demand. He staid again all night.

Sept. 6, Saturday. Genl. and Mrs. Worthington [89] breakfasted with me;—also Gen. McDowell and Mr Haven.[90]

After Breakfast, Genl McDowell read me the draft of

his letter, which I thought excellent, but suggested one or two modifications which he adopted. I then went to the Department.

Soon after, the President came in, and asked what Mc-Dowell had determined to do. I told him. 'Where is the letter?' 'He took it, intending to have it copied I suppose.' 'Well, it ought to be done immediately, for the corps must march, and Gen. Halleck feels that he must be releived [*sic*], at all events, from command. Where can he be found?'—'I cannot tell. An orderly, no doubt, can find him.'—The President went away, and, later in the day, I heard that Gen. McDowell had been relieved at his own request. He came in himself, afterwards, stating the fact and adding, 'I did not ask to be relieved—I only asked for a court.' I explained as well as I could, and he left me.

Afterwards, I started to War Department, but met Seward, who said Stanton was not there. Went to President's, where Stanton was. He spoke of McDowell's letter, and praised it in the strongest terms.

Mr. Barney came this morning about the labor contract in New-York,[91] about which quite a difference of opinion and interest exists—one or two of our most influential journals being concerned in its continuance. The question was, whether the Contract, by its own terms, was not limited to three years, and whether an extension of it beyond that time would be, in reality, a new Contract. Doubting on the point, I referred it to the Attorney-General, who returned an answer expressing a decided opinion that the Contract was so limited and could not be extended without a new Contract.—Before receiving this opinion, I telegraphed Mr. Field to come on, if he desired to say anything further.

In the evening, Gen Pope came in. He expressed strong indignation against Fitz-John Porter and McClellan, who had, as he beleived [sic], prevented his success. He wanted his Report published, as an act of justice to himself and his army. I stated my objection to present publication, on the ground of injury to service at this critical time; but said that a General Order, thanking his Army for what they had done ought to be promulgated. He said this would be satisfactory (partially so, at least) but that Halleck would not publish one. I said, I would see the President and urge it.

Mr. Barney and others also called,—B. having declined invitations to breakfast, but said he would come at nine, to meet Field who telegraphed he would come and call at that hour.—Maj. Andrews [92] came in and spoke so of Col. Crook,[93] that I agreed to ask that he be made a Brigadier-General. Major Andrew [sic] wrote a statement of what Crook did in Western Virginia.

Sept. 7, Sunday. Mr. [David Dudley] Field called after breakfast, and proposed to go to War Department, and we went together. Met Gurowski, who denounced what he called military usurpation, saying that Franklin's corps, marching out, cheered McClellan. Found Stanton, Pope, and Wadsworth [94] uneasy on account of critical condition of affairs. Spoke to Stanton about Crook, and he promised to give him a Commission. Saw Halleck, and he approved.

Went to President's, and spoke of General Order commending Pope's Army. He thought it due, and said he would speak to Halleck.

Coming home met McDowell and T. C. H. Smith. Smith came home with me and spoke of battles,—eulogizing in strong terms both Pope and McDowell. Referring to my omission to reply to his letter of a year ago, I explained it as well as I could.—Field and Barney came, and I sent for Harrington. Had long talk about Labor Contract, and dissatisfaction of our friends with Mr. Barney. So far as I could see, the dissatisfaction was unreasonable. I said I could not hold the contract to be continuing, unless the Attorney-General should reverse his opinion, of which there was too little probability to warrant postponement of action, and so virtual continuance, until his review of his decision. Said I would gladly oblige party friends, but not at the expense of any breach of public duty.—Field and Barney left together, and soon after Harrington.

Received to-day telegram from Paymaster-General of New-York: 'Cannot forward troops for want of means to pay State bounty. Will you exchange smaller U. S. Notes for $1000s and 500s, to enable State to do it?'—Answered, 'Yes! Be as prompt in sending your troops;' and sent necessary directions to Mr. Cisco.

In the afternoon, McDowell called to say Good bye. The Court of Inquiry demanded by him had been postponed, and he had fifteen days leave of absence. He went away feeling very sad indeed.

In the night, a large part of the army moved northward, following the force already sent forward to meet the rebels invading Maryland. Generals Burnside, Hooker, Sumner and Reno [95] in command (Burnside chief) as reported.

Sept. 8, Monday. Jay Cooke came to breakfast, after which we talked on financial matters. He thought gold could be easily obtained on deposit at 4%; [96] and that, by and by, on a more favorable turn of affairs, 5-20s could be negotiated.—Clay [97] came in, and Cooke left. Clay and I rode towards Department in wagon. Clay said he had made up his mind to take [a] Department and that the President and Stanton were willing he should take that beyond the Mississippi. 'Would I go with him to see Halleck?'—'Certainly.'—Halleck received us kindly, but was unwell. Showed no favor to the new Department project.

Returned to Department and attended to general business. Nothing of special financial moment. Barney came in, and said that Stanton and Wadsworth had advised him to leave for New-York this evening, as communication with Baltimore might be cut off before tomorrow. He would be governed by my advice. Told him I did not think the event probable, but he had best govern himself by the advice received.

After he had gone, Gen. Mansfield came in and talked very earnestly about the necessity of ordering up, from Suffolk, 1st. Delaware and 3 and 4 New-York, trained and disciplined now 14 months, each 800 strong, say 2400 men; and from Norfolk 19th. Wisconsin and 48th. Pennsylvania, say 1600 men; leaving, at Suffolk, Forey's Brigade of four diminished Regiments, say 1800 men in all, late of Shields' division; 11th Pennsylvania Cavalry (a full and good Regiment) say 900 men;—and Dodge's Regiment of mounted Rifles except one Company; and at Norfolk, 99th New-York, and one Company of Dodge's, sufficient for military police. He favored leaving Keyes [98] and Peck [99] at Yorktown.—He said the defences of the city were weak on the Eastern side; and that there ought to be at least 65,000 good men to hold it if McClellan is defeated—to improve victory, if he is successful.—He referred to old times. Was in Texas the Winter before Rebellion broke out. Saw Twiggs,[100] who hated him because he was on Court-Martial. Was then told by officer in Council of War of K. G. C.[101] that Floyd and Cobb, in Cabinet, and Jeff Davis and Breckinridge,[102] were members. In this Council of War, Orders were given to seize Navy-Yards, Forts, &c., while its members were yet Cabinet officers and Senators. The Order of the K. G. C. ramified throughout the South. First offered services to Juarez,[103] who refused them because too dangerous. They then plotted the invasion of Cuba, which failed. Then declared themselves Protectors of Southern Rights and levied a contribution upon all planters and slaveholders—some giving $5 and some $10, and some more or less. In this way they got large sums and commenced operations. They designed to seize Washington and inaugurate Breckinridge; and with reference to this Mason wrote Faulkner [104] advising him not to resign—this letter being now in Seward's possession. This plot only failed through the bringing of troops to Washington, and the unwillingness of leaders to make a bloody issue so early.—He spoke of Gen Scott. Said he had not treated him well—had placed McDowell in command over the river last year, superseding himself, and when he had asked for explanation he simply replied that his orders had been given. He felt himself wronged, but did his duty to the best of his ability. He was afterwards treated badly by Gen Wool who did not like him, though he treated him civilly. Had lately been in command at Suffolk (an insignificant post) until summoned here to Court of Inquiry.—Wanted active employment but was unable to get any. Had sent for his horses, and proposed to visit all the fortifications around the city on his own account.—I was a good deal affected by the manifest patriotism and desire to do something for his country manifested by the old General; and could not help wishing that he was younger, and thinking that, perhaps, after all, it would have been better to trust him.

After the General left, went to War Department, where found the President, Stanton and Wadsworth. The President said he had felt badly all day. Wadsworth said there was no danger of an attack on Washington, and that the man ought to be severely punished who intimated the possibility of its surrender. The President spoke of the great number of stragglers he had seen coming into town this morning; and of the immenses losses by desertion.

Returned home. Maj. Andrews and others called.

Sept. 9, Tuesday. Maj. Andrews came to breakfast. Told him I had seen Secretary of War, who had assured me that Col. Crooks' commission as Brigadier had been sent him.

Went to Departmaent. Directed Commission for 10th New-York district to be sent to Hyatt.[105] Directed Mr. Rogers [106] to proceed to New-York and expedite alterations in Exchange and Custom House, and make proper contracts for the same.

Went to President's to attend Cabinet meeting, but there was only a talk. I proposed the creation of a Department beyond the Mississippi and that Clay be placed in command, with whom Frank P. Blair [107] should be associated; and that an Expedition should be organized to Petersburgh and afterwards to Charleston.

Genl Van Ransellaer [108] called to ask my interest for him as Paymaster-General; and Mr Carroll, to ask the same for Genl. Griffin.—Went to War Department, where Watson told me that Gen. McClellan had telegraphed expressing doubt if there was any large rebel force in Maryland, and apprehension that their movement might be a feint.—Watson dined with me. Read him Denison's letter from New-Orleans about evacuation of Baton Rouge— Butler's black Regiment—&c., &c.[109]

Just after dinner, Capt. [word omitted by copyist] came in with Mr. Green [?], who had been arrested near Soldiers' Home as a suspicious character—taken before Gen Wadsworth, to whom he said he was known to me—sent by Gen. W. to me—identified and discharged. He is an Englishman of a Manchester House, who brought a letter from Mr. Layard to Acting Minister Stuart,[110] by whom he had been commended to me. Riding around to gratify curiosity he had fallen into trouble.

Sept. 10, Wednesday. Mr. Skinner [111] at breakfast. Soon after, Mr. Hamilton (James A.)[112] came, and we conversed about the condition of things. He said the Committee from New-York had arrived, representing the views of the five New-England Governors who met lately;[113] and that they would insist on the resignation of Messrs. S[eward]. and B[lair].—I told him I thought the mission vain—that it might be useful if all the Heads of Departments were to resign, and that I was not only ready but anxious to do so, either with my associates or alone.—He criticized severely some passages in Mr. Seward's Diplomatic Correspondence—especially those in the Letter of April 10, to Mr. Adams, which concede the proposition that the Federal Government could not reduce the seceding States to obedience by conquest, and affirm that 'only an imperial or despotic Government could subjugate thoroughly disaffected and insurrectionary members of the State.' [114] He said in them was the key to the whole temporizing policy, civil and military, which had been pursued. I could make no reply to this, except to say that I had never known Mr. Seward object to any *action*, however vigorous, of a military nature; though his influence had been cast in favor of harmonizing the various elements of support to the Administration, by retaining Genl. McClellan in command, and by avoiding action which would be likely to alienate the Border States. I added that in his wishes for harmony I concurred; and that I credited him with good motives in the choice of means to ends, though I could not always concur with him in judgment as to their adaptation.

After this conversation, I went to the Department and transacted the routine business. I also examined the Tax Law for insurgent States; sent for Commissioner Boutwell; read and approved Regulations drafted by Judge Smith;[115] and determined to overcome the difficulties in the way of putting the law into operation, arising from the omission of any appropriation for the purpose by Congress, by applying, so far as the District of South-Carolina is concerned, the necessary amount from a small fund legally at my disposal.

Received letter from Birney,[116] desiring that his brother should command Kearney's corps and sent it to War Department with strong commendation.

Genl. Kane [117] called to thank me for my support to his appointment as Brigadier, to which I answered, most sincerely, that he 'was indebted for the appointment, not to my support, but to his own merits.' Indeed, while I will most gladly aid merit to place, and seek it out in order to give it place, I am resolved never from sympathy or weak compliance, to help unfit persons to position. The condition of the country is too critical for it now, were it ever excusable.

At dinner, Mr Hamilton told me of the interview between the New-York Committee and the President. The Committee urged a change of policy. The President became vexed, and said, in substance, 'It is plain enough what you want—you want to get Seward out of the Cabinet. There is not one of you who would not see the country ruined, if you could turn out Seward.' [118]

After dinner, rode to Mr. Cutts', proposing to invite Mrs. D. to ride; and was very sorry to learn from her mother that she was much indisposed—Went to the War Department. No satisfactory information yet from army and no satisfactory account of numbers or position of the enemy.—David Taylor [119] called with Mr. Northcott, of Champaign, who wants to be Commissary. Endorsed his paper, '*Recommended.*'

Received telegram from McDowell asking if it was not just to publish his letter. Answered, 'Will see it done.'

4

Antietam and Emancipation

[SEPTEMBER 11–OCTOBER 12, 1862]

SEPTEMBER, 1862, was a critical month. While Kirby Smith and Braxton Bragg threatened Louisville and Cincinnati, Lee's veterans pushed forward into Maryland. Frederick City was occupied, the Federal garrison at Harpers Ferry was surrounded, and Lee moved toward Hagerstown. The approach of the invaders brought panic and terror to Northern cities, and war governors demanded that Lincoln oust McClellan, emancipate the slaves, and reorganize his cabinet.

The morale of the Federal army was sadly shaken by recent defeats and shifts in command, and Chase had no confidence in McClellan's ability to check the Confederates. Even when McClellan was given a copy of Lee's army orders, accidentally dropped by one of the Southern commanders, he seemed unable to move swiftly. The engagement at South Mountain (September 14) was inconclusive, and the battle of Antietam three days later has been called a "defeat for both armies." Then, while McClellan rested, Lee's army recrossed the Potomac to the safety of Virginia.

"We have spent large sums of money and sacrificed a

vast number of precious lives," Chase lamented, "and yet we seem to be still far from the final issue." Conversations with his cronies confirmed Chase's view that the fault was largely McClellan's. The Secretary paid assiduous court to "Fighting Joe" Hooker, wounded at Antietam and afterward hospitalized in Washington, and that ambitious commander fed his hostility toward McClellan. Lincoln, too, was becoming impatient with the general's slowness, and, after a visit to the army in October, he determined that McClellan must go. On November 5th Ambrose Burnside was given command of the Army of the Potomac.

The ousting of McClellan seemed to Chase, and to other Radical Republicans, a major step forward. Equally encouraging was the President's decision to issue his Emancipation Proclamation. Chase's record of the cabinet discussions on September 22nd is the most important single entry in his diaries. With emancipation announced and McClellan removed, the Secretary looked confidently forward to a season of victories.

〜 〜 〜

Sept. 11, 1862, Thursday. Two weeks since Hooker drove Ewell at Bristow Station [1]—and what weeks! Ten days of battle, and then such changes,—changes in which it is difficult to see [?] the public good! How singularly all our worst defeats have followed Administration cr— no, blunders! McDowell defeated at Bull Run, because the Administration would not supersede Patterson by a General of more capacity, vigor and devotion to the cause. McClellan defeated at Richmond, because the Administration recalled Shields and forced Frémont to retire from the pursuit of Jackson, in order that McDowell's force

might be concentrated at Manassas to be sent to Mc-
Clellan before Richmond. Pope defeated at Bull Run because the Administration persisted in keeping McClellan
in command of the Army of the Potomac, after full warning that, under his lead and influence, that army would
not coöperate effectively with Pope.

After breakfast this morning Mr. Hamilton took leave
of me, and I prepared to go to Fairfax Seminary to visit
Butterfield,[2] who, according to the papers, is sick there.
Before starting, however, I thought it best to send Bannister[3] to the War Department to learn if anything of
importance had occurred. He returned with a note to the
effect that nothing important had come from the army but
that an important question was for consideration and decision, and if I would come up he would send for Genl
Halleck and the President. Went up immediately. It
rained. On arriving at the War Department, found Gen
Wright,[4] of Penna., there; with a request from Gov. Curtin[5] to call into active service all the able bodied men of
the State. The President, Gen. Halleck and Mr. Stanton
submitted the question, 'What answer shall be returned to
Gov Curtin?'—Gen. H. thought the important thing was
to mass all the force possible on this side the enemy, and
defeat him; and that a general arming of Pennsylvania
would not be sufficiently available to warrant the vast expenses sure to be incurred.—Mr. Stanton expressed no
opinion as to defeat of the enemy from this side, but
thought Gov. Curtin's proposal too large to be entertained,
and stated that the arms for a general arming could not be
furnished.—I asked Gen. H., 'What force, in your opinion,
has the enemy?'—'From the best evidence I have—not
satisfactory, but the best—I reckon the whole number in

Maryland and the vicinity of Washington, at 150,000.'—
'How many in Maryland?'—'Two-thirds probably, or
100,000'—'What, in your judgment as a soldier, are the
designs of the enemy?'—'Impossible to judge with certainty. Suppose he will do what I would do if in his place
—rest, recruit, get supplies, augment force, and obtain all
possible information; and then strike the safest and most
effectual blow he can—at Washington, Baltimore or Philadelphia. If not strong enough to strike a blow, he will,
after getting all he can, attempt to re-cross into Virginia.'
—'You think, then, there is no probability of an advance
into Pennsylvania at present.'—'None, unless a raid.'—
Upon these statements, I expressed the opinion, that, considering the situation of our troops sent out to attack the
rebel army, it was not impossible that a raid, at least,
would be attempted into Pennsylvania, and that Gov.
Curtin was wise in making provision for it; that the proposition to arm the whole people was, however, too broad;
and that I thought it would be well to authorize the Governor to call out as many troops as could be armed with
the arms he reported himself as having—say 30,000. The
President said he was averse to giving the order, on the
score of expense; but would think of it till tomorrow.

The President and Secy. Stanton having left the room,
I took occasion to ask Gen. Halleck what, in his judgment,
were the causes of the demoralization of the troops. He
replied, there were several causes; first, the incapacity of
officers from inexperience, or want of ability or character;
second, the want of proper discipline; third,—a political
cause—the action of the late Congress in its abolition and
confiscation measures,[6] which were very distasteful to the
Army of the West, and, as he understood, also to the Army

of the Potomac. I expressed my conviction that the influence of the last was exaggerated, and dropped the subject.

I abandoned the idea of visiting Butterfield and returned to the Department, where I transacted usual routine business.

In the evening, called to enquire for Mrs. Douglas,
taking some [word omitted by copyist].

Sept. 12, Friday. Breakfasted alone. After breakfast
went to Department, putting carelessly in my pocket a
roll of papers, consisting, in part, of some sheets from an
Account of McClellan's Course till the junction of the
Army of the Potomac with that of Virginia,[7] and of others
containing the first draft of my Journal of the 10th. and
in part of the 11th. On reaching the Treasury, I was a
little alarmed on missing my roll; and still more annoyed
when, on sending Thomas and Mr. Plantz to look along
the street and at the house, nothing could be found of it.
What if it should fall into the hands of somebody who will
make public what is not designed for publication, but
simply in memoriam?

Fortunately the roll was picked up in the street and
brought to me.

Little of interest occurred at the Department to-day.
Expenses are enormous, increasing instead of diminishing;
and the ill-successes in the field have so affected Government Stocks that it is impossible to obtain money except
on temporary deposit, and these deposits very little exceed
[word omitted by copyist]. We are forced, therefore, to
rely on the increased issue of U.S. Notes, which hurts
almost as much as it helps; for the omission of Congress to
take any measures to restrict bank-note circulation, makes
the issue of these notes a stimulant to its increase so that

the augmentation of the currency proceeds by a double action and prices rise proportionably. It is a bad state of things; but neither the President, his counsellors nor his commanding generals seem to care. They rush on from expense to expense and from defeat to defeat, heedless of the abyss of bankruptcy and ruin which yawns before us— so easily shunned, yet seemingly so sure to engulf us. May God open the eyes of those who control, before it is too late!

Went over to the War Department about two. Found that no important intelligence of rebel movements had been received. The Secretary informed me that *he had heard* from Genl. H. that the President is going out to see Gen. McClellan; and commented with some severity, on his humiliating submissiveness to that officer. It is, indeed, humiliating; but prompted, I believe, by a sincere desire to serve the country, and a fear that, should he supersede McClellan by any other commander, no advantage would be gained in leadership, but much harm in the disaffection of officers and troops. The truth is, I think, that the President with the most honest intentions in the world, and a naturally clear judgment and a true, unselfish patriotism, has yielded so much to Border State and negrophobic counsels that he now finds it difficult to arrest his own descent towards the most fatal concessions. He has already separated himself from the great body of the party which elected him; distrusts most those who most represent its spirit; and waits. For what?

Before I left the Department, the Secretary kindly promised me a Paymastership for Wm. D. Bickham; which will, when given be a great gratification to a very

worthy friend.—We talked also of Port Royal and matters
there. I advised the removal of Brannan,[8] who is hostile
to the plans of the Department and the measures of Saxton. He said he would be ordered to the North; but did
not seem inclined to talk much about it.

Speaking of the number of rebels, he said he thought it
could not exceed 100,000; but that his judgment was
founded upon possibilities of supplies and transportation—
not on reports.

Called at President's, and spoke to him of leave of
absence to Cameron. He referred me to Seward, to whom
I went, and was informed that leave was sent by last
steamer.—We talked on many things—Barney's appointments, conduct of the war, &c., &c.—Engaged to go together tomorrow, and urge expedition to C[harlesto]n.—
He said some one had proposed that the President should
issue a Proclamation, on the invasion of Pennsylvania,
freeing all the Apprentices of that State, or with some
similar object. I thought the jest ill-timed.

Judge Adams (6th. Auditor), Mr. Burnam (of Kentucky Legislature, now a refugee from his home)[9] and
Mr. Case (formerly of Patriot, Ia., now of Portland, Me.)
dined with me. The Kentucky Slaveholders were more
against Slavery than the Northern Conservative. Strange,
yet not strange!

In the evening, Maj. D. Taylor, Mr. O'Harra[10] and
Mr. Cooke called—later Mr. Cummings.[11] General talk
and not very profitable. Cooke and O'Harra want introduction to Gen. Mitchell for Pitt Cooke[12] and O'Harra,
who want to buy cotton at Port Royal.—Col. Kane called
and left note about McDowell.—Mr. Cummings talked

about '*Bulletin*'—about removal of one of the Editors from
Custom House—about support to himself for Assembly—
about distribution of stamps, &c.—I got tired.

Sept. 13, Saturday. Breakfasted alone. What has become
of Mr. Skinner? Went to Department and attended to
some matters of routine.

Went to Navy Department with Gov. Seward, according to appointment, about expedition to Charleston. Examined chart with Secretary Welles and Asst. Secy. Fox.[13]
Learned that the '*Ironsides*' and '*Passaic*' will be ready for
sea by the 1st. October; which is more than two weeks
longer than Mr. Welles gave me to understand ten days
ago. Fox thinks that James Island [14] ought to have been
held and that Hunter was wrong in withdrawing our force
from it; but it is now commanded by our gunboats, so
that a landing upon it is easy, and a force of 10,000 or
15,000 men would suffice for the reduction of Charleston.
A land force, however, would have to act mainly inde-
pendently of the naval; and no naval force but ironclads
could act with any efficiency, because, the harbor being a
cul de sac, wooden vessels entering it to bombard the town
would be exposed to fire from all sides, and could not pass
and repass the enemy's batteries, as at Port Royal, and, by
motion, make the enemy's fire comparatively ineffectual.
Ironclads, however, such as the '*Passaic*' and the '*Ironsides,*' could go right into the harbor, with little or no risk,
and destroy the Forts, batteries, and the town itself, if not
surrendered. After all, it seemed to me that it would contribute greatly to the certainty of the result if a land force
should be organized, and I determined to confer with the
Secretary of War on the subject, as soon as possible. No
time should be lost in making every arrangement for such

overwhelming blows, just as soon as the ironclads are ready, as will effectually annihilate the possibility of rebel success.

From the Navy Department, we went to Head Quarters where we found Genl. Cullum,[15] who said: 'We have got whipped again. We have just received a telegram that the rebels have defeated our people in Fayette County, Va., and are driving them down the Kanawha. The trouble is that our men won't fight.' The style of remark did not suit me; but it is too common among our generals. In my opinion, the soldiers are better than the officers.—Genl. Halleck came in, and we asked the situation. There was nothing new, he said, except confirmation that Burnside drove the rebels out of Frederick yesterday, and had renewed the fight to-day. Heavy firing had been heard from the direction of Harpers Ferry and the Frederick and Hagerstown Road. We left Headquarters, and I returned to the Department.

Gave O'Harra and Pitt Cooke letter of introduction to Gen. Mitchell. Visited Mr. Clark's [16] Sealing and trimming machines for the ones and twos and found them a perfect success; and the ones and twos are sealed and trimmed by machinery, attended for the most part by women, with such prodigious advantage to the Government that it seems difficult to imagine that coining, except in large masses, can be of much utility hereafter.

Jay Cooke writes that he has visited New-York and conversed with Bankers; and thinks that $10,000,000 in Gold will be gladly deposited at 4%. I think that, in this way, all the Gold needed can be obtained at very small cost and without affecting the market in any way. If it succeeds, it will form not the least remarkable chapter in the history of the financial success which has attended me thus far.

Wrote to Katie and Nettie, and to Horton—to Katie, advising her not to return immediately; to Horton about Pope.

In the evening, went to Willard's to call on Genl. Schenck,[17] but did not see him. Met Weed, and went to his room and talked of sundry matters. He says I have done as well in the New-York appointments as was possible, and advises care as to securities taken; which advice I think very good. He thinks the time has come for vigorous measures South; and is for freeing the slaves, and arming them as far as useful, without noise or excitement. He saw Hunter in New-York; who says that if he had been sustained, he would have emasculated the rebellion [in] South-Carolina before now—which he seemed to believe and which I believe absolutely.

Went to War Department. Telegraph men told me that telegraph was built to Point of Rocks and several miles beyond the Monocacy towards Frederick, and that heavy continuous firing was heard, by the operator at the former place, from the direction of Harpers Ferry, till between three and four this afternoon; and that firing, though not so heavy, was also heard from the direction of Middleton, between Frederick and Hagerstown. There was also a rumor that we had captured a large wagon-train, with a considerable number of prisoners. The inference from the firing heard is that an attack has been made on Harpers Ferry by a large rebel force, and a stout defense with unknown result; and that a less important conflict has taken place between the advance under Burnside and the rebel rear falling back towards Hagerstown or Harpers Ferry (probably the former) and that the rebels have been worsted.

Telegram from Gov Curtin yesterday states that a reliable gentleman of Maryland, who had opportunities to converse freely with officers of the rebel army, says that the rebel force in Maryland is 190,000, and on the other side of the Potomac 250,000—in all 440,000. This is a specimen of information collected and believed! [18]

Came home and Cooke called with Mr. Davis, General Birney's partner, who wants him made a Major-General with command of Kearney's corps. I think this should be done. We must advance all our Republican officers who have real merit, so as to counterpoise the too great weight already given to Democratic officers, without much merit. They have been more pushed than the Republicans and we have been more than just—more than generous even— we have been lavish towards them. It is time to change the policy.

Sept. 14, Sunday. Went to Methodist Church. Mr. Brown [19] preached good sermon.—Afterwards called to enquire for Mrs. Douglas, who, I found, had passed a bad night, but was better.

Went to War Department. Despatches from McClellan to the President—also to Gen. Halleck. First, complimentary—respects to Mrs. Lincoln; ladies enthusiastic welcome of McClellan and his army 'us.' The second states getting possession of Lee's Order to Hill of 10th.—troops from various directions to attack Martinsburgh and Harpers Ferry on the 12th.—capture both—and then reunite at Hagerstown. White [20] had anticipated the enemy by joining Miles at Harpers Ferry, where the enemy made vigorous attack yesterday;—courier from Miles says he can hold out two days, but enemy is in possession of Maryland Heights;—McC. hopes before two days to relieve Miles —is already in possession of Middleton and Jefferson;— estimates rebel force in Maryland at 125,000;—thinks defeat of his army would be ruinous, and therefore better to spare all troops from Washington than suffer it;—anticipates great battle tomorrow, Monday;—enemy don't mean to go back to Virginia, but thinks Lee has blundered, and hopes to make him repent of it.—Watson rode with me.

Read several books, especially article in 'Revue des deux Mondes' on the soul.[21]—In the evening, Mr. Case called and talked of Politics and Spiritualism—especially the last, in which he is a firm believer. Says he receives letters from the inhabitants of the Sixth and other Spheres, among whom are Calhoun, Brutus and others; that there is a Council in the 6th., presided over by Washington, to which the control of this war is committed; that Richmond will be taken about Dec. 1st., and Charleston early in the Spring.—Dr. Rabe called and talked over California matters. Seems to have been very unfairly and unjustly dealt with. Thinks Hoffman an excellent man—also Sharp, Dist. Atty. Thinks Phelps or [word omitted by copyist], a partizan of Frémont, will be elected Senator. Rand, new Marshal, is one [of the] Palmer, Cook & Co. set.[22] Advised him to examine papers, and, if possible, refute charges and be restored.

Mr. Varnum, of N. Y., and his cousin, from Mass., came in and talked a little. Nothing important

Sept. 15, Monday. Went to Department soon after nine, stopping at Franklin's[23] to buy glasses. Got a pair, not I fear exactly the best for me. Received letters from John

Sherman,[24] O. Follett,[25] Horace Greeley,[26] and others. Greeley's assured me that the 'Tribune' had no interest in the Labor Contract, which I was very glad to learn.— Called on Attorney-General about citizenship of colored men. Found him averse to expressing official opinion.— Met Eliot [27] and [Isaac C.] Taber, Mayor of New Bedford, and invited them to dine with me.—Commenced letter to Greeley; when I was reminded of my promise to accompany Mr Case to the President's. Went with him. Found Eliot and Taber in antechamber. Went in and found Blair with the President discussing affairs. Told him of the gentlemen outside and was permitted to bring them in. Did so. Introduced Case, who shook hands, and we two came away.

Parted from Case at Department. Finished letter to Greeley, and wrote Judge Mason about Rodney,[28] promising to do what I could for trial. Several callers—among them, Col Lloyd [29] of Ohio Cavalry, and Col Mason [30] of [Fourth] Ohio Infantry, with two Captains. Lloyd said that the cavalry was very badly used; that forage was insufficient and irregular and needlessly wasted; that sometimes a squadron, company or regiment, was ordered out early in the morning, and left all day without any further orders. Pope, he said, had nominally about 2000 cavalry when he went South, and when he returned had not 500 fit for duty. Sometimes the cavalry was ordered to march, when five or six horses in a Company would die from sheer exhaustion. Artillery horses better cared for. Lloyd desired Mason to be made Brigadier-General. Promised to make inquiries, and if found all right, promote object.

Mr. Wetmore [31] called about Cotton and Tobacco. Proposed that Government should take all cotton at 20 cents

and tobacco at [figure omitted] cents—pay this price—
send it to New-York—sell it for Gold—keep account with
each owner, and, at the end of the war, pay him the difference, if loyal. The idea struck me very favorably, and I
promised to see him again tomorrow.

Weed called and we had a long talk. He expressed again
his conviction that more decided measures are needed in
an Anti-Slavery direction; and said there was much dissatisfaction with Seward in New-York because he is supposed to be averse to such measures. I told him, I did not
doubt Mr. Seward's fidelity to his ideas of progress, ameli-
oration and freedom; but that I thought he adhered too
tenaciously to men who proved themselves unworthy and
dangerous, such as McClellan; that he resisted too per-
sistently decided measures; that his influence encouraged
the irresolution and inaction of the President in respect
to men and measures, although personally he was as decided as anybody in favor of vigorous prosecution of the
war, and as active as anybody in concerting plans of action
against the rebels. Mr. Weed admitted that there was
much justice in my views, and said he had expressed similar ideas to Mr. Seward himself. He said he would see
him again, and that Seward and I must agree on a definite
line, especially on the Slavery question, which we must
recommend to the President. We talked a good deal about
our matters—about the absence of proper Cabinet discussion of important subjects—about Tax appointments in
New-York, with which he is well satisfied, &c., &c.

Went to War Department between 3 and 4, and saw
telegrams of McClellan. They state that the action of yesterday resulted in a decided success, that the enemy,
driven from mountain crest, did not renew the action this

morning but retreated in disorder—that Lee confessed himself 'shockingly whipped,' with loss of 15,000 killed, wounded, missing and prisoners—that he has 700 prisoners at Frederick, and that 1000 have been taken by Hooker and held—that he proposed pursuit as rapidly as possible—that Franklin on the right in advance towards Harpers Ferry, had succeeded as well as the troops on the right. News from the West also good. Nothing from Miles at Harpers Ferry but it is believed that he still holds out.

Returned to the Department, closed the business of the day, and went home. Eliot, Taber and Harrington dined with me. After dinner, rode with Harrington. Stopped at Mr. Cutts, to enquire for Mrs. Douglas—glad to hear she was better. Stopped also at War Department. No further news. Stanton thinks Halleck begins to realize his mistake. Said he intended to make Birney Major-General, but Halleck (or rather McClellan) had designated Stoneman.[32] Told him that Birney had sent his letter of resignation to me, but I had declined to present it. Nothing new from the army, except report from Operator at Point of Rocks of firing apparently between that place and Harpers Ferry— which may indicate Franklin or Miles in that position. Nothing from McClellan since noon.

Dropped Harrington at Ebbitt House, and called on General Schenck at Willards. Helped dressed [sic] his wound which looked very bad, but the surgeons say he is improving rapidly and will be able to sit up in two or three days. His daughter is with him, and most assiduous and devoted.

Home. Friend Butler and Benedict [33] called, wishing to be introduced to the President, in order to present Petition for exemption of society from draft. Promised to go with

them, or write note, tomorrow morning.—Gov Boutwell
called and we talked of Tax Law, Stamp distribution, etc.

Sept. 16, Tuesday. Bannister at breakfast. Went to
Department, and from Department with deputation of
Friends from Mt. Pleasant, O., and Wilmington, Del., to
the President and introduced them. Asked, for Bishop
McIlvaine,[34] the appointment of Revd. Mr. Tolford [35] as
Chaplain at Camp Chase—which the President directed.

Went to Navy Department and advised Expedition up
the James River; and said if Gen Wool or other good
General could be sent I would go myself as Volunteer aid.
Mr. Welles seemed pleased with the idea; and said the
'Ironsides' and 'Passaic' would be ready by the time troops
could be, and might take Richmond as preliminary to
Charleston.—Spoke to the Secretary of Commodore Barb-
head's [36] remark to Harrington, that the Government
ought to be superseded by McClellan.—Went to War De-
partment   Surrender of Harpers Ferry is confirmed. Mc-
Clellan's victory of Sunday was probably over the rear of
Longstreet's [37] Division, which made a stand.

Weed called with Morgan,[38] who wished to enquire
about Texas Bonds issued under authority of the Rebel
Government. Told him they would not be recognized and
promised him copies of papers relating to the subject, from
files and records of the Department. Told Weed that we
must have decided action and that he could ensure it. Was
going to Meeting of Heads of Department, not to Cabinet.
Went over to White House. Met Seward, who said the
President was busy with Gen Halleck and there would be
no meeting.

Returned to Department. Rode out to Sigel's [39] Camp,
by way of Chain Bridge, with Harrington and Dr. Schmidt.

Saw Sigel and Schurz.[40] They want to have corps organized for operations in the field. Sigel said scouts returned from Drainesville report large rebel force at Leesburgh.

Home to late dinner—Harrington with me. Sent message to War Department for news. Nothing of importance.

Sept. 17, Wednesday. Bannister breakfasted with me. At Department finished Proclamation declaring States in insurrection, without the exception formerly made, with view to taking exclusive control of all purchases of cotton, sugar, tobacco and rice in insurgent States.

Judge Hoadley [41] came. Went to War Department with him. Stanton promised the Generals he wanted, but could promise nothing else.—Went also to Genl. Halleck's. Found the President and Reverdy Johnson there, talking with a Union Captain who was at Harpers Ferry at the time of its surrender. Says Maryland Heights were surrendered to the surprise of every one; that Miles was struck by a shell after surrender of the post, just as he had put the white flag in the hands of an orderly, that there was no necessity whatever for the surrender, and that the officers were very indignant.

Warrants to-day enormous—over $4,000,000—and unpaid Requisitions still accumulating—now over $40,000,-000. Where will this end?

Gen. Hunter came to dine with me. Expressed his decided opinion that if his Order had not been revoked, he would now have had the whole coast lined with disciplined loyal Southern men—black, to be sure, but good soldiers and true.

Sept. 19, Friday. Recd letter from Robt. Dale Owen [42] (addresed [*sic*] to the President) eloquently urging General Emancipation; which I handed to the President at Cabinet.

Stanton showed me Halleck's telegram to McClellan, dated Aug. 31, which was substantially as follows:—

'I do not know the terms of Order. I expected to leave you in full command, except of troops temporarily detached to Pope. I beg you to come up and give me the benefit of your talents, experience and judgment at this critical moment. Am completely tired out.' [43]

This telegram announced the surrender of Halleck to McClellan. It saddens me to think that a Commander in Chief, whose opinion of his subordinate's military conduct is such as I have heard Halleck express of McClellan's, should, in a moment of pressure, so yield to that very subordinate. Good may come of it, but my fears are stronger than my hopes. How differently old Gen. Scott would have acted! When up all night at the critical period immediately following the first Battle of Bull Run, he was never heard to complain of being 'completely tired out,' or known to try to shift any part of his responsibility upon another.

Sept. 20, Saturday. Katie came home this morning, looking very well.—Nothing of special importance in any Department.—Mr. Garrett called expressing great uneasiness about the B. and O. R.R., and the probable invasion of Western Virginia if the enemy is not followed up.—Genl. Mason dined with me. He is extremely anxious to have a trial in the case of Rodney Mason, who was lately dismissed the service for the surrender of Clarksville.—Received letter from Mr. Hamilton. He will come on Monday to see the President about Proclamation.

Received a letter from Miss Virginia Smith, asking my

interest for Col. Bulow's appointment as Brigadier; to
which I replied that I would say a good word for the
Colonel, and thought the prospect not desperate as no man
is safe, now-a-days, from being made a Brigadier—not
even a man of merit.

Sept. 21, Sunday. At home to-day, under orders from
Dr. F.[44] Mr. Montgomery of Philadelphia dined with us.
—Called on Harrington, to have Dr. F. go to see Gen.
Hooker, if possible. Harrington made arrangements.—
Towards sundown, called at Mrs. C's. to enquire for
Mrs. D., and was much gratified to find her so far re-
covered as to be in the parlor. Mr. Montgomery went to
church with Katie.—Bannister, Taylor and others called.

Dr. F. spoke of having been to the President's, who, being very busy writing, could not see him.

Thought to myself, 'Possibly engaged on Proclamation.'

Sept. 22, Monday. To Department about nine. State
Department messenger came, with notice to Heads of De-
partments to meet at 12.—Received sundry callers.—
Went to White House.

All the members of the Cabinet were in attendance.
There was some general talk; and the President mentioned
that Artemus Ward [45] had sent him his book. Proposed to
read a chapter which he thought very funny. Read it, and
seemed to enjoy it very much—the Heads also (except
Stanton) of course. The Chapter was 'Highhanded Outrage at Utica.' [46]

The President then took a graver tone and said:—

'Gentlemen: I have, as you are aware, thought a great
deal about the relation of this war to Slavery; and you all
remember that, several weeks ago, I read to you an Order
I had prepared on this subject, which, on account of ob-

jections made by some of you, was not issued. Ever since then, my mind has been much occupied with this subject, and I have thought all along that the time for acting on it might very probably come. I think the time has come now. I wish it were a better time. I wish that we were in a better condition. The action of the army against the rebels has not been quite what I should have best liked. But they have been driven out of Maryland, and Pennsylvania is no longer in danger of invasion. When the rebel army was at Frederick, I determined, as soon as it should be driven out of Maryland, to issue a Proclamation of Emancipation such as I thought most likely to be useful. I said nothing to any one; but I made the promise to myself, and (hesitating a little)—to my Maker. The rebel army is now driven out, and I am going to fulfil that promise. I have got you together to hear what I have written down. I do not wish your advice about the main matter—for that I have determined for myself. This I say without intending any thing but respect for any one of you. But I already know the views of each on this question. They have been heretofore expressed, and I have considered them as thoroughly and carefully as I can. What I have written is that which my reflections have determined me to say. If there is anything in the expressions I use, or in any other minor matter, which anyone of you thinks had best be changed, I shall be glad to receive the suggestions. One other observation I will make. I know very well that many others might, in this matter, as in others, do better than I can; and if I were satisfied that the public confidence was more fully possessed by any one of them than by me, and knew of any Constitutional way in which he could be put in my place, he should have it. I would gladly yield it to him. But though I believe that I have not so much of the confidence of the people as I had some time since, I do not know that, all things considered, any other person has more; and, however this may be, there is no way in which I can have any other man put where I am. I am here. I must do the best I can, and bear the responsibility of taking the course which I feel I ought to take.'

The President then proceeded to read his Emancipation Proclamation, making remarks on the several parts as he went on, and showing that he had fully considered the whole subject, in all the lights under which it had been presented to him.

After he had closed, Gov. Seward said: 'The general question having been decided, nothing can be said further about that. Would it not, however, make the Proclamation more clear and decided, to leave out all reference to the act being sustained during the incumbency of the present President; and not merely say that the Government "recognizes," but that it will maintain, the freedom it proclaims?' [47]

I followed, saying: 'What you have said, Mr. President, fully satisfies me that you have given to every proposition which has been made, a kind and candid consideration. And you have now expressed the conclusion to which you have arrived, clearly and distinctly. This it was your right, and under your oath of office your duty, to do. The Proclamation does not, indeed, mark out exactly the course I should myself prefer. But I am ready to take it just as it is written, and to stand by it with all my heart. I think, however, the suggestions of Gov. Seward very judicious, and shall be glad to have them adopted.'

The President then asked us severally our opinions as

to the modifications proposed, saying that he did not care much about the phrases he had used. Everyone favored the modification and it was adopted. Gov. Seward then proposed that in the passage relating to colonization, some language should be introduced to show that the colonization proposed was to be only with the consent of the colonists, and the consent of the States in which colonies might be attempted. This, too, was agreed to; and no other modification was proposed. Mr. Blair then said that the question having been decided, he would make no objection to issuing the Proclamation; but he would ask to have his paper, presented some days since, against the policy, filed with the Proclamation. The President consented to this readily. And then Mr. Blair went on to say that he was afraid of the influence of the Proclamation on the Border States and on the Army, and stated at some length the grounds of his apprehensions. He disclaimed most expressly, however, all objection to Emancipation *per se,* saying he had always been personally in favor of it—always ready for immediate Emancipation in the midst of Slave States, rather than submit to the perpetuation of the system.

After this matter was over, I stated to the Cabinet that it had been strongly recommended that all Cotton, Sugar, Tobacco and Rice should henceforward be purchased only by Government officers, paying to the owners, loyal or disloyal, a certain proportion of the price in New-York amounting to nearly or quite the full price in the producing States; and giving a Certificate which would entitle the owner to the remainder of the proceeds, deducting taxes and charges, at the end of the rebellion, if loyal. Having made this statement, I said I would like to have the matter reflected on, and that I should bring it up at our next meeting.

Before going to Cabinet, and on my walk to Mr. Seward's room, I met Judge Pierrepont,[48] and invited him to dinner. Coming from Cabinet, I found a letter from Barney about Wadsworth's nomination and Weed's willingness to make it unanimous, if it is not to be considered as a triumph over him; and wrote a note to the General, asking him also to dine. Both he and the Judge came, and we had a pleasant time. Wadsworth has but one objection to saying he would be Governor, if at all, of the State and not of a section of a party; which was, that it might be considered as in some sort a pledge, which he would not give to anybody. Told Wadsworth, in confidence, that the Proclamation might be expected tomorrow morning—which surprised and gratified him equally.

Mr. [Delano T.] Smith, Chief-Clerk of the Third Auditor's Office; his brother, associated with Fowler; and Dr. Schmidt, called. Also Donn Piatt.[50] A good deal of speculation about Proclamation, of which some said a rumor was current a day or two since. I said I thought we need not despair of one yet. Chief Clerk Smith said he had eagerly looked at the newspapers one morning lately, on the strength of the rumor, for it, and was really disappointed. I told him to keep looking.

Donn Piatt wanted young Este [51] made Clerk. Told him I would be glad to do so, but could not promise. Mr. Platt called to learn about Col Hays, and Dr. Harkness about his son-in-law.

Sept. 23, Tuesday. At breakfast this morning, I proposed to Katie to ride over to the Insane Asylum and see Genl. Hooker,[52] to which she agreed; and she having provided a basket of grapes, peaches, &c., we went. We were very kindly received by Mrs. Nichols who ushered us into the General's room. He was lying on a couch, but suffering no pain. He talked very freely, as far as time would permit, of the recent events. He said that at Richmond, when the order came to withdraw the army, he advised McClellan to disobey, and proposed a plan for an advance on Richmond. McClellan gave him the order to advance, but before the time for movement came recalled it, and gave orders for evacuation. When Hooker expected to march to Richmond, therefore, he found himself, to his surprise, compelled to fall back to the Chickahominy on his way to Aquia. I said to him, 'General, if my advice had been followed, you would have commanded after the retreat to James River if not before'—He replied, 'If I had commanded, Richmond would have been ours.'—He then spoke of the Battle of Antietam, where he received his wound, and expressed his deep sorrow that he could not remain on on [sic] the field three hours longer. 'If I could have done so,' he said, 'our victory would have been complete; for I had already gained enough and seen enough to make the rout of the enemy sure.' After he had been carried off, he said, McClellan sent for him again to lead an advance. The General impressed me favorably, as a frank, manly, brave and energetic soldier, of somewhat less breadth of intellect than I had expected, however, though not of less quickness, clearness and activity.[53]

While we were conversing, Dr. Nichols came in and I had some talk with him in an adjoining room. He said the General's wound was as little dangerous as a foot-wound could be, the ball having passed through the fleshy part just above the sole and below the instep, probably without

touching a bone. I suggested the trial of Dr. Forshés
[Forsha's] Balm. He made no special objection, but said
the wound was doing as well as possible, without inflama-
tion [*sic*] and with very little matter; and he thought it unnecessary to try any experiments. I could not help concurring in this, and postponed Dr. F. and his Balm.—The
Doctor said he first knew him when encamped below him
last year; that he became deeply interested in him; that
when he heard he was wounded, he went up to Frederick,
seeking him; that he missed him; but that his message
reached him, and he came down to the Asylum himself.
I asked, 'What is your estimate of him?'—'Brave, energetic, full of life, skilful on the field, not comprehensive
enough, perhaps, for plan and conduct of a great campaign; but at least equal in this respect, if not superior
to any General in the service.[']

Mr. Rives (of the Globe)[54] his daughter and son-in-law
came in and we took our leave; Dr. Nichols having first
strongly recommended to me to secure the appointment
of Col. Dwight,[55] of Mass., as a Brigadier-General.

Returned home and went to Department. Found Genl.
[William] Robinson, of Pittsburgh, there: and Mr. Platt
and Dr. Harkness. Got Harrington to go with P. and H. to
War Department.—Mr. Welles came in, about appoint-
ment of Pease,[56] in Wisconsin, and I asked him to write a
note about it.—Attorney-General Bates called, with Mr.
Gibson[57] of St. Louis, about pecuniary aid to Gov. Gam-
ble[58]—both telling a very different story from Farrar and
Dick.[59] Promised to look at papers and answer tomorrow.
—Stanton came in about payment of paroled soldiers at
Camp Chase, which I promised to provide for. Said that
he proposed to make the Department of Florida, with

Thayer [60] as Governor and Garfield as Commanding General, if I approved of Garfield. I said I approved heartily. Said he had insisted on removal of Buell, and leaving Thomas in command. I could not disapprove of this, though I think less highly of him than he seems to think.— He went, and Barney came in Asked him to dine. Declined, but promised to call in the evening.—Mr. Hamilton, on invitation, came to our house to stay while in town.

In the evening, many callers—Miss Schenck, Genl. and Mrs. McDowell, Genl. Garfield, and others. Young Mr. Walley [61] came, with letters from his father, and I brought him in and introduced him to Katie and our guests.

Sept. 24, Wednesday. The President called a special meeting of the Cabinet to-day, and asked our judgments on two questions:

First, as to the expediency of Treaties with Governments desiring their immigration, for voluntary colonization of blacks.

Second, As to the proper answer to be returned to the letter from John Ross,[62] excusing the Treaty of the Cherokees with the Rebels, and asking the protection of the United States and the fulfilment of old Treaties.

On the first question, there was the usual diversity of opinion. I, not thinking Colonization in itself desirable, except as a means of getting a foothold in Central America, thought no Treaties expedient; but simple arrangements, under the legislation of Congress by which any persons who might choose to emigrate would be secured in such advantages as might be offered them by other States or Governments. Seward rather favored Treaties, but evidently did not think much of the wisdom of any measures for sending out of the country laborers needed here. The

President asked us to think of the subject, and be ready to express our opinions when we next come together.

As to the Cherokee question there seemed to be a general concurrence that no new pledges should be given them but that, at the end of the war, their condition and relations to the United States should have just consideration.

After Cabinet, went with Stanton to War Department, and laid before him sundry applications for positions, with such verbal support as I thought due to them. Returning to the Department, I found there young Mr. Walley, and gave him an earnest recommendation to Stanton; and was surprised, an hour or so after, to receive a note from him, thanking me for my kindness, but saying that Mr. Stanton told him there was no likelihood of his receiving an appointment; and that he was going to enlist as a private. Wrote note to Mr. Walley (his father) expressing my regret.

Nothing at Department but routine—except direction to Cisco to receive deposits of Gold, and a call from Eli Thayer about his project for colonizing East Florida, with which I sympathize.

Had proposed to Gen. Garfield to take him over and call on Genl. Hooker but it rained and he did not come. After dinner, however, the sky cleared somewhat, and Katie and I rode out and called on him. He was still improving.

An hour or two after our return, a band of music, which had just serenaded the President by way of congratulation on the Proclamation, came to my house and demanded a speech—with which demand, I complied briefly. Gen. Clay, who was with me, responded more at length. After the crowd had passed on, Gen. Clay; Mr. Clarke,[63] of

Mercer, Penna.,; Genl. Robinson, of Pittsburgh; and Mr. Wm. D. Lewis,[64] of Philadelphia, came in and spent a little time with me.

Sept. 25, Thursday. At Department as usual. The President sent for me to meet the Secretary of War. Found he had nothing to talk about except the supply of an additional sum to Gov. Gamble, of Missouri, to be used in defending the State against invasion and guerillaism. Agreed to confer with the Secretary of War on the subject.—Enquired as to progress of the war. No information, and nothing satisfactory as to what is to be expected. Coming out, Stanton told me that McClellan wants bridges built across the Potomac and Shenandoah, as preliminaries to movement; to which Halleck won't consent. Dan helps Zeke doing nothing.

Delighted this morning by news of Genl Wadsworth's nomination for Governor of New-York on the first ballot.

In the afternoon, went with Garfield to see Hooker, who was very free in his expressions about McClellan. He said it was not true that either the army or the officers were specially attached to him; that only two corps, whose commanders were special favorites and whose troops had special indulgences, could be said to care anything about him; that other officers—he himself, certainly—thought him unfit to lead a great army; that he is timid and hesitating when decision is necessary; that the Battle of Antietam was near being lost by his way of fighting it, whereas, had the attack been simultaneous and vigorous on the enemy's right, centre and left, the rout would have been complete; that our force in the battle exceeded the enemy's by 30,000 men, and that the defeat of the enemy should have been final. He said, also, that when Pope had drawn off a large part of the rebels from Richmond and orders came to McClellan to withdraw, he urged him to give, on the contrary, orders for advance ; that the orders were actually given and then revoked, much to his chagrin. This recalled to my mind a conversation with Gen Halleck at that time. I said to him that it seemed to me our people could now certainly take Richmond by a vigorous push, as Pope had 60,000 of the rebels before him, and at least half of the remaining 60,000 were South of the James, leaving only 30,000 with the fortifications on the North side ; to which Gen Halleck replied, that it was too dangerous an undertaking. I said, 'If this cannot be done, why not return to Fredericksburgh, leaving Richmond on the left?' 'This, he said, 'would be quite as dangerous—a flank movement, in which our army would be exposed to being cut off and totally lost.' Gen Hooker said that the movement I suggested could have been executed with safety and success. He said, also, that he was somewhat reconciled to leaving the Peninsula, by being told that it was a plan for getting rid of McClellan, and the only one which it was thought safe to adopt. This he thought so essential, that anything necessary to it was to be accepted.

Returning from Gen Hooker's, as well as going, Genl. Garfield gave me some very interesting portions of his own experience. This fine officer was a laborer on a canal in his younger days. Inspired by a noble ambition, he had availed himself of all means to acquire knowledge—became a Preacher of the Baptist Church [65]—was made President of a flourishing Literary Institution on the Reserve—was elected to the Ohio Senate, and took a conspicuous part as a Republican leader. On the breaking out of the War he became a Colonel—led his regiment into Eastern Kentucky—fought Humphrey Marshall near Prestonburgh [66]—gained position rapidly—was made, at my instance, a Brigadier—fought under Buell at Shiloh—and was now in Washington by direction of the Secretary of War, who proposes to give him the Department of Florida. A large portion of his Regiment, he said, was composed of students from his College.

Went to Seward's to dinner, where I met the Marquis of Cavendish, and his brother, Col. Leslie of the British Army; [67] Mr. Stuart and Mr Kennedy [68] of the British Legation; Genl. Banks, and Mr Everett.[69] Genl Banks earnest against more separation of forces until the rebel army is crushed.

Home. Found there Genl. and Mrs. McDowell. Soon after, Capt. and Mrs Loomis came in. Could not help the Captain who wished to be Quartermaster of Genl. Sigel's Corps.

To bed, tired and unwell.

Sept. 26, Friday. Received note from Gov. Seward, asking me to name Consul to Rio. Named James Monroe.[70] Another note from Fred Seward asked me to call at State Department before going to Cabinet. Called, but Gov. Seward had already gone.

Went to Cabinet. Talk about Colonization. I said nothing. All the others except Welles (Stanton not present) in favor of treaties.

Several of the loyal Governors came to-day,[71] and in the evening I called on them. Saw Yates at the National, and left card for Berry of N.H.—Saw Kirkwood at Kirkwood house.—Saw Saloman at Willard's and left cards for Andrew, Bradford, Sprague, Tod, Blair and Pierpont. At Gov.

Yates' room saw Genl. McClernand,[72] of Ills., who made a very favorable impression on me.

Sept. 27, Saturday. Gov Andrew came to breakfast. Laughed—vexed too—at Report in Herald of proceedings of Governors at Altoona,[73] which he ascribed to the exclusion of reporters. While at breakfast, Col. Andrews and Lieut. Barber, both of Marietta, came in from battleground. The Colonel handed me Cox's [74] Report, and informed me that Col. Clark [75] was killed, which left him Lieut-Colonel in actual command He gave a very interesting account of Cox's (late Reno's) corps, both at South Mountain and Antietam. The Reports, however, were more full, and reflected the highest credit on Cox and the officers and men of his troops. Andrews said that McClellan and Burnside would recommend Cox for Major-General—an object which I assured Col. A. I would most gladly promote.

Gov Andrew said he had called on Gen. Hooker the evening before, and met Stanton and Tod. Hooker was unequivocal in condemnation of McClellan's inactivity. At Department, McClernand called and my favorable impression of last evening was strengthened. Many things in a plan of campaign which he urged seemed admirable, especially the Eastern movement from the Mississippi River.

Saw the President, and asked him his opinion of McClernand Said he thought him brave and capable, but too desirous to be independent of every body else.

Later in the day, received telegram from Bliss,[76] Paymaster General of New-York, asking for $300,000 in small notes in exchange for the same amount of large ones to enable him to forward eight regiments. It occurred to me

that, by having these regiments sent to Louisville and
Mitchell's and Garfield's bridgades brought from Louisville and sent to Port Royal, with one or two brigades in
addition, a successful expedition against Charleston might
be immediately organized; and I determined to speak to
Stanton in relation to it tomorrow. Garfield spent the evening with me and accepted invitation to make my house
his home while in town.

(The Chapter in Artemus Ward's Book, read by the
President as introductory to his Proclamation, was 'High-
handed Outrage in Utica.')

Sept. 28, Sunday. At Dr. Pyne's [77] in morning—sermon
excellent. Home in afternoon. In the evening went to War
Department, about Expedition to Charleston; my idea
being to have New York regiments sent to Louisville, and
Mitchell's and Garfield's brigades withdrawn thence and
sent to Port Royal with Garfield; when an immediate attack should be made on Charleston which would be sure
to fall. Did not find Stanton at Department. Went to Halleck's and found him there. Had some general talk. Was
informed by Halleck that the enemy was moving to
Martinsburg. 'How many?'—'150,000.' 'How many has
McClellan?'—'About 100,000.'—'Where [are] Pennsylvania troops, said to have joined him though raised only
for emergency?' 'All gone back.'—Had talk about draft.
He showed me a letter to Gamble, insisting that all officers
of drafted militia above regimental should be appointed
by the President. I expressed the opinion that the principle of drafting Militia was erroneous—that the law should
have provided for drafting from the people an army of the
United States. He agreed.—I asked him his opinion of
McClernand. He said he is brave and able but no discipli-

narian; that his camp was always full of disorder; that at Corinth he pitched his tents where his men had been buried just below ground, and with dead horses lying all around. The cause of the evil was that his officers and men were his constituents.

Leaving Halleck, Stanton and I rode together to Columbia College [78] and back to his house. I stated my wish concerning the two brigades and Charleston. He said nothing could be done. The New-York Regiments must go to McClellan, who absorbs and is likely to absorb everything and do nothing. At Stanton's saw, for the first time, Genl. Harney [79] who mentioned several circumstances to show Frank Blair's misconduct in Missouri matters. He said it was not necessary to fire a gun to keep Missouri in the Union. I thought him evidently mistaken.

Sept. 30, Tuesday. The papers this morning confirm the news of Nelson's [80] death. He died as the fool dieth. How sad! His early services to the Union cause in Kentucky—his generous and manly nature—his fine talents and great energy—compelled my admiration and esteem; while his cruelty and passion and tyranny, especially when excited by drink, often excited my indignation. Nothing from any quarter of much importance in a military point of view.

Genl. Garfield, at breakfast, related this: When Gen. Buell's Army was on the march to Nashville, a Regiment passed in front of the house of Gen Pillow's [81] brother, where was a spring of good water and a little stream issuing from it. As the soldiers quenched their thirst and filled their canteens and watered their horses at the stream, Pillow came out and cursed the men, forbidding them to take water and saying that if he were younger he would fight against the Yankees until the last man of them was killed or driven home. A Lieutenant commanding the Company then having expostulated with him without effect and finding the army likely to be delayed by his interference, directed him to be put under arrest, and sent him to the Colonel. It happened that this Colonel was an admirer of Miss Stevenson—a young lady of Nashville, a niece of Pillow and a violent Secessionist—and had been in the habit of sending the Regimental Band to serenade her with 'Dixie' and the like, not playing any National Airs. As soon as he understood who Pillow was, therefore, he discharged him from arrest and apologized for it; and at the same time arrested the young Lieutenant. Pillow returned to his house, mounted his horse and rode to Genl. Buell's Head Quarters and complained that a slave of his had escaped and was somewhere in the army. Buell gave him leave to hunt for him and with this warrant he rode where he pleased. After fully satisfying himself, he went on to Corinth and gave Beauregard [82] a full account of Buell's force and rate of advance. This information led to the attack on Grant's division, which Beauregard hoped to destroy before Buell should come—and he almost succeeded in doing it.

At Department, received a Note from Seward, with Memorandum by Stuart, Acting British Minister, of Conversation with Seward about cotton. From this Memorandum, it appears the [that?] Butler's Order of August authorizing free purchases even from Slidell,[88] and Grant's Order annulling Sherman's prohibition of payments in gold,[84] were, if not motived by Seward, fully approved by him and made the basis of assurances that no hindrance to purchase and payment on cotton from rebels would be interposed by this government. Afterwards, or about the time of these Orders, Seward proposed the same policy of substantially unrestricted purchase for money, to me; and I was at first, in view of the importance of a supply of cotton, inclined to adopt it; but reflection and information from Special Agents in the Mississippi Valley changed my views. The subject was also brought up in Cabinet, and Seward proposed liberty to purchase 500,000 bales. Stanton and I opposed this, and the President sided with us; and the subject was dropped. I then proposed to frame Regulations for trade to and from Insurrectionary Districts, in which was included prohibition of payments in gold.

To this prohibition Stuart now objects, as in contravention of Seward's assurances connected with Butler's and Grant's Orders.

After considering the whole subject, I addressed a letter to Seward declining to change the existing Regulation as to payments in gold.

Received letter from [Mellen?] himself, stating difficulty between himself and Agent Gallagher [85] as to Confiscation—Mellen thinking that antecedents of cotton, as to liability to confiscation in prior hands and notice to present holders, should not be investigated; Gallagher contra. Wrote Mellen that his view is approved—thinking this may relieve Seward.

Oct. 1, Wednesday. Seward came to Department and we talked over foreign relations, particularly as connected with cotton. Showed him my Reply to his Note of yesterday. He thought it would not answer, as his assurances, coupled with Butler's and Grant's Orders, committed us too far. I said I would modify it. After he left, altered my reply and sent it.

Examined Regulations concerning trade with block-aded ports, and War Orders.

Oct. 2, Thursday. Seward came to my house with Letter to Stuart, vindicating the course of the Treasury Department concerning Trade Orders and Regulations. I approved the whole; but suggested that as the Regulations embraced the Coal Order substantially, and as Great Britain took exception to that as particularly intended for her, he might say that, to prove the absence of such intention and as a proof of the entire absence of any wish to vex trade, the Coal Order would be rescinded.

Oct. 3, Friday. The President still absent at McClellan's Army. I expect little good from this visit.

Oct. 4, Saturday. Mr. Harrington left this morning for New-York. He is instructed to hasten increase of issue of Postage Currency to $100,000 per day. Expects to go to Boston in 'Miami.'

Oct. 5, Sunday. At home to favor foot. Much better in the afternoon, and rode over to Insane Asylum to see Hooker Was glad to find him much improved. He said we had plenty of good officers, and that all the courage, ability and genius we needed could be found among our Volunteer Colonels. He then said that an *aide* of McClellan had been down to see him with an enquiry as to how soon he would be able to take the field, and expressing his confidence with hints of important command of army moving from Washington. He expressed the belief that no decisive victory would be achieved so long as McClellan had command.

Before starting on this visit, John A. Stevens, jr.,[86] called wishing me to see Col. Hamilton [87] about Texas; and I asked him to bring him to dinner. Accordingly both came.

Secretary Stanton also, by accident, and Mr. Montgomery, by Katie's invitation. After dinner, Col. Hamilton spoke fully of Texas—described his escape and hiding in the woods—said that many hundred loyal Texans were now concealed in Texas or refugees—declared that the War was a war of the Oligarchy upon the People—that Slavery was the basis of the Oligarchy, but that the perpetuation of slavery was not more their object, than the despotic power of the Class over the Mass. I entered fully into his feelings; and promised to go with him to the President's tomorrow.

After he went, Gov. Morton [88] came in and spoke very earnestly of the condition of matters in Indiana. Apprehends State defeat on the 14th., and loss of all the Congressional Districts except Julian's, Colfax's, and perhaps Shanks'. Wants Indiana Regiments in the State furloughed so that they can vote. Thinks Buell utterly unfit for command of the great army under him—is slow, opposed to the Proclamation, and has bad influence every way. Wishes me to go with him to President's about the regiments which I promised to do tomorrow.

Oct. 6, Monday. Maj. Garrard [89] called to speak about North-Carolina and Genl Foster.[90] Foster has now 3d. N. Y. Cav., and of Infantry, 17, 24 and 25 Mass, 9 N.J., 2 Md. and 5 R.I.; supported by Albemarle and Pamlico Fleet, say Ten Gunboats. Foster wants reinforcements,— several Regiments of Infantry and another Regiment of Cavalry. Maj Garrard desires that if another Regiment of Cavalry is sent, Col Mix [91] should be made Brigadier.

Genl Keyes and Maj. Bannister, with Genl. Garfield and Major Garrard formed our breakfast party. Genl. Keyes spoke of the disposition in the army (McClellan

&c.) to disfavor Republican officers. Genl. Garfield mentioned the case of a young Republican officer ordered to Kansas in 1856, who was told by his Colonel that he would not allow him to remain in the Regiment if he remained a Republican. Genl Keyes spoke of the Chaplain at West Point, as the most perfect specimen of a Northern man with Southern principles he ever knew; and said that when the new Regiments were organized under Jeff Davis, as Secretary of War to Pierce, eleven out of fifteen officers were appointed from the South, and when he remarked upon it he was challenged to select eleven better men.

Went to Department, and with Gov Morton to see the President about furlough to enable Indiana soldiers in camp to vote; which he promised. Left the Governor with the President. Saw Col. Hamilton and arranged interview for him. Met Wadsworth and Cochrane.[92] Asked Cochrane to breakfast.

Oct. 7, Tuesday. Genl. Cochrane breakfasted with me, and after breakfast conversed freely about McClellan. He said McClellan would like to retire from active command if he could do so without disgrace—which could be accomplished and a more active General secured by restoring him to the chief command, where he would now act in unison with myself. I explained frankly my relations to McClellan—my original admiration and confidence—my disappointment in his inactivity and irresolution—my loss of confidence and conviction that another General should replace him—my constant endeavor to support him by supplies and reinforcements, notwithstanding my distrust, when the President determined to keep him in command —my present belief that I had not judged incorrectly, but my entire willingness, also, to receive any correction which facts would warrant; and my absolute freedom from personal ill-will, and my entire readiness to do anything which would ensure the earliest possible suppression of the rebellion He said that Col. Key had often expressed his regret that McClellan had not conferred with me, and acted in concert with me. I replied that I thought, if he had, the rebellion would be ended now; but that I feared concert between us impossible, our views, dispositions and principles harmonizing so little. He said he would talk with McClellan and write me. I answered that I should be glad to hear from him, and was quite willing he should report to McClellan what I had said.

At Cabinet, the President spoke of his visit to the Army at Sharpsburgh, and the battle-fields of Antietam and South Mountain. He said he was fully satisfied that we had not over 60,000 men engaged; and he described the position of the enemy and our own—the enemy's being much the best, his wings and centre communicating easily be [by] the Sharpsburgh road parallel with the stream. He expressed no opinion as to Generalship, nor of results.

Seward asked what new of the Expedition to Charleston? Secretary Welles [said] the necessary iron-clads could not be ready in less than a month. I was much disappointed by this statement, remembering that ten days of a month were up; and said at once that I hoped then we should not wait for the Navy but at once organize a land force sufficient to take the city from James' Island. Mr. Stanton agreed in the importance of this, and proposed to order Mitchell's and Garfield's Brigades from the West— send Garfield at once to South Carolina with these Brigades and two more regiments—and let Mitchell go to work immediately. He said also that he proposed at once to organize an Expedition to open the Mississippi and give the command of it to McClernand. The President seemed much pleased with both movements—but Halleck remained to be consulted. Would he oppose the President and Stanton? I thought not.

I left the Cabinet with more hope than I have felt for months.

At the President's, I met W. H. Aspinwall and invited him to come and dine with me, which he did. In conversation, I enquired what he thought of the idea of selling some $50,000,000 of Five-twenties at about the Market rate? He thought it should be done but doubted whether more than 97½ could be obtained. I said I hoped to get 99 or 99½. He then spoke of his visit to McClellan and seemed greatly to desire my coöperation with him. He mentioned that Burnside had heard that I blamed him for having Porter restored to command; but thinks I would not if I understood all the circumstances.

Oct. 10, Friday. Went to Cabinet, taking Mr. Whittlesey [93] to Department. Found the President reading telegrams from Kentucky. McCook's [94] division engaged with Bragg's Army on the 8th. and hard pressed, but was reinforced and the enemy repulsed. All the Corps up at night and in position. Slight engagement with enemy's rear guard yesterday, but main body retreated to Harrodsburgh. This from Buell at Perryville yesterday morning. Stager [95] p[er]. Cleveland telegraphs another great battle yesterday, and no mistake about victory this time. This came this morning at ten. So we hope the best.

Nothing of much importance was discussed except Norfolk. I favored opening the Port. Nothing was decided.—

Asked Stanton what he had done about McClernand's Army for clearing the Mississippi, and he replied 'Nothing.' Seward said he thought something had been done, and the President that something had been agreed on. It turned out that orders for the organization of the expedition had been given but that nothing of importance was yet done.

Home. Signed official letters and Warrants—Directed Regulations of Trade with open ports to be sent to the Secretary of War.

In the evening, Genl Hunter, Maj. Halpin,[96] Mr. Cowan,[97] Judge and Mr. Maxwell of N.Y., Genl. McDowell, Maj. D. Taylor and others called. Before Dinner, Bannister came about Col. A. J. Hamilton, of Texas, going to Ohio. Urged him to have him go if possible.

Directed $10,000 Postage Currency sent to Cincinnati.

Oct. 11, Saturday. Surprised to read this morning that Stuart's Cavalry have taken Chambersburgh, Penna.[98] What next?

Recd. letter from John Cochrane, saying that McClellan appreciates my support while not approving his command, and would gladly coöperate with me and see me; and that there is no substantial difference between us on the Slavery question.—Also received letter from Aspinwall about Five-twenty Loan, which he advises—He thinks 98 may be obtained—equivalent to, say, 75 in gold.— Also a letter from Cisco sending a $10 U.S. Note, purloined from National Bank Note Company and falsely filled and sealed.—Wrote Cisco about detective; and enclosed Aspinwall's note and asked his opinion.—Sundry other letters received and answered.—Needham (Ky) [99] called I accepted [Harrison A.] Williams' declination as Assessor Louisville District, and agreed to appoint Needham in his place—he to resign Collectorship.

Genl. Hunter, Maj. Halpin, Mr. Jay [100] and Genl. Garfield (still our guest) at dinner. Maj. Halpin mentioned that McClellan had telegraphed Head Quarters that not one of the rebels who have invaded Pennsylvania shall return to Virginia. Hope it may be so, faintly. Too many Bills of the same sort protested for the credit of the Drawer.

After dinner talked a good deal with Genl. Hunter, who is very well read. Asked him his opinion of Halleck. He said, 'He has ability and knowledge, but does not make an earnest study of the War—does not *labor* to get clear ideas of positions, conditions and possibilities, so as to seize and press advantages or remedy evils.'—I then asked what he thought of the President? 'A man irresolute but of honest intentions—born a poor white in a Slave State, and, of course, among aristocrats—kind in spirit and not envious, but anxious for approval, especially of those to whom he has been accustomed to look up—hence solicitous of support of the Slaveholders in the Border States, and unwilling to offend them—without the large mind necessary to grasp great questions—uncertain of himself, and in many things ready to lean too much on others.' What of Stanton?—'Know little of him. Have seen him but once, and was then so treated that I never desired to see him again. Think from facts that have come to my knowledge that he is not sincere. He wears two faces; but has energy and ability, though not steady power.' The conversation then turned on Douglas whose ardent friend and constant supporter

Hunter was—also on other persons and things. I found him well read and extremely intelligent.

Gen Hunter tells me that he desires to retire from the army, and have some position in New-York which will enable him to resume his special vocation as a writer for the Press. He says he has written lately some leaders for the 'Republican,' and has *aided* the Proprietor of '*Wilkes' Spirit of the Times.*' [101]

Oct. 12, Sunday. At home all day, nursing inflamed foot—reading, and conversing with Katie and friends.

5

An Available Candidate

BETWEEN October, 1862, and August, 1863, Chase seems not to have kept a diary. These important months formed a period of growing tension within the administration. The replacement of McClellan by Burnside led in December, 1862, to the catastrophe at Fredericksburg. With repeated failure, Congressional outcry against Lincoln's administration grew angrier, and information was fed to the critics by the disgusted Secretary of the Treasury. To him, as to the other Republican Radicals, it appeared that the blame for the wavering policies and the unsuccessful military strategy of the President rested upon Secretary of State Seward, who had become a symbol of what was wrong with the administration. "While they seemed to believe in my honesty," Lincoln said of his critics, "they seemed to think that when I had in me any good purpose or intention Seward contrived to suck it out of me unperceived."

On December 19th a delegation of Republican Congressmen met with the President and demanded that he oust Seward. With characteristic skill, Lincoln avoided a direct response but arranged another meeting at which the Congressmen confronted the cabinet with their criticisms. Chase was thrown into an ambiguous position. He had tried to function both as an adviser to the Congressional junto and as a member of the cabinet. It now became clear that he could not serve the one without being disloyal to the other, and the Secretary on December 20th wrote out his resignation. Lincoln, who already had Seward's offer to resign, seized Chase's letter eagerly. "Now I can ride," he said in his homely fashion; "I have got a pumpkin in each end of my bag." By compelling his cabinet to assume a united front, he had warned Congressional Radicals that further attacks on Seward would lead to the withdrawal of Chase, and he had notified Seward's friends that assaults on the Secretary of the Treasury could only weaken the Secretary of State. Then Lincoln refused to accept either resignation. Both Seward and Chase remained in a cabinet where the President had clearly emerged as the dominant figure.

There is no known diary record by Chase of these events, or of his important Treasury Department duties during the first months of 1863. Thanks to Jay Cooke's staggering promotional campaign, the 5–20 loan was selling rapidly, and the Treasury officials worked overtime to supply the bonds as fast as they were needed. In February, 1863, the National Banking Act was forced through a reluctant Congress. Though Chase was far from satisfied with the provisions of the act, he at once installed as first Comptroller of the Currency Hugh McCulloch, of Indiana, who energetically supervised the new banking system. During these months, also, as Northern armies advanced, the Secretary's responsibilities for trade with the Southern states became increasingly heavy. Some wanted to cut off all commerce with the seceded states; others advocated unlimited trade with any area reconquered by Federal troops; but Congress decided upon a system of licensing, designed to keep money and supplies from falling into Confederate hands, and entrusted the enforcement of the regulations to the Treasury Department. The restrictions on trade were especially vexatious to merchants at St. Louis, Cincinnati, and other ports which had always depended on river commerce, and they complained loudly against Chase's administration.

Criticisms of Chase's policies during these months were closely related to the Secretary's political aspirations. In typical politician's idiom, he had declared himself "available" for the Republican nomination in 1864:

What the country may think proper to do with me is of far less consequence than what it is my duty to do for my country. . . . Of course, I have very little inclination for any political arrangement which has reference to my personal future, but prefer to leave that to the disposition of events and the will of the people, being quite as willing to resume the post of private citizen as to continue in my present, or be transferred to any other public position.

So open an announcement meant that the Secretary's every move would be regarded as a political maneuver. "I'm afraid Mr. Chase's head is turned by his eagerness in pursuit of the presidency," Attorney-General Bates concluded. "For a long time back he has been filling all the offices in his own vast patronage, with extreme partizans, and contrives also to fill many vacancies, properly belonging to other departments."

Chase's role as an avowed presidential aspirant naturally strained his relations with the President. The Secretary's correspondence assumed an increasingly critical and patronizing tone toward Lincoln. The failure of his own protégé, Hooker, at Chancellorsville in May did not lessen the Secretary's eager interest in military affairs, and he still complained that "the war moves too slow and costs too much." Even after George Gordon Meade, Hooker's successor, checked Lee's invasion of Pennsylvania at Gettysburg and after Grant captured Vicksburg, Chase still distrusted the President's military wisdom. And, beyond victory, he foresaw the dangers of reconstruction with which Lincoln would not be able to cope.

The President, in turn, was kept well informed of Chase's attitude. Representing border-state suspicion of Chase's radicalism, the Francis Preston Blair clan now strongly opposed the Secretary of the Treasury, and in the cabinet itself Montgomery Blair openly exhibited his hostility. Suspicion bred suspicion, and busybodies helped widen the breach. Lincoln was warned of the "Treasury rats," who were "busy night and day and becoming more and more unscrupulous and malicious." When Lincoln interfered with Chase's appointments, the Secretary in March and again in May threatened to resign. An uneasy truce was maintained, but the real test of political strength lay just ahead.

❧ ❧ ❧

Aug. 29, 1863, Saturday. Received from A. C. Wilson, President of the Continental Bank Note Company, his charges against Mr. Clark, and referred them to Mr. C. for explanation or answer. The charges seem to be inspired by no public reason, but by hostility to Mr. Clark because of his supposed animosity and injustice to the Company.

Conferred with Mr. McCulloch on the subject of deposits with the National Banks, and determined that the clerk having special charge of this business and its correspondence, shall take a desk under Mr. McC. and be attached to his Bureau.

Mr. Smith Chief Clerk of the 3d. Auditor's Office,[1] was consulted on the subject of the selection of the Chief Clerk in his place, in view of his probable appointment to some outside position.

In the afternoon the President came in with letters from Generals Grant and Banks in relation to the arming of negro troops, and read them to me. Gen. Banks stated that he had already about 12,000 in about 25 regiments of 500 each, which number he regarded as most likely to secure good discipline and drill, and the greatest efficiency of the regiments when filled to their maximum, which he expected to accomplish by degrees. He tho't he had now organized about all the blacks who could be obtained till a larger extent of country should be occupied. Gen. Grant's was much to the same effect, except that he did not contemplate any other original organization as to numbers than that of the white regiments, nor did he specify the numbers actually enlisted. Both Generals express confidence in the efficiency of these troops and clear opinions in favor of using them. These letters gave much satisfaction to the President, and I suggested to him that not only was the public sentiment of the loyal people of Louisiana in favor of negro troops, but also in favor of the revocation of the exception in his Proclamation of the two Districts, including New Orleans, from its operation, and told him that some weeks ago, after talking with him on this subject, tho' more particularly in reference to the excepted Virginia Districts, I had prepared the draft of a Proclamation revoking the exceptions, which, with his permission, I would hand to him. He received it kindly, and said he would consider it further.

In the evening Mr. Mellen and Mr. Risley [2] came to my house, and we read through the new Regulations of trade and concerning abandoned property, and completed their revision. Mr. Mellen will now return to his Agency, and Mr. Risley will supervise the printing of the new Regulations.

Aug. 30, Sunday. Mr. Covode called at my house after church and desired to know my opinion as to the proper course, to be taken in Pennsylvania. I replied that there seemed to me but one course to be taken, and that was to give a hearty support to the re-election of Gov. Curtin. He thought Gov. Curtin and his friends designed that he should be brought forward as a candidate for the Presidency, and that, if elected Governor he would shape matters in Pennsylvania so as to secure its delegates in the Convention, while a majority of the loyal men of Pennsylvania preferred me, and that the vote of the State controlled by Curtin would not be given to me unless under some arrangement which would pledge to Gov. Curtain and his friends the patronage in Pennsylvania. To this I replied that no speculations as to Gov. Curtin's future course could excuse the loyal men from supporting him now; that the future must take care of itself; that I was not anxious for the Presidency; that there was but one position in the Government which I really w'd like to have, if it were possible to have it without any sacrifice of

principle or public interest, and that was the Chief Justiceship, and that should the wishes of our political friends
incline to me as a nominee for the Presidency, those
wishes must be entirely of a public nature, for I certainly
would never consent under any circumstances to make
pledges as to appointments to office, but would insist upon
being left entirely free to avail myself of the services of
the best men in the country. Mr. Covode approved of
these sentiments, and said that he would confer with a
number of prominent citizens opposed to Mr. Curtin tomorrow evening, at Philadelphia, and endeavor to secure
united action in his favor. After he left, Mr. Mellen came
in and dined with me. We had some conversation in relation to the duties of his Agency from which I hope some
good. He is active, intelligent, and faithful, and if any one
can accomplish the work of regulating trade without prejudice to military operations, and at the same time to the
satisfaction of honest people engaged in it, and for the
benefit of the people of the rebel states within our military
lines, I think he will do it.

Aug. 31, Monday. Business at the Department for to-
day was chiefly routine. Wrote to Mr. Cisco directing
him to ascertain whether the Banks and Bankers of New
York would subscribe 35,000,000$ for 5 per cent. Treas-
ury Notes payable in a year and made a legal tender for
their face.[3] Addressed similar letters to the Assistant Treasurers at Boston and Philadelphia, asking for a subscription of ten millions at Boston and five millions at Philadelphia. I am not at all sanguine in the expectation that
success will attend these applications. It is substantially
a proposition to the capitalists to loan money to the Government for a year at about 5¼ per cent., with a privi-

lege, however, of being repaid at any time after 30 days when the Treasury Notes can be delivered.

A Note from Senator Henderson [4] apprised me that a delegation from St. Louis desired to call upon me with reference to the regulations of the River trade. I replied that I would see them to-morrow at 10 or 2 o'clock as best suited them. I afterwards received a note from the Senator, saying they would call at 2 to-morrow afternoon.

In the afternoon I called at the President's, and found him listening to representations of Senator Bowdoin [5] and Representatives Chandler [6] and Segur [7] of Virginia and Dr. ———, of Northampton county, concerning the tax imposed by order of the War Department on the people of that county to pay for the re-building of a Light-house lately destroyed by rebels. The object of these gentlemen was to induce the President to revoke that order, on the ground that the people of Northampton were thoroughly loyal, and that the destruction of the Light-house was without the least privity of theirs, but by rebels who came from that portion of Virginia still controlled by rebels. After these gentlemen took their leave, the President said to me that he felt inclined to suspend the order. I suggested that perhaps it would be well to revoke the exception of Northampton and the other counties of Virginia from his [Emancipation] Proclamation, and accompany that revocation by the revocation of the order imposing the tax, inasmuch as the first revocation would insure the loyalty which the people of the county professed.

Turning from this subject I asked the President to appoint Mr. Shellaberger [8] Governor of Dacotah if he should determine not to give that place to Judge Bliss, [9] and if he should then to give the Chief Justiceship to Mr. Shellaberger; and I also asked him in case Mr. Bingham [10] should decline the Judgeship at Key West to give it to Judge Lawrence [11] of Logan county, Ohio. He received these requests favorably, but promised nothing.

I then called at the War Department, and not finding the Secretary, left a request that he would call at the Treasury Department, and went myself to the Navy Department, to inquire if there was any immediate necessity for a Judge at Key West. Secretary Welles was absent at the North, but Assistant Secretary Fox informed me that the want of a Judge at Key West occasioned great inconvenience and risk of public and private injuries, but that he thought Judge Marvin [12] would hold the Court if requested until his successor could arrive in November. Mr. Fox informed me that there were now between sixty and seventy naval vessels undergoing repairs at New York, and the loss in consequence of the poor timber necessarily employed in their construction was enormous. I inquired if any steps had been taken toward purchasing tar, pitch, turpentine and ship timber in North Carolina, the export of which I had prohibited in order to give the Navy Department an opportunity to buy at reasonable rates. He replied that orders had been given to purchase except as to ship timber. I inquired the cause of such frequent violations of the blockade at Wilmington, to which he answered that the blockade there was now weak in consequence of the withdrawal of so many of the ships for Charleston and for repairs, but that in a few days [it would] be greatly strengthened. After I returned to the Department, Mr. Stanton came in and I suggested to him to propose to the President the revocation of the Proclamation exceptions in Virginia in connection with the suspension or revocation of the Northampton tax order. He seemed disinclined to connect the two, but was disposed to insist on the tax. We discussed the question briefly and left it unsettled. I represented to him the great importance of prompt and vigorous military action, that tomorrow the amount of suspended requisitions, including the pay of the whole army for July and August would approach 35,000,000$, of which I could not command in ordinary ways over 5,000,000$, and that unless the war could be pushed more vigorously and greater certainty of early and successful termination there was cause for serious apprehension of financial embarrassment. He replied that the delay of Gen. Rosecrans [13] was the principal cause of difficulty; that he commanded a full third of all the effective force of the country, and did nothing comparatively with it. That in a week's time he could if he would penetrate those portions of Georgia and Alabama in which the negroes had been taken by their masters, and where the gathering of large bodies of negro troops would be easy. He said that he had represented these things to the President, but so far without much effect.

At the house in the evening Major Taylor, Doctor Schmidt, and Mr. Wright [14] of California, called. Dr. Schmidt warned me, in his way, against Mr. Clark and Dr. Gwinn [14a]; to which I answered that if facts were presented to me instead of vague generalities, they would be considered.—Mr. Wright said he should like some position at my hands some fourteen months hence, to which I replied that at that time it was not likely I should have any to give. He then went into a statement of his connection with the Fremont campaign in '56, and of the election of Mr. Lincoln in '60, and expressed his conviction that I would be the nominee in '64, and that it was his wish to promote that result. I replied that nothing could be more uncertain than the currents of popular sentiment; that I was by no means anxious that they should turn towards me, and that if they did, and the result should be such as he predicted, it must be without any pledges from me in relation to appointments, for no man could honorably take charge of the administration under any other obligations than those of duty, and exercise its powers for the best good of the whole country in conformity with the principles upon which, and in general with the aid of the best men by whom, he had been elected.

Sept. 1, Tuesday. The Committee from Saint Louis called, and after some conversation on the subject of the Relations of Trade Mr. Breckinridge,[15] who appeared to be their chairman, handed me a letter and they withdrew. On reading the letter I found it an indictment against the course of the Government in respect to Western trade with a demand that the river be opened to the same freedom of trade as in times of peace, except so far as restriction might be necessary at points of distribution within the rebel States. I sent for Mr. Barnitz [16] and consulted with him on this subject. He prepared a draft of a of [*sic*] Reply to the Committee.

I directed Mr. Plantz to prepare an abstract of the papers relating to the compensation of Jay Cooke as General Subscription Agent for the sale of 'Five Twenties.' [17]

Note. This draft was not used.

Sept. 2, Wednesday. Nothing of note transpired during the day.

In the evening General Schenck called and conversed

fully about the Court of Inquiry called nominally to investigate the conduct of General Milroy,[18] but which subjected to its investigations *his* conduct as well as all the circumstances connected with the evacuation of Winchester. He was much dissatisfied with these proceedings which gave him no notice and allowed him no opportunity for proper defence. He said he should call upon the President and have the matter set right. I tendered him my services so far as they might be useful.

Sept. 3, Thursday. Mr. Risley came to breakfast, bringing with him the still unfinished regulations. I could give but little attention to them, being compelled to prepare an answer to the Saint Louis Committee, which I wrote after breakfast and took to the Department to be copied.

Gov. Pierpont called and talked about Virginia affairs. He thought a majority of the members of the Legislature would be in favor of calling a Convention to amend the Constitution so as to make it a free-labor State. He said he had not yet sent a written request to the President for a revocation of the exception of the South Eastern counties in his Proclamation, and that though he had originally asked for this exception, he become [*sic*] fully satisfied that it was unwise, and had represented to the President his wish to have it revoked. I told him that if he would put this wish in writing and place his request on grounds of military necessity, the revocation would probably be made; and I suggested to him some grounds of military necessity which seemed to me important. He replied that if I would make a draft of a letter he would use it in framing a request to the President for the revocation. I told him I would do so within the next half hour. At the expiration of that time he called, and I handed him the draft.

Judge Whittaker [19] of New Orleans dined and afterwards took a ride with me. We conversed fully about the state of things in Louisiana, and he expressed himself as being satisfied that Slavery was virtually abolished, and that the Constitution of the State should be so framed as to prohibit it permanently. He was not at first as decided in these sentiments as he became towards the end of our conversation. Indeed, I had expected to find him, from the representations of Mr. Denison and Mr. Plumley, [20] much further advanced than I did.

In the evening, Messrs. McJilton, Meredith, [21] Turner and Snowden, called to converse about matters in Maryland. They stated that Mr. Swan [22] would probably be a candidate against Mr. Davis, [23] on the part of the Conservative Union men, and that on the other hand the Radicals would probably nominate candidates in the several Districts where the Conservatives had succeeded in carrying the Conventions. All these gentlemen seemed to belong to the Conservative side, but were desirous that Mr. Swan should not be a candidate, and on the other hand that the candidates who had been nominated by the Conservatives should not be opposed. I expressed my great regret that the division had occurred, but said that I felt it was founded in differences too radical to be overcome. I could see no remedy, unless both sides could agree to call a Convention upon a platform satisfactory to each and support the candidates that were already or might be nominated and accept it in good faith. Mr. McJilton thought if some of the leaders would come together and talk matters over in a patriotic spirit of accommodation that some good might come of it, and some common ground be found. I begged him to do what he could to accomplish this result, and especially to call with some others of Mr. Swan's friends and represent to him the impossibility of supporting him if he should be a candidate, and induce him, if possible not to consent to such a use of his name.— He promised to do this, and the gentlemen left me.

Mr. Taft [24] and Mr. French of Cincinnati also called to talk over Ohio affairs and political matters generally.— Mr. Parker [25] of St. Louis also called about his Express Company, with a letter from Mr. McKee.[26] Sent word to him to call at the Department to-morrow.

Sept. 4, Friday. At the meeting of the Cabinet (so-called) to-day, Mr. Bates stated that the restrictions on trade created a great deal of inconvenience; that he thought the River should now be free to trade as in times of peace except at points occupied by our troops, and that care should be taken that supplies did not reach rebels. He admitted that some few thousands of dollars worth of goods would get to them under the system he proposed, but he thought this evil would be trivial compared with the evils of restriction. I stated briefly the law and the executive action on the subject and that the change proposed by Mr. Bates was disapproved by Generals Banks and Grant. I added that I had been revising the Regulations, and hoped soon to have them complete; that they had been modified in favor of trade as far as the improved condition of affairs will allow, but wd. not, I feared, meet the sanction of the Generals, whose views and wishes were entitled to the greatest consideration. Mr. Stanton stated that a letter had been recently received from General Grant, in which he proposed to prohibit all trade except in certain articles through Post-Sutlers; that he did not agree with General Grant in this view, believing that the sutlers should be confined to furnishing supplies to the Army, and that all trade with citizens should be under the Regulations of the Treasury Department. After some observations from the President and others the subject was dropped.

The President then called the attention of Mr. Stanton to the order prohibiting the export of arms, and after some conversation, it was agreed that all arms imported into the country should be allowed to be exported to the place from which they were shipped. I then called Mr. Stanton's attention to the order prohibiting the exportation of live stock, and he consented that the order should be modified so far as to allow exportation from ports on the Pacific. On returning to the Department, in order to avoid delay I drew up an executive order, modifying the former order so as to allow exportation of imported arms to the place from which they were originally shipped, and the exportation of live stock from the ports of the Pacific, and sent them to Mr. Stanton for his approval, and then to the President for his signature; and I then telegraphed the Collector at San Francisco that the exportation of live stock was permitted.

Mr. Scudder, of Memphis, called; to whom I read the letter of the St. Louis Committee and my reply. He approved the letter and expressed the opinion that no greater liberty of trade than I proposed could at present be safely allowed.

Mr. Tilton [27] of the New York *Independent,* came to dinner, and rode with me afterwards. I endeavored to impress upon his mind that there were but two practical ways of reconstructing the Proclamation States so as to [protect?] them against the re-establishment of Slavery: One, by the organization of Provisional Governments; the other, by encouraging the loyal citizens to re-establish State Governments under constitutions prohibiting slavery. He inquired much concerning men and things, and I endeavored to give him correct information. The Rev. Mr. Turner [28] (colored) called for a letter to Mr. Stanton recommending him as Chaplain; which I gave him. Professor Hedrick [29] also called to talk about North Carolina matters.

Sept. 5, Saturday. Telegraphed the Collector at San Francisco, congratulating him on the result of the California election.

Received a telegram from Judge Bond [30] desiring to have an interview arranged with the President for Mr. Goldsborough,[31] and other Maryland gentlemen.—Sent to the President a commission for Mr. Stewart,[32] in place of Mr. Ridgeley, who was removed, because of his hostility to the President's policy.

Sept. 6, Sunday. Mr. Heaton [33] came to breakfast, and gave me a full account of the progress of the emancipation sentiment in North Carolina. He represents the hostility to the Proclamation to be confined principally to the former slave owners, who wish to re-enslave the emancipees, but the poorer classes, and many of the middle class, desire freedom, and with it, education and progress. On talking with men who came in to sell a barrell [*sic*] of turpentine, sometimes bringing it in a boat for several miles, or to sell water-melons from an old cart, he found them always quick to understand the cause of their troubles, and their poverty, and anxious for the removal of slavery

in order that their children might have the advantages
of education, which had been denied to them by the aris-
tocracy.

In the afternoon Mr. Stickney [34] called. He had just
arrived from Florida, and lastly from Morris Island.[35] He
says that it is easy now to take possession of Florida; that
five thousand men can accomplish it. Gen. Saxton desires
the command, and Gen. Gilmore [36] approves the expedition, and is willing to spare one or two regiments to aid it.
If the business can be promptly taken hold of, and pushed
vigorously, Mr. Stickney is confident that Florida can be
restored as a Free State by the first of December.

Sept. 11, Friday. Mr. Galloway [37] breakfasted with me.
We talked of Ohio affairs. He speaks encouragingly of our
political prospects at home.

Called on the President immediately after breakfast to
obtain his approval of the revised Regulations of Trade.
He referred me to the Secretary of War, wishing that the
Secretary's order to officers to observe the Regulations,
should precede his approval. Going then to the War Office,
I obtained Mr. Stanton's order, and at the Navy Department obtained that of Secretary Welles. Returned to the
President's. He read me the rough draft of a letter to Andrew Johnson of Tennessee, urging immediate measures to
re-constitute that State, and to so amend the Constitution
as to insure emancipation, and promising him that the re-
constituted State Government, so framed as to exclude the
possibility of rebels regaining the ascendancy, would be
recognized and sustained by the National Government.[38]
Immediately after this, Secretaries Stanton and Fox, and
General Halleck, came in. Some conversation took place
about the further steps for the reduction of Charleston.

Fox expressed the opinion that the harbor outside of Charleston had been closed by the rebels so as to be inaccessible to our ships, except through a narrow passage in which they kept a ship ready to be sunk, so as to close it completely. He said he thought that if such proved to be the fact, the only course would be to reduce the batteries on Sullivan's Island,[39] so as to command that portion of the inner harbor outside of the obstructions. Gilmore had told him, he said, before going on the expedition, that he could reduce Fort Moultrie from Cumming's Point.[40] Mr. Stanton doubted the existence of the obstructions, and said that the Admiral should try immediately what could be done. After Fox left, the President mentioned the resignation of General Burnside, received yesterday.—He said he was not willing to accept it at present, at any rate, as Burnside was now doing very well, and was very loyal and true-hearted. He proposed to say to him that he could not be spared at present, but that after awhile, should success still attend us and his private affairs should make his retirement necessary, his resignation would be accepted. Gen. Halleck then spoke briefly of affairs in and near Tennessee. He thought Rosecrans should advance so as to hold the mountains between him and Atlanta, but not attempt to advance on Atlanta until the movements of the rebels were more fully developed. That Burnside should also hold the country towards the eastern limits of Tennessee, but not attempt a further advance till more certain intelligence concerning the enemy and their designs.

(While I was at the War Department, Mr. Stanton told [me] he should endeavor, to-morrow, to prevail on the President to revoke his exceptions in Virginia, and to adopt some settled principles respecting the enlistment of negroes held as slaves, and that he wanted me to be present. He wished me also to see Seward, and ask him to use his influence with the President to have Farragut sent to Charleston.)

After Stanton and Halleck had left, I explained briefly the Trade Regulations to the President, who said: 'You understand these things: I do not,' and signed the approval.

At the Department, little of interest occurred.—Gen. Blair called with Col. Sanford, and I promised to speak to the Secretary of War in Sanford's behalf. Gen. Cameron called, and told me he was about leaving town, and could not dine with me. I gave him a designation for Mr. Minor. Directed payment of the ten per cent gold loan in full. Called on Gov. Seward. Spoke to him about sending Farragut to Charleston, and he promised to see the President on the subject.

In the evening several callers as usual. Among others, Reese,[41] who promised to bring Judge Edmunds,[42] which I told him to do at any time; and Brand,[43] whom I promised to assist in obtaining promotion if practicable, and Field who gave me an account of the Bank discussions in the Bank Meeting about the Loan.

Sept. 14, Monday. Governor Andrew came in to breakfast. Afterwards I went with him to the President, where I found Secretary Stanton, to whom I recommended 'Scotty'[44] for a medal, as I had promised him. Stanton said he would order one engraved, as soon as I sent him the name and inscription. At eleven a meeting of Heads was held. The President said that the applications for discharges by drafted men and deserters were very numerous, and were granted under circumstances which show that the Judges are disposed to defeat the objects of the law. He expressed the opinion that State Courts had no authority to issue a Writ of Habeas Corpus for any person in the custody of United States officers, claiming to act under the national law. He proposed, therefore, to direct officers holding persons in such custody, to make a return of the fact that they were so held, and to refuse to obey the writ, and if force should be used to overcome it by force. Mr. Seward favored this action, and there was no expression against it, till I remarked that I had always been accustomed to regard the Writ of Habeas Corpus as a most important safeguard of personal liberty. 'It has been generally conceded,' I went on to say, 'or at least such has been the practice, that State Courts may issue Writs of Habeas Corpus for persons detained as enlisted soldiers, and to discharge them. Several cases of this kind have occurred in Ohio, and the proceeding of the State Court was never questioned, to my knowledge. Of course, a proper exercise of the power does not justify its improper exercise. If the Writ is abused with a criminal purpose of breaking up the Army, the persons who abuse it should be punished as any other criminals are. But before taking any action, which even seems to set aside the writ, a clear case should be made, which will command the concurrence of the people and their approval. I suggest, therefore, that the Secretary of War should make a statement of the number of persons discharged from military service under the Writ, with such notes of the circumstances as will show the abuse of it. After which such action can be taken as the case requires.' Mr. Blair and Mr. Usher coincided substantially with these views, Mr. Blair remarking that he had often, when a judge in Missouri, discharged soldiers on Habeas Corpus. The President thought there was no doubt of the bad faith in which the Writ was now being used; Mr. Seward thought it indispensable to assert the authority of the Government at once; and Mr. Bates expressed the opinion that the President as head of the Army could not be interfered with by any civil authority whatever; but was in his action as Commander-in-Chief superior to any process, and might properly instruct his officers and disregard such process; and this without any suspension of the Writ of Habeas Corpus, except as incidental to the exercise of his legitimate authority.—Mr. Stanton thought prompt action necessary. The President ended the discussion by saying he would prepare such an order as he thought best, and would see us again tomorrow at half-past two. The conversation then turned upon Writs of Habeas Corpus issued from Federal courts, when it appeared that the number of discharges made by two Federal Judges in Pennsylvania, Cadwalader at Philadelphia, and McCandless at Pittsburgh,[45] largely exceeded the number discharged by all the State Courts put together. So it at once became evident that an order to reach the State Courts only would be inefficient.

After leaving the President I returned to the Department, and attended to its ordinary duties; the principal to-day being that of drawing upon the Banks for ten per cent. of their subscription for Treasury Notes, and the beginning of the distribution of the revised regulations concerning trade.

Sept. 15, Tuesday. Went to the President's at half-past nine, and met there young Mr. Steven,[46] nephew to the English lawyer, and Mr. Gillespie,[47] of Illinois.

Most all the Heads of the Departments having come in, the President read his order. It was a direction to the military officers holding persons in custody as soldiers, deserters or drafted men, to make return to the Writ of Habeas Corpus from any Court, that the principal in the Writ was so held and refuse obedience; and that if force should be used to compel obedience, to overcome it. After the order was read, the Secretary of War made a statement showing the great number of persons discharged by Habeas Corpus principally by the two Federal Judges Cadwalader and McCandless, and stated some very gross proceedings under color of judicial authority, manifestly intended to interfere with the recruiting and maintenance of the Army. The President remarked that the order he had read was the same he had proposed yesterday, only modified so as to apply to Federal as well as to State courts. I then remarked: 'This is an important matter. The statement made by the Secretary of War clearly shows a design to defeat the measures which Congress and the Executive have thought necessary to maintain the Army. The only question then is, in what mode should this attempt be met. You, Mr. President, have believed that you have the power to suspend the writ of Habeas Corpus without being authorized by Congress, and in some cases have acted on this belief. After much consideration I have come to the conclusion that your opinion and action are sanctioned by the Constitution. Whatever doubt there may have been as to your power to suspend the Writ, it has been removed by express legislation. The act of the 3d March last,[48] approved by you, authorizes you to suspend the Writ in any case during the existing rebellion when in your judgment the public safety may require it. The order you have just read does not suspend the Writ in terms, though it probably does in effect.—It leaves the question of suspension open to debate, and will lead to serious collisions probably, with the disadvantage on the side of the Federal authority. In my judgment, therefore, instead of this order there should be a Proclamation distinctly suspending the Writ of Habeas Corpus so far as may be necessary to prevent the great evil of virtually disbanding the Army, and when once issued any attempt to interfere with the organization should be punished under the Act of Congress promptly and decisively, no matter who the offender may be, whether Governor or Judge, or any less conspicuous personage. By this bold and direct action, I think you will command the confidence of the public, avoid collisions upon uncertain grounds, and secure most completely the great objects you have in view.' This I said in substance. The President seemed to be struck with the force of it; took the law to which I had referred, and came to the conclusion that the best move was to issue a Proclamation under it, suspending the Writ.[49] Some conversation then took place as to the proper return to be made by the officer to whom the Writ was addressed. As this matter, however, seemed to be sufficiently provided for by the law, the subject was not pursued. I was surprised to find that in a matter of this importance, no one but myself seemed to have read the Act of March 3d with reference to the subject under discussion, and that its provisions were unfamiliar to all.

Mr. Field [50] left for New York to-day. I offered to make him Chief Clerk, with $3,000 a year, and to make him Second Assistant Secretary in case Congress would give me such an officer. He will consider it and reply.

I was much gratified to find by reports of the proper officers that the arrearages in the issue of 5–20 bonds was nearly made up, and that there was reason to expect that in the course of the present month we shall be prepared to issue fractional currency and Treasury Notes in sufficient quantities for the public demand.

Sept. 16, Wednesday. Nearly my whole time was consumed by callers. Endeavored to examine the papers in relation to Jay Cookes agency, but made small progress. Some claims for cotton surrendered to Yeatman,[51] the Agent, the largest of which was represented by Colonel Letherman,[52] came in. Mr. Moore,[53] from Washington Territory, called. He is a candidate for the Collectorship vacated by Major Goldsborough. He explained the transaction relating to the *Herald of Progess* and Dr. Allyn,[54] showing that Victor Smith had no connection with Dr Allyn's contribution to the *Herald*. His explanation was entirely satisfactory on this point. He also denied positively on behalf of Mr. Smith, the statement of Henry and others, that Smith asserted that I was indebted to him. In the evening, Mr. Pierce [55] and Mr. McKim [56] called. Also Major Smith and Mr. Green, the latter of whom said that he was requested by Judge Balcom [57] of the Court of Appeals of New York to tender his respects to me and say that the Court had agreed upon a decision in the legal tender cases before them, affirming the constitutionality of the law. Major Giddings [58] and Captain Ilgis [59] also called, who, in the course of conversation made these remarkable statements about the condition of the Regular Regiments. They said that the Twelfth, now in New York, had 600 men, and about twenty-seven officers; that the Fourteenth at [had?] 400 men, and twenty seven officers, the full complement. These two regiments are of the new organization, 2400 men each; that the Third had 180 men and eight officers; the Fourth 22 men and nineteen officers; the 6th 130 to 140 men and fifteen officers; the 10th 31 men and nearly a full complement of twenty-seven officers. The 3d, 4th, 6th and 10th are old regiments.

Sept. 17, Thursday. Went to the President's immediately after breakfast.—Found Governor Newall [60] and other New Jersey gentlemen interceding with the President for the pardon of a deserter. Said to the President that I feared some injustice had been done in removing Mr. Ridgeley, who had in conversation with me the day before expressed the most decided support of the Administration, saying that the ground of complaint against him was that he had supported Mr. Webster [61] for nomination to Congress, and that Mr. Webster was as decided a friend to the Administration as himself. Mr. Ridgeley had asked me for a pass to go to the Army to see Col. Webster, and I suggested to the President the propriety of allowing him to go. The President said he could go after a few days, but that just now the army might be moving. I mentioned to the President the message of Judge Balcom, and he said that Judge Davies had given him similar information. I again referred to the case of Gen. Hamilton, and he told me that General Hamilton had been sent for, and wd probably return to Texas, as Brigadier General and Military Governor. Referred again to the subject of revoking the exceptions of the South-Eastern counties of Virginia from his Proclamation, and he read to me the draft of an unfinished letter he had begun to me on that subject,[62] the argument of which was very strongly put, but based entirely upon the idea that the military necessity which justified the Proclamation did not now exist in regard to these counties.—I questioned the correctness of this view and referred to the letter of Gov. Pierpont, urging the revocation upon the distinct grounds of military necessity. He then remarked that the revocation, at all events, was not expedient at present, and should be deferred until after the Fall elections. We then talked on the suspension of the Habeas Corpus. He said that I was quite right in recommending it rather than the order which had been prepared, and that he had been convinced of it as soon as he heard my statement of the law. I also spoke to him about the promotion of Col. Davies,[63] saying that I thought he deserved it by his gallantry and ability, and that I should be particularly glad to have it done because of the Judge's steady support of the Government. He intimated that it had been already decided upon, which I was very glad to hear.

I then went to the War Department. Mr. Stanton stated a curious circumstance. Yesterday, he said, a shot or shell from the Navy Yard fell into a cavalry camp on the Maryland side of the Potomac, killing one man and doing considerable injury to the Camp. He directed a report of the facts to be made to Secretary Welles, with a request to change the direction of the guns; to which the Secretary replied that he paid $200 a year for the privilege of firing on that piece of ground! Mr. Stanton said that he was going to offer him $600 a year to make such a change as would save his camp.

After returning to the Department, Mr. Plumley called to talk about matters in Louisiana, and I invited him to breakfast to-morrow morning.

Sept. 18, Friday. Mr. L. E. Straughn,[64] of the Cambridge (Maryland) Intelligencer, called. He had been recommended for assessor in place of Russell,[65] and naturally thought the change a desirable one. He impressed me very favorably: indeed, I had already been satisfied by his paper, of his activity and patriotism, and should be very glad to show my sense of it, but am not prepared to make the desired removal.

Plumly [sic] breakfasted with me, and gave quite a clear inside view of military and civil affairs at New Orleans. He represents General Banks as very friendly to me.

Gen Hamilton called and bid me 'good bye,' being about to leave for his new position in Texas. Shurz [sic] also called.

Sept. 20, Sunday. Having been impressed, by somewhat careful study, with apprehensions for the condition of Rosecrans' army, I was a good deal alarmed by the telegrams in the morning papers, and went immediately to the War Department after breakfast, where I found two telegrams, one from Rosecrans himself, and one from Dana,[66] both dated at Chattanooga, and both reporting serious disaster. Later in the day another telegram came from Dana, saying that Thomas had successfully resisted the enemy's advance, but left room for serious forebodings.

Sept. 21, Monday.[67] At War Dept. Rosecrans' and Dana's telegrams look bad. Chickamauga.

Sept. 22, Tuesday. Harrington left for Europe today. May he come back fully restored! Went to Hallecks Headquarters—

At the meeting of the Heads of Departments, the President gave an account of the battle of Sunday. Results are less unfavorable than was feared, although the losses are great in killed, wounded and prisoners, and some fifty guns captured by the enemy on the center and right. On the left Thomas and Granger [68] and Garfield, who had joined Thomas at great personal risk, had distinguished themselves greatly.

Received a letter from Shurz [sic], enclosing a printed scheme for a Testimonial to McClellan, which was being circulated in the army for subscriptions, with the sanction of the Commanding General and his Staff. Called Stanton's attention to it, who agreed with me in thinking it an insult to the President. I also showed the letter and the paper to the President, who took the paper and promised to see Stanton about it.—Harrington left to-day for Europe, hoping to recover his health, impaired by over-exertion.—Received a telegram from Mrs. Charles Jones [69] that her brother, and my brother-in-law, Lieut. Ludlow, was wounded and a prisoner at Chickamauga. I telegraphed Garfield, at Chattanooga, and received a reply confirming the report, and urging prompt reinforcements.

Sept. 23, Wednesday. Spoke to Stanton about promoting Charles A. Cooledge,[70] who enlisted as a private and has been promoted Lance Sergeant in the Sixteenth Regulars.

Sept. 24, Thursday. Having gone home last evening very weary, was called up from my bed about midnight by a messenger from the War Department, who said I was wanted there immediately. The summons really alarmed me. I felt that disaster had befallen us; that the army of Rosecrans had been attacked before his defences were completed, and had been compelled to surrender, or had been defeated with great loss in another bloody battle, and its remains driven across the Tennessee. Great was my relief when, reaching the War Department and asking 'more bad news?' Stanton replied 'No, what there is,

is favorable.' He then handed me a telegram from Garfield to myself which stated that Rosecrans could hold
out ten days where he was, but earnestly urged reinforcements. Other telegrams from Rosecrans and Dana gave
encouraging expectations that he could hold out still
longer time. Both also urged re-inforcements. After a little
while the President and Mr. Seward also came in. General
Halleck was already there. Mr. Stanton then opened the
conference by inquiring of Gen. Halleck, what reinforcements Burnside could add to Rosecrans and in what time.
Halleck replied twenty thousand men in ten days, if un-
interrupted. The President then said, 'before the ten days
Burnside will put in enough to hold the place (Chattanooga). [']

Stanton to Halleck—How many in eight days?

Halleck—12000.

The President—After Burnside begins to arrive, the
pinch will be over.

Stanton—Unless the enemy, anticipating reinforcements, attacks promptly.—(To Halleck)—When will
Sherman's [army] reach Rosecrans?

Halleck.—In about ten days, if already moved from
Vicksburg. His route will be to Memphis, thence to Corinth and Decatur, and a march of a hundred or a hundred
and fifty miles on the north side of the Tennessee River.
Boats have already gone down from Cairo, and every
available man ordered forward, say from twenty to twenty-
five thousand.

Stanton.—Are any more available elsewhere?

Halleck.—A few in Kentucky; I dont know how many.
All were ordered to Burnside.

Stanton.—I propose then to send 30,000 from the Army of the Potomac. There is no reason to expect that General Meade will attack Lee, although greatly superior in force; and his great numbers where they are, are useless. In five days 30,000 could be put with Rosecrans.

The President.—I will bet that if the order is given tonight, the troops could not be got to Washington in five days.

Stanton.—On such a subject I dont feel inclined to bet; but the matter has been carefully investigated, and it is certain that 30,000 bales of cotton could be sent in that time by taking possession of the railroads and excluding all other business, and I do not see why 30,000 men cannot be sent as well. But if 30,000 cannot be sent, let 20,000 go.

Much conversation followed, the President and Halleck being evidently disinclined to weaken Meade's force, whilst Seward and myself were decided in recommending the re-inforcement of Rosecrans. It was at length agreed that Halleck should telegraph Meade in the morning, and if an immediate advance was not certain, the Eleventh and Twelfth Corps, supposed to make about 13,000 men, should be sent Westward at once, under Hooker, with Butterfield as his Chief of Staff.

Sept. 25, Friday. By telegram after we separated last night, the Secretary of War called the officers of the Baltimore and Ohio, the Philadelphia and Baltimore, and the Pennsylvania Central Railroads to Washington. They were in conference with him the greater part of the day. The movement of the troops was arranged. It was found that the number would exceed 15,000, but no doubt was expressed that the movement would [and] could be accomplished promptly, though not quite as soon as Stanton had anticipated. In the evening I found myself quite unwell.

Sept. 26, Saturday. Having been kept awake most of the night, with severe pains, I telegraphed Garrett and Smith [71] that I could not come to Baltimore and visit Mr. Hopkins [72] as I had proposed. A little before 11 I received a reply from Mr. Smith to the effect that Mr. Hopkins had notified some twelve or fifteen of the leading financial men to meet me at dinner, and that the disappointment would be great if I did not come. I concluded therefore to risk the journey, and answered that I would come on the 11:15 train. I arrived in Baltimore; met Mr. Garrett and Mr. Smith, who insisted that I should take a ride with them through Federal Hill and Fort McHenry before going to Mr. Hopkins's: to which I consented. We reached Mr. Hopkins's about four o'clock. Only two or three of the guests had arrived, and Mr. Hopkins proposed to show us his place. We therefore accompanied him on a walk around the grounds, which are very spacious and beautiful. Extensive graperies with every variety of grapes in rich clusters; a pleasant fruit orchard, the trees of which were loaded with fruit; a vegetable garden, conveniently situated, with commodious and handsome farm buildings near, together with a lake so artistically contrived with islands, trees and shores, as to give it the appearance of great extent,—formed the principal features of this beautiful place. The whole extent of the grounds is about four hundred acres, of which perhaps sixty are used for the purpose just mentioned, while the rest are devoted to farm cultivation. Mr. Hopkins insists that though a gentleman farmer, he contrives to make both ends meet, at the close of each year. His dinner was simple, but excellently prepared and in the best taste. His dessert of grapes exceeded in beauty and variety and flavor anything I had ever seen. My indisposition condemned me to almost total abstinence, much to my regret. The guests were intelligent and substantial men, constituting, as Mr. Hopkins said, the best part of the Baltimore merchants and capitalists. And all of them earnest Union men. And nearly all, if not all, decided Emancipationists. It was about nine o'clock when we left his hospitable mansion and returned to the city, where I soon found myself established in comfortable quarters at Mr. Garrett's.

Sept. 27, Sunday. I slept better last night than the night before, tho' still far from well. A slight fever made me fancy myself beset with matters of public concern, when I was sure I was not so engaged; and would try to dispel the illusion, and sometimes succeeded for a moment, only to find it coming back the next. This was unpleasant enough, and I was glad when the morning came to my relief. After breakfast, of which I partook very slightly, I found myself sufficiently well to accompany the family to Church; where I heard an excellent sermon and spent two pleasant hours. On coming out, Judge Bond asked us to go with him to see a dress parade of a colored regiment at Camp Birney. They asked Mr. Garrett if he would go, and he assented. A little after five o'clock we rode to the Camp. The regiment was already in line, nine hundred strong, besides the guards on duty. Behind it was another line; three or four hundred new recruits. These were rough and ragged in their negro clothes, fresh from the plantations. I directed Mr. Garrett's attention to the spectacle, saying that the front line in uniform and the rear line in negro clothes soon to come forward also into the front ranks in uniform, was very suggestive. Mr. Garrett looked and said nothing. The sight could hardly be palatable to one so recently, if not still, thoroughly pro-slavery in his sentiments. After some conversation with Col. Birney,[73] in charge of the recruiting service, and Col. Duncan [74] (whose graduation I witnessed some years ago at Dartmouth College), commanding the uniformed, we returned to the city.

Sept. 28, Monday. I slept pretty well last night under the hospitable roof of Mr. Garrett. After breakfast he and Mr. Smith accompanied me to Mr. Swann's, with whom I exchanged kind greetings; thence to the hat-store of Mr. Smith's father-in-law, Mr. Van Zandt,[75] where I supplied myself with something more suitable to the season than my 'straw'; thence to the Custom House where I exchanged salutations with the officers and clerks, and thence to the cars where I found Judge Jewett, with whom I proceeded to Washington, and resumed my duties at the Department.

Mr. Garrett informed me that the movement of the troops was going on successfully, which was confirmed by Mr. Stanton, who is greatly delighted by its success. He told me that the number to be moved had been found to reach 20,000, and yet the whole had been put in motion without disturbance and in perfect order. The last were expected to reach Washington to-day, and would be immediately sent forward. Thus in five days the men who, as the President was ready to bet, could not be got to Washington, would be already past that point on their way to Rosecrans, while their advance had reached the

Ohio River. If this whole movement is carried through to the end as well as it has been thus far, it will be an achievement in the transportation of troops unprecedented, I think, in history.

Sept. 29, Tuesday. Nothing occurred of much interest to-day. At the President's neither Mr. Seward nor Mr. Stanton were present. They seemed, reasonably enough, to have given up attendance on these meetings of the Heads of Departments as useless. And for aught I see I may as well follow their example.—Received a note from Miss Walker, asking the promotion of Bryant Walker to be an Assistant Adjutant General with the rank of Captain, and sent a note to Mr. Stanton, begging that the favor might be done, which was promptly and kindly done.

Sept. 30, Wednesday. Received a note from Mr. Stanton, notifying me that young Walker's commission would be sent to him as soon as possible. I enclosed the note to Miss Walker, New York. There was the usual number of callers, and the usual variety of talk and business, but nothing of special importance.

In the evening, I entertained at my house, a delegation of 'Radicals' from Kansas and Missouri, with Mr. Charles D. Drake [76] as their Chairman, come hither to ask of the President such a change in the conduct of military affairs in that Department as shall better secure the loyal men in their rights and homes.

Oct. 1, Thursday. [77] Mr. Field takes his place as Asst Secretary. Genl. de Alna [78] called with strange story—He says a letter came from Richmond, with $3000 from Benjamin. [79] The money was to be used by one Chs. d'Arnaud [80] formerly on Fremont's staff to corrupt Col. Percy Wyndham [81] an officer of one of our cavalry regiments and induce him to betray his command to the enemy—for which he was to receive some addl. compensation. This letter came to a Mrs Van Camp, wife of a Mr. Van Camp [82] said to have the confidence of the Prest. and to claim to hold a license to buy cotton granted by him[;] thro' some mistake of personal identity this letter of Benj. came to de Alna, who communicated with Hogan, a detective employed by the Treasy. Dept., who communicated it to me; and I to the Secy of War: who agreed with me that I should see de Alna and hear his story. It was little else than the above—he showed me Benjamin's note which promd. compensation for 'artillery' meaning I suppose 'horses'—he also paid over to Hogan $2000 of the money sent by Benjamin which I directed Hogan to deposit with Jay Cooke & Co. De Alna was told to discover, if he could, what was being done in complicity with the rebels, and advise me or the Secy. of War.

Mr. Field entered on his duties as Asst. Secy. today.

Oct. 2, Friday. Camp called with letter from Greeley,—proposed plan for collecting public sentiment in my favor as candidate for Prest.—told him that people must do as they pleased in this matter—I would not interfere. Sickles,[83] Cartter [84] and others also called—had pretty hard nights work on business of Dept.

Oct. 3, Saturday. Mr. Camp called introduced by Mr. Greeley—proposed plan for collecting public sentiment in reference to next Presidency—told him I could take no part—people must do as they pleased.

Oct. 4, Sunday. Mr. Barney called. Went to Church with me. Sermon on Christ in us—grand theme ill handled—much talk on coming home with Barney—is my friend certainly—but does not like to show preference if Mr L—— desires renomination.

Oct. 5, Monday. Barney called at breakfast—seems not exactly to know his own mind—but will go for Mr. Lincoln if he desires reelection—Risley came in with Trade forms which I revised.

6

Chase's Resignation

[JUNE 24–JULY 6, 1864]

THE WINTER of 1863–64 forms another long break in Chase's diary record. It was a period more distinguished for political than for military maneuvers. In March, 1864, Lincoln named Grant lieutenant-general and called him to Washington as general-in-chief of the Federal armies. Deciding to accompany the Army of the Potomac himself, Grant entrusted the armies at Chattanooga to Sherman. In early May the two forces simultaneously moved forward, Sherman forcing the wily Joseph E. Johnston back toward Atlanta, and Grant grinding away at Lee in the bloody battles of the Wilderness. Unsuccessful, Grant had to shift his base to City Point, east of Richmond, and it seemed that his summer campaign had resulted in nothing but disastrous casualty lists. Then in June, to relieve pressure on Richmond, Lee sent Jubal A. Early into the Shenandoah Valley, where he routed the troops of David Hunter, and Washington again was in danger.

Such bleak military news naturally had political repercussions. In January Chase had formally announced his presidential candidacy, and the following month a com-

mittee of Congressional Radicals issued the famous "Pomeroy Circular," an open letter which declared that Lincoln
could not be reëlected and claimed that Chase had "more
of the qualities needed in a President, during the next four
years, than are combined in any other available candidate." Though the author of the Circular asserted that
*"Mr. Chase was fully informed of this proposed action
and approved it fully,"* Chase hastened to assure Lincoln
that he "had no knowledge of the existence of this letter"
before its publication, and he offered to resign. Doubtless
realizing that the Secretary's ambitions could better be
muted inside the cabinet than outside, the President again
declined to accept his resignation. Both the people and the
politicians regarded the cabinet member's candidacy as
open disloyalty to his chief, and the Chase boom quickly
subsided.

While Chase was thus checked, Lincoln's friends were
active. Both General F. P. Blair, Jr., and Montgomery
Blair vituperatively attacked the Treasury administration, and Lincoln seemed to give tacit approval. As Chase
was weakened, the Lincoln forces gained strength, and in
state after state his managers procured endorsements for
the President's renomination. When even the Ohio Republicans came out for Lincoln, Chase abandoned the
race. "It becomes my duty," he wrote stiffly, "to ask that
no further consideration be given to my name." Though
Lincoln was told that Chase's withdrawal was only a
"shrewd dodge," and though the Secretary openly grumbled that the Republican National Convention which
nominated Lincoln and Andrew Johnson was only "a
Blair-Lincoln Convention," Chase had clearly been out-
maneuvered.

In financial affairs, too, the Secretary met with reverses during these months. Despite his insistence, Congress failed to levy taxes adequate to meet the minimal Treasury needs. Political pressure did not permit the reappointment of Jay Cooke as general agent, and Chase had great difficulties in promoting his new bond issue. Meanwhile, as the currency depreciated, the premium on gold skyrocketed. At the Secretary's demand, Congress passed a law designed to outlaw speculation in gold, but it only hampered honest businessmen while gamblers continued to profit by the constantly climbing premium.

At this harried moment, Chase heard of the resignation of John J. Cisco, Assistant Treasurer of the United States at New York. His position was one of the richest patronage plums in the Federal government, and Chase did not intend to have it fall to his party opponents.

∽ ∽ ∽

June 24, 1864, Friday. Another anxious day. What will be the result of the Summer Campaign? Can we keep Grant and Sherman so furnished with men and means that they can inflict decisive blows on the rebellion?

My part is to supply if possible the means—and where am I to find them. The currency is depreciated less—though much—by surcharge than by the distrust which seems to be gradually pervading the public mind; especially the mind of that class whose conclusions,—half instinctive, half reasoned,—determine the degree of confidence in Governments and Constitutions.

Under these circumstances, to increase the circulation will merely aggravate our greatest financial evil—that of disordered commerce and prices unnaturally high. It should be diminished rather than increased. Can this be done? Not without large taxes or large loans.

A committtee from New York, introduced by Senator Morgan, called this morning to urge modification or repeal of the Gold Act. Their arguments should, I said, be addressed to Congress rather than to me; but I was glad to hear their views. Some, especially Mr. James Brown, of Brown Brothers & Co, Mr. [Charles B.] Hoffman, of Colegate [*sic*] & Hoffman, Mr. [George C.] Ward, of Ward Campbell & Co argued for repeal; if repeal impossible for modification. Their arguments were substantially these (1.) Absolute freedom of trade secures lowest prices. True in certain conditions of market individuals or combinations may monopolize whole supply and exact their own prices from those who must have the article monopolized as gold for example but this evil less than restrictive regulation. (2) Convenience to merchants of public sales even those of gold gambling room as giving a standard of price. The complaints of practical inconvenience were principally of the supposed necessity to pay notes in hand for gold bought when check would be much more convenient and of the supposed prohibition against buying exchange for gold. I could not see that license to gambling was essential to freedom of trade; and said that under the act as I understood it there could be no objection to *public* sales; or to the use of checks, if real checks on active deposits and paid during the day; or to direct purchases of exchange for gold. One gentleman suggested that Congress should expressly authorize loans of gold to be repaid in gold and sales not of exchange only but of all merchandize for gold. I saw no objection to loans of gold for gold but sales such as proposed would repeal the legal tender law.

The conversation was good tempered on both sides and to me instructive.

The Internal Revenue bill remains with the Committee of Conference, but it is expected they will report tomorrow. It is apprehended that the bill will not impose taxes enough to bring the residue of expences within the reach of loans. Mr. Orton [1] came tonight from New York at my request and will devote himself to careful examination of the bill and amendments and estimate the probable revenue as nearly as possible.

Spent some time with Mr. Taylor [2] who by my direction has been engaged in preparing a bill or measure to authorize the sale of gold and silver lands. I cannot but think that fee simple titles in mines will tend powerfully to their most productive working. He has conferred with Senator Conness,[3] Commissioner Edmunds and others and has finally prepared a bill which seems to me adequate. I directed him to put it into the form of a section to be added by way of amendment to a bill authorizing sales of lands embracing coal mines which has passed the Senate and is in the House.[4] This was done and I prepared letters to Mr. Julian [5] Chairman of the Public Lands Committee and to Senator Conness and instructed Mr. Taylor to confer with Senator C—— and the California delegation and if they approved the amendment take it with my amendment to Mr. Julian and try to have the bill adopted. If the measure succeeds it will work quite a revolution.

Note. The amendment was approved and came very near success. It is possible,—had not the necessity for my resignation arisen—I might have carried it through. It will probably engage the attention of Congress at the next Session and become law.

June 26, Sunday. This day was given to what seemed necessary labor. It was extremely important to know whether a gentleman invited to accept the Asst. Treasrship at New York [6] would consent to do so and to set in motion the advertising for the new loan and to prepare for an appeal to Congress to make up the deficiency in taxes. The day was therefore mainly devoted to these objects. Dr. Elder [7] came in and dined with me—no one at home besides myself.

June 27, Monday. Called on Senator Morgan to consult about Asst. Treasurer at New York—told him I had concluded to recommend Mr. Field. He thought I had better name Mr. Gregory [8] or Mr. Blatchford.[9] I replied that either gentleman would be entirely acceptable to me personally but I thought the public interests would on the whole be best consulted by the appointment of Mr. F. He said that Mr. [Charles] Jones of Brooklyn Chairman of the Union Committee had brought a list of clerks and officers under Mr. Cisco and that there were but some half dozen Union men among them—all the rest being democrats I replied that I thought the statement erroneous and that on fair enquiry it would be found that of the persons called democrats the largest proportion are of the same class with Andrew Johnson—but I would think the matter all over and decide today. At the Dept. Mr Freeman Clarke [10] called and I talked the matter over with him. He seemed to prefer Mr. Field. I told him if he would take it, I would send his name to the President at once. He said his health would not allow him to do so and even if it would he could not on other grounds. I asked him to confer with the Senators and report, telling him I must decide today. Having waited to hear from him till about four and having in the

meantime conferred fully with Mr. Field, whom I found
even a more decided supporter of the Admn. than Johnson was at the time of his nomination, I went to the Capitol to see him. He was neither in the House nor Senate and
I then sent to the Department thinking that in the meantime he might have gone thither. The Messenger returned
reporting that he had not been there and I at once sent
Mr. Fields name to the President, about [?] half past
four.[11]

In the course of the morning, Mr. Orton whom I had
summoned from New York to examine the Internal Revenue bill and ascertain what revenue might be expected
and to give me also his judgment as to the sources from
which the deficiency if any might be raised made his report. He estimated the net product at 220 mills for the
next fiscal year and submitted a paper showing how the
deficiency of eighty millions could be made up. I directed
him to have a bill prepared for the taxes suggested by
him. I have repeatedly assured the Committee and the
President that we cannot even sustain the existing or even
somewhat reduced rate of expenditure without a revenue
from taxes and duties of $400 000 000. In a recent letter
upon the assumption, admitted to be improbable that
Expenditure might be reduced to 750,000,000 I fixed the
amount with which we might get along at one half or
375 000 000. I mean to send the bill for the additional
taxes to Congress and the President and insist on it.[12]

These were the most important matters of the day.
Talk about Trade regulations, various applications for
permits and positions, revision of Spragues proposed remarks about Blairs charge against him of Cotton Specula-

tion;[13] correspondence and conversation about gold act occupied most of the day.

One thing merits record. Having received a telegram from Mr. Barney about 6 P.M. enquiring when the operation of the Joint Resolution increasing duties for 60 days would cease, and having satisfied myself that on the construction already given it took effect on the day of its approval, it would cease today at midnight I conferred with Mr. Hooper who happened to be with me, and, having ascertained that Congress had taken no step to extend its operation except to put such a provision in the Tariff bill not yet passed, requested him to introduce a Joint Resolution to extend the time till the first of July. He drew one immediately and promised. The result was the introduction of this Joint Resolution,[14] its passage through the House and Senate—its approval by the Senate and its communication by telegraph to all the Collectors before midnight.

June 28, Tuesday. How beautiful and excellent is the order and progress which St Paul enjoins and illustrates in his letter to the Ephesians! Oh if the world could but learn that lesson, how anxieties, and perplexities would lighten and pass away with the clashes, and jars, and wars which bring them. May God in His infinite mercy send us peace with union and freedom.

This morning I read part of Paul to the Ephesians and as usual endeavored to reach God in prayer. Oh, for more faith and clearer sight! How stable is the City of God! How disordered is the City of Man!

At the Department received a note from the President,[15] saying that Senator Morgan strongly opposed the nomination of Mr. Field in place of Mr. Cisco—replied asking an interview, but received no answer. He may not wish one or what is more probably allows himself to forget the request. He asks the nomination of R. S. Blatchford or Dudley S. Gregory, neither of whom, I fear, is the proper man to take charge of the office at this critical juncture; though either would be entirely acceptable to me personally. I fear Senator Morgan desires to make a political engine of the office, and loses sight in this desire of the necessities of the service.

Received a note from Senator Morrill [16] informing me that the Trade Bill [17] has passed the Senate, and from Mr. Hooper that the Loan bill [18] passed the House by concurrence in all the Senate amendments. He had vainly endeavored to procure a modification of one, so as to let the Govt. pay for stock used in engraving its notes instead of allowing the same stock to be used, if it had been previously so used, in preparation of other circulation, and to exclude the use of green pigment from all notes and bonds, letting [the] Govt. remunerate any patentee. Congress preferred to risk the evils to the National Note Circulation.

Went to House and talked with Mr. Hooper and Mr. Washburn [19] about Trade Bill and urged importance of it. I do this reluctantly because of the labor it will impose on me and because of the odium which its interference with private speculation and naval enterprize [?] will be sure to excite against me. I wish we could have good Commissions to manage these things and also Loans. But the President would almost certainly put in men from political considerations and after all the responsibility would still be on me.

Returning to Dept. conferred with Mr. Orton and

Actg. Comm. Rollins [20] (Int. Rev.) about Supplementary tax bill. Both agreed that the Revenue for fiscal year commencing next Friday would not exceed 220 or 225 millions whereas 300 mills at least is necessary. In accordance with my instructions they had prepared a new bill which with their statements and a letter of my own I propose to send to Congress tomorrow—another great and painful responsibility!

Telegraphed Mr. Cisco urging him to withdraw resignation and serve at least another quarter; and wrote to President what I had done and why I could not honestly, in duty to him or the country, recommend at this time either of the names he had suggested.[21]

In the evening went up to the Capitol. The Senate was holding an evng session and Garrett Davis [22] was making a rambling, violent speech for slavery, abusing the President, against the Freedmen's-Bureau Bill [23] then under consideration. Talked to some of the Senators—found that the House was not in session and so came home.

The 3d Auditor Mr. [Robert J.] Atkinson resigned today. Mr. Sills [24] of Iowa is to take his place. Atkinson has been an excellent officer; but has been much disliked by our friends on account of his politics. I advised him to resign therefore, proposing to use his services in another place where the same hostility wd. not manifest itself His health too requires a change. Hence his resignation.

The day has been one of great anxiety and distress. What can be done to avert the decline of public credit? I see nothing effectual except taxation which will make excessive borrowing unnecessary and military success which will make necessary borrowing possible on reasonable terms. Had the first object of this Campaign been the suppression of rebellion west of the Mississippi I think our prospects now would have been much brighter. Had artificial reconstruction by amnesty proclamations and military power been let alone and actual reconstruction left to the loyal people—loyal enough to recognize in every real loyalist a man and a citizen, and had the Army of the Gulf been put under a real military but at the same time thoroughly loyal leader—the trans-Mississippi rebellion might and probably would have [been] suppressed with the force actually engaged.

I must not omit to mention that the President and faculty of Otterbein College, travelling together in vacation called on me this evening.

June 29, Wednesday. Last evening I received Mr. Ciscos reply to my telegram consenting to withdraw his resignation. This morning I received the Presidents reply to my note. He says he did not accede to personal interview because useless—complains of the difficulties occasioned by his retention of Mr. Barney and the appointment of Judge Hogeboom,[25] both considered as of the radical side and says he cannot go further in that direction by the appointment of Mr. Field[;] desires appt. made acceptable to Gov Morgan and those who think as he does. Will await Mr. Cisco's action. I replied that I made no general distinction in appointments except friend and opponents of his administration and among the former none except degrees of fitness—that Mr. Cisco's reply relieved the present difficulty; but as I could not help feeling that my position here was not agreeable to him and there was nothing in my office making me wish to retain it, I enclosed my resignation and should feel really relieved by its acceptance. I added that I would give my successor all the aid I could for his entrance upon the duties of the office. With this note I enclosed my resignation.[26]

All the time I could command today was devoted to the preparation of a letter to the Chr. of the Com. of Ways and Means urging additional taxes—sufficient to ensure a revenue from Internal Duties of 300,000,000, and representing strongly the necessity of such provision in order to reduce circulation and diminish the increase of debt—the former depreciating currency and the latter damaging public credit. It was finished and sent with letters and statements supporting it from Collector Orton of New York, about six oclock in the afternoon. I also directed copies of the letter and all the documents to be prepared for the Chn. of the Com. on Finance (Senate) and of all except the bill and the letters of Collector Orton and Rollins to be prepared for the President.

One of the last acts today was to send to the President nomination of captains [?] and other officers in the Revenue Service.

Coming home Mr. Day and his daughter called—the former asking a place for the latter. I was vexed and I fear rude which was wrong. The man however does not impress me as true and honest.

Risley called and Orton came to the House to spend the remainder of his time in the city with me. Risley and Harrington went to the House to promote, if possible, the passage of the Insurrecting District Trade Bill Washburn of Ill told me today that it would be very difficult to set the bill before the House.

June 30, Thursday. Immediately after breakfast this morning I went to see Gen Schenck about the enrollment law; and found him with Gen Garfield and a gentleman who was a stranger to me at breakfast. In view of the difficulties which embarrassed the action of the Senate and House I suggested and somewhat earnestly pressed the expediency of leaving the whole subject very much to the discretion of the President, authorizing him to draft for not less than one or more than two years and to allow commutation, if he should deem it expedient, at rates not less than $300 nor more than $500. Under this law the discretion would I thought be judiciously exercised by the Secretary of War and the Lieutenant General who would doubtless be allowed to act upon their own judgment, and the rule being flexible could be adjusted to circumstances with great advantage. The idea seemed to strike both gentlemen favorably, and as they are both on the Military Committee some good may come of it.

On going to the Department I found that Mr. Fessenden had been there and left word that he desired to see me at the Capitol. So after signing the letter to the President, commending to his attention my letter to the Committee of Ways and Means and the statements and estimates of Mr. Orton I went to the Capitol. Fessenden had not yet returned; but I had read [?] on my way a letter he had left for my perusal from a Mr Dole urging the repeal of the gold bill. When he came in we talked on this subject, and he desired my views. I told him I never expected great benefits from such legislation; but that I thought it hardly wise to yield to the clamor of the opponents of this particular act; that the rise of gold did not in my judgment come from this law as a permanent cause, though doubtless its tendency in the particular condition of the market was to cause a rise; and that as there was no prohibition of sales in it nothing but simple restrictions upon gambling and restraint of operations to legitimate channels, I thought it best to let it alone at this session; but should be entirely satisfied whatever the Committees and Congress might do.[27]

Mr. Morrill [28] of Vt. came in during our conversation and spoke of the proposition I had made to increase taxes. He was adverse to it. In his opinion the bill already passed would yield some 30 millions more than Orton's Estimate. I replied that admitting there might be such improvement or increase, still the revenue would fall far short of half the expenditures and it would be impossible to borrow the remaind[er] on fair terms. On conversation with Mr. Orton afterwards I found that Mr. Morrill had omitted to take into the account the important circumstance that the increase he expects next year will if realized [not] go into the next fiscal year but into the year following.

While we were talking a Messenger came in to summon Mr. Fessenden to the Senate. The Messenger said something privately and he came back to me saying 'Have you resigned. I am called to the Senate and told that the President has sent in the nomination of your successor.['] I told him I had tendered my resignation but had not been informed till now of its acceptance. He expressed his surprise and disappointment and we parted—He to the Senate and I to the Department. There I found a letter from the President accepting my resignation, and putting the acceptance on the ground of the difference between us indicating a degree of embarrassment in our official relations which could not be continued or sustained consistently with the public service.[29] I had found a good deal of embarrassment from him but what he had found from me I could not imagine, unless it has been created by my unwillingness to have offices distributed as spoils or benefits with more regard to the claims of divisions, factions, cliques and individuals, than to fitness of selection. He had never given me the active and earnest support I was entitled to and even now Congress was about to adjourn without passing sufficient tax bills, though making appropriations with lavish profusion, and he was notwithstanding my appeals taking no pains to assure a different result.

Among those who called during the day was Mr. Hooper who related a conversation with the President some days ago, in which the President expressed regret that our relations were not more free from embarrassment, saying that when I came to see him he felt awkward and that I seemed constrained. At the same time he expressed his esteem for me and said that he had intended in case of vacancy in the Chief Justiceship to tender it to me and would now did a vacancy exist. This he said, he remarked, to show his real sentiments toward me; for he remembered that not very long after we took charge of the Administration I had remarked one day that I preferred judicial to administrative office and would rather, if I could be Chief Justice of the United States than hold any other position that could be given me. Mr. Hooper said that he thought this was said to him in order to be repeated to me and that he had sought an opportunity of doing so but had not found one. I said it was quite possible had any such expressions of good will reached me I might, before the present difficulty arose, have gone to him and had a frank understanding which would have prevented it: but I did not now see how I could change my position.

Indeed if such were the real feelings of Mr. Lincoln he would hardly have refused a personal interview when I

asked it or have required me to consult local politics in the
choice of an officer, whose character and qualifications
were so vitally important to the Department. Besides I
did not see how I could carry on the Department without
more means than Congress was likely to supply and amid
the embarrassments created by factious hostility within
and both factious and party hostility without the Department.

So my official life closes. I have laid broad foundations.
Nothing but wise legislation—and especially bold yet judicious provision of taxes—with fair economy in Admn. and
energetic yet prudent military action, (the last of which
seems to be evidenced by the position of Grant at the
head [of] our armies—oh may he have troops and supplies
enough!) seems necessary to ensure complete success. The
Insurrectionary District Trade bill will give the Department the power to regulate trade more efficiently than
heretofore and to take to the use of the Government the
profits of purchase and sale of the staples of the Rebel
States. Not only can many abuses be now corrected—but
a pecuniary benefit can be derived to the Govt of not less
I think than $25,000,000. The Tax bill it is true is inade-
quate but Congress may give to my successor, under the
alarms created by the change, what would not be yielded
to me. And even if taxes are not increased a tolerable showing can be made. The provisions I have secured with so
much difficulty in the Tax bill requiring monthly returns of
banks and monthly collection of taxes and high taxes on
excess beyond existing circulation, or any circulation beyond ninety per cent of capital, will, I think, certainly
prevent increase of bank note circulation and secure some
slight reduction. This to be sure leaves almost the whole

burden of reduction upon loans; but something at least
can be done in this way also; for the next six months when
Congress will have been again in session a month and will
have had an opportunity to supply what is now lacking.
With these advantages and with all the great work of administration already inaugurated and blocked out, and
especially with the still greater advantage of not having
the inside and outside hostility to encounter, which I have
been obliged to meet, my successor, I think, can get on
pretty well. If he fails any where, without his own fault,
it will be on the side of loans or under the pressure of military disaster. What I can do to help him, I will, for the
country's sake, do most gladly.

July 1, Friday. This morning the papers contained telegrams answering that Gov Tod [30] declines to take the
Treasury Department. On receiving this information the
President sent to the Senate the name of Mr. Fessenden—
a wise selection. He has the confidence of the country and
many who have become inimical to me will give their
confidence to him and their support. Perhaps they will do
more than they otherwise would to sustain him in order
to shew how much better a Secretary he is than I am. If
so the country will gain even by hostility to me transmuted
into friendship for him.

Gen Moorhead [31] called and related briefly an interview between himself and Mr. Williams,[32] and the President. They had attempted to induce him to send for me
with a view to my return to the Department; but he would
not consent to this. He thought we could not agree and it
was without use; and in this he was I think right. I cannot sympathize with his idiotic notion more than once
expressed to me and others that the best policy is to have

no policy and he cannot sympathize with my desires for positive and energetic action. It is best that he try somebody else. They had then mentioned to him Mr. Howe [33] of Pittsburgh as a proper person for Secretary; but found him not inclined to this. The conversation preceded Tod's declination; and had reference to the possibility that the Senate might not confirm the nomination.

The day was given to writing letters and to conversation with others who called. In the evening Fessenden came in immediately after dinner, or rather just before finishing dinner. Nobody but Senator Sprague and myself were at the table and he introduced the subject of his nomination. He expressed an extreme aversion to acceptance—fears of inability to carry on the Department—and especially strong apprehensions that his health would give way. He had he said begun a note declining, but had been prevented from finishing it by constant interruptions—and had received so many and such urgent appeals to accept that he was greatly embarrassed and wanted my advice. I told [him] I thought he ought to accept—that all the great work of the Department was now fairly blocked out and in progress—that the organization was planned, in many parts complete, and in all in a state which admitted completion—that is so far as completeness could be said of any thing needing constant supervision and allowing constant development and improvement. His most difficult task would be to provide money. He would now see, I thought, how important sufficient taxation was and that the Department ought to have been helped by some legislation, asked but denied. But he would have advantages which I had not. I had been obliged to inaugurate the National Banking System and to claim the circulation for the whole country through their Association and had necessarily encountered the ill will of those whose prejudices or interests bound them to the support of the old System. And I had necessarily also given offence to many whose counsels I had not been able to follow or whose wishes I had not been able to satisfy. These persons would have no cause of ill will against him; and would very probably come to his support with zeal increased by their ill will to me. So my damage would be his advantage, especially with a certain class of capitalists and Bankers; and I thought nothing more probable than that he would be able to obtain loans easier than I could. At any rate this would be his chief and so far as I could see the only real difficulty in his administration. He expressed great apprehension lest his health might give way and said that if he took the place to which he was much urged in Congress and by callers and telegrams from various parts of the country, he should look to me for counsel and all the help I could give. I told him that I thought he would want very little of either; but that all I could give was at his service. He referred to the longstanding relations of confidence and friendship between us and said he felt he had a right to depend on me. And I told him that I would stand by him and with him and whether he needed me or not that my friendship and affection would continue the same as ever. Judge Spalding [34] came in— and we all three rode to the Capitol together. Fessenden stopped at the Senate Wing, but Spalding and I rode a few minutes longer together, talking of the resignation[,] of Todds [sic] appointment and declension &c when I left him also at the Capitol and returned home.

July 2, Saturday. The bill giving the Secretary of the

Treasury effective control control [sic] over trade in rebel states and power to purchase their products for resale for the benefit of the Government, and authority to lease abandoned property and care for the freedmen passed the House today having previously passed the Senate. How much good I expected to accomplish under this bill! Will my successor do this work? I fear not. He had not the same heart for this measure that I had.

I spent the day in writing letters and in receiving calls, not going out at all. My letter to the Com of Ways and Means appeared in the Intelligencer and Chronicle. I am glad of it. It will prove at least that I desired no inflation.

July 3, Sunday. Attended Church at Wesley Chapel where I heard an excellent Sermon on Orphanage, supported by the death of a young girl member of the Church killed lately with twenty others by an explosion of powder at the Arsenal.

July 4, Monday. Cries of all kinds except cries of pain filled the air this morning, with explosions of cannon, ringing of bells, and whiz-whiz snap-snap of crackers and awakened me. It is the Anniversary of the Independence of the United States. How little most of those who celebrate it are thinking of the difference between the United States which declared it and the United States which celebrate it—the thirteen United States—just resolved no longer to be colonies—and battling for Independence and Union—now twenty three of the United States struggling, with divided counsels, to compel to obedience to the National Constitution and laws, eleven others, in which counting all classes and colors there is a majority of loyalists, but a majority controlled by the master class, and, so far as the colored portion of it is concerned, treated by the Government of the Union as inferiors and aliens rather than as equals in natural rights and as citizens. What will be the end? It is hidden from me. The Twenty three are vastly stronger than the Eleven, and must prevail if they persevere unless Divine Providence takes sides against them. Surely if the Government had been willing to do justice and had used its vast powers with equal energy and wisdom the Struggle might have been happily terminated long ago.

Congress adjourned today without having passed an additional tax bill except five percent on incomes, which may produce 22 mills. There must be great reduction of expenditure, or better success in borrowing than I antici-pate or inflation must continue. The President pocketed the great bill providing for the reorganization of the rebel States as loyal States.[35] He did not venture to veto, and so put it in his pocket. It was a condemnation of his Am-nesty Proclamation and of his general policy of reconstruc-tion, rejecting the idea of possible reconstitution with Slavery; which neither the President nor his chief advisers have, in my opinion, abandoned.

Called at Mr. Hoopers and found nobody in; but left a note inviting Gov. Andrew and himself to come down and dine with me. Mr. Sumner called and remained to dinner with Mr. Hooper and Gov. A. He said Gov. Sprague had made a statement of great force and power in relation to the Blair charges which was listened to with breathless attention. He said also that there was intense indignation against the President on account of his pocketing the Win-ter Davis or Reconstruction bill. Gov. Andrew hopes to have the controversy of back pay of Negro troops enlisted

by Massachusetts settled on just principles. This Justice
has been too long and too cruelly withheld.

After dinner many others called. Mr. Fessenden came
in about next. He had already been with me in the Morning and had told me that he had received a letter from a
certain individual (the same who proclaimed the most
indecent joy on my leaving the cabinet) recommending
Gov Morgans special choice for the successor of Mr. Cisco
and he expressed his intention not to have either of them
for when it was sought to make me choose appoints [?]
and had told me that he should call on the President and
before acceptance have it distinctly understood that the
appointments of subordinates in his office, for whom he
was to be responsible, must be made only with his full
consent and approval, if not made directly on his own
nominations. He now came in to say that the President
had at once acceded to this, only requiring that should he
himself desire any particular appointment made that his
wishes in that regard should be fully considered. He said
too that he hoped Mr. F—— would not without a real
necessity remove any friends of Gov. Chase. Had the President in reply to my note tendering his [my] resignation
expressed himself as he did now to Mr. F—n, I should
have cheerfully withdrawn it. Why did he not? I can see
but one reason, that I am too earnest, too antislavery, and,
say, too radical to make him willing to have me connected
with the Admn., just as my opinion that he is not earnest
enough; not antislavery enough; not radical enough,—
but goes naturally with those hostile to me rather than
with me,—makes me willing and glad to be disconnected
from it.

We parted—I promising to meet him at the Depart-

ment in the morning and introduce him to his work and
his Chief Officers.

July 5, Tuesday. Called on Fessenden and took him to
the Department and spent sometime in explaining the
State of the Finances and the general working of business.
About half past ten Judge Wayne [36] came in and administered the oath of office. Fessenden read it from the
printed form from the State Department very distinctly
and pronounced the adjunction So help me God! with
great earnestness. The conclusion of the oath struck me
'I will faithfully administer [37] the duties of the office on
which I am about to enter.' There was no such clause as
is commonly added 'to the best of my ability.' At eleven or
a little after the Heads of the Bureaus came in and I introduced them to the new Secretary. Most of them were
already known to him and the greeting on both sides was
cordial. After this was over I left him promising to call
again in the morning and confer about the practical business of borrowing money.

From the Department I returned home; and used the
remainder of the day in writing letters and receiving visitors. Mr. Durant called and talked over La matters. Garfield, Schenck and Wetmore rode with me—all were bitter against the timid and almost proslavery course of the
President. Strange story by Garfield about Col. Jaques.[38]

July 6, Wednesday. Senator Pomeroy [39] came to breakfast—he says there is great dissatisfaction with Mr. Lincoln, which has been much exasperated by the pocketing
of the reorganization bill. Garfield said yesterday that
when the news of the intention of the President to pocket
this bill came to the House on Monday, Norton [40] of Ills.
the special friend of the Presidents said it was impossible

[?] and would be fatal. G—— told him, if he desired to prevent it he should go to him at his room in the Capitol at once and remonstrate. Norton started, almost running; but returned after a little. 'Did you see him.' 'Yes' 'Will he sign.' 'No—great mistake but no use trying to prevent it.' Pomeroy says he means to go on a Buffalo hunt and then to Europe. He cannot support Lincoln, but wont desert his principles. I myself [am] of the same sentiments; though not willing now to decide what duty may demand next fall. Pomeroy remarked that on the news of my resignation reaching the Senate several of the democratic Senators came to him and said 'will go with you now for Chase.' This meant nothing but a vehement desire to overthrow the existing Administration; but might mean much if the Democrats could only cut loose from Slavery and go for freedom and the protection of labor by a national currency. If they would do that I would cheerfully go for any good man they might nominate.

Several other gentlemen called while Pomeroy was with me, but about nothing of much consequence.

Went to Department and talked about loans with Fessenden. The problem to provide means without further inflation and with gradual reduction. Condition, Immediate demands in requisitions about $94,000,000, &c &c. Means (1) proceeds of late loan received mainly in 5% Coupon Legal Tenders (2) receipts from temporary loans also most[ly] in same Legal T. (3) receipts from Internal Revenue—(4) Miscellaneous receipts sales of Exchange &c.

The condition is by no means so difficult or rather by no means so apparently difficult as at the close of the last session of Congress. Then the unpaid requisitions

amounted to $72,171,189.41 ; and the funds on hand were
[blank]. At the close of the recent session the requisitions
amounted to [blank] Then Congress had passed the National Banking act and had repealed the conversion clause
of the loan act ; but had provided no essential increase of
revenue. But with these aids, notwithstanding a very un-
promising military condition I succeeded in disposing so
rapidly of public securities that within four months the
whole amt. of unpaid requisitions had been discharged
and all demands were promptly met. The same can be
done now, but Mr. Fessenden will be obliged to pay
higher interest for less value. The Tax Legislation is better than then—far better—though not what it should be.
The power of the Department over the Trade in Insurrectionary Districts is now complete and may be made
very productive. The Military situation is far better. All
things combine to make financial success comparatively
easy.

Left T[reasur]y Dept. and went to see Stanton at War.
Found him concerned about Raid to Martinsburgh and
Harpers Ferry—thinks Sigel inefficient and that Hunter
went too far off. Hunter however yesterday at Parkersburg
and will probably today reach the vicinity of the rebels. I
cannot see from the statements made why they may not be
cut off and signally defeated or captured. Told Stanton
that everything looked favorable to me only I wished Grant
could have more men. Sherman at Marietta and rebels
forced back on the Chattahooche—Danville Railroad
broken up and Grant holding fast and on the whole gaining
—Hunter soon to drive the rebels again from Shenandoah
Valley and the glorious victory of the Kearsarge in the
combat with the Alabama,[41] which came ought [out] to

fight and went to the bottom. All looked well—The last event particularly worth millions in the improvement of our prestige and credit in Europe.

Walked home under an intensely hot sun. Soon after Mr. Wetmore came in and we went to Freedmens Village. What a striking result of the War and illustration as well as result it is. There it stands, a semicircular village extending round a sort of ravine; wooden houses—about 1800 people—mostly old and infirm or women and children—with schools—a church—good order—though much sickness and poverty—all refugees from slavery and not one wishing to return, unless free after the war.

Ewing,[42] Ashley, Hosmer,[43] and Taylor called. H is going as Chief Justice to Montana. Taylor just from Northwest Ohio—says opinions there much divided about my resignation and some inclined to blame me.

Reid [44] came in with letters from Greeley who wishes me to succeed Pendleton.[45] Told him I thought nothing gained unless we could have radical change of men and policy. He goes to New York soon. People, of course, think little of any thing in comparison with the war.

7

A Summer of Discontent

[JULY 13–NOVEMBER 26, 1864]

CHASE'S diary for the months following his departure from the Treasury Department is both cryptic and revealing. The least coherent of all his Civil War journals, it is full of abbreviations and unclear references. Much of the time Chase was traveling, and he jotted down the names of people he met, many obscure and most of not the slightest historical importance. Free from the responsibilities of office, he spent a good part of the summer visiting relatives in New Hampshire, carrying on an unimpassioned flirtation with Mrs. Carlotta Eastman of Beverly, Massachusetts, and resting with the Sprague family in Rhode Island.

Under his desultory record of apparently aimless wandering, however, one may detect a significant purpose: Chase was still a potential presidential candidate. At first thought, any such hope would seem absurd, for Lincoln had been renominated by the Republican National Convention in June. But the summer of 1864 was a period of turbulent discontent, and the President had few friends. Democrats, of course, blamed the President's antislavery policies for prolonging a useless war. Republicans, too, were in open opposition to their own presidential nominee. Some of the extreme Radicals bolted the party entirely and at a convention in Cleveland nominated John C. Frémont for President. Others remained in the party but did not stir to help reëlect Lincoln. As Congress adjourned, Ben Wade and Winter Davis issued a pronunciamento against the President's pocket-veto of their Radical reconstruction bill: ". . . if he wishes our support he must confine himself to his executive duties—to obey and execute, not make the laws—to suppress by arms armed rebellion, and leave political reorganization to Congress." Representing another element of discontented Republicans, Horace Greeley believed the President did not sincerely desire peace and reminded Lincoln that the country could not bear "fresh conscriptions, . . . further wholesale devastations, and . . . new rivers of human blood." Even the chairman of the National Union (Republican) Executive Committee despaired. "I find everywhere a conviction that we need a change," Henry J. Raymond lamented, "that the war languishes under Mr. Lincoln and that he *cannot* or *will* not give us peace." Lincoln himself lost hope. "This morning, as for some days past," he wrote on August 23rd, "it seems exceedingly probable that this Administration will not be re-elected."

Against this background of despair the movement to replace Lincoln as Republican candidate becomes understandable. Such New York Radicals as Horace Greeley, Theodore Tilton, George Opdyke, William Curtis Noyes, and Parke Godwin concluded that the President was hopeless, and on August 18th they sent out a circular letter, signed by John Austin Stevens, to party leaders throughout the country suggesting that a new Republican National

Convention be called "to concentrate the union strength on some one candidate who commands the confidence of the country, even by a new nomination if necessary." At a meeting of this committee in New York on August 30th, letters from Charles Sumner, Henry Winter Davis, Daniel S. Dickinson, and other Republican notables were read, and the committee agreed "that it was useless and inexpedient to attempt to run Mr Lincoln, in the hope of victory. . . . A National Convention was therefore called to meet at Cincinnatti [*sic*] on the 28th Sept to consult upon the affairs of the country, and, if need be, to nominate some candidate who can unite the entire loyal vote."

Chase's connections with this anti-Lincoln movement are not so clear as one might wish. As his diary shows, his New England trip had political implications. "Chase is going around," Samuel Bowles of the Springfield *Republican* reported, "peddling his griefs in private ears and sowing dissatisfaction about Lincoln." A list of the people he visited in New York and New England would make an almost complete roster of the backers of the new convention project, many of whom openly favored the ex-Secretary for President. In a letter to the New York committee Chase gave guarded approval of their scheme, and, as his diary reveals, he conferred freely during this period with William Curtis Noyes, who attended the August 30th meeting as Chase's personal representative.

For many reasons the plan to replace Lincoln did not work out. Some Republicans supported the project only on the condition that Lincoln should first voluntarily withdraw from the race. This the President showed no indication of doing. Instead, he increased his control over the party machinery, and, after elaborate negotiations, during which the Conservative Montgomery Blair resigned from the cabinet and the Radical Frémont withdrew his independent candidacy, even such Radicals as Zachariah Chandler fell in line behind the President. Another blow at the New York junto was the action of the Democratic National Convention, which nominated General George B. McClellan on a platform condemning the war as a failure and calling for peace. To many loyal Northerners, the Democratic program meant disunion, and a reaction in Lincoln's favor set in. Finally, and most influential of all, in early September Sherman's army occupied Atlanta, and suddenly it seemed silly to talk about the hopelessness of the war or the imbecility of Lincoln's administration.

These developments helped cool Chase's enthusiasm for a new Republican convention, and when he reached New York in September, he advised his friends there to drop the project. Though the Republican party contained "a great deal that is far from any tolerable standard of either ethics or politics," the Democrats, filled with "hatred of the humblest of God's poor—the colored race—and much subserviency to the slave-holding class," were worse, and he ceased his complaints about Lincoln. Presently he himself took the stump for the Republican nominees.

Such belated loyalty, it is clear, was not altogether unrelated to the imminent death of Chief Justice Roger B. Taney, whose increasing feebleness had become apparent as the summer went by. Since spring, Senator Charles Sumner had been begging the President to name Chase as Taney's successor, and when the Chief Justice died on October 12th, many other Republicans supported Sumner's demand. With his strict views of propriety and his sense of the high dignity of the position, Chase was un-

willing to solicit the appointment, but on October 19th
he did write to Sumner: "It is perhaps not exactly *en
règle* to say what a man will do in regard to an appointment not tendered to him; but it is certainly not wrong to
say to you that I should accept." Sumner sent a copy of
Chase's letter along to Lincoln, but until after the election
the canny President gave no inkling of his plans.

⌒ ⌒ ⌒

July 13, 1864, Wednesday. Half of my fifty seventh year
is ended. Today I leave Washington a private citizen. Saw
Stanton before leaving, warm and cordial as ever—no
other Head of Dept has called on me since my resignation.
Stanton said the rebels have left and have probably gone
towards Baltimore. There were probably 30,000 in front
of city and 5000 more with [*sic*] region roundabout—
Breckinridge,[1] Early and Gordon [2] dined above Rockville
Saturday and were here [?] and of course their main body.
He mentioned a curious misunderstanding. Capt. [T. S.]
Paddock of Cleveland, commanding at Fort Lincoln sent
Message to Dept.—'The enemy is approaching I desire
instructions'—Stanton sent the message to Gen. Halleck
and to Gen. Augur.[3] Three hours later another message,
of similar purport, came which was sent to the same Generals. But becoming uneasy Stanton desired Col Fry [4] to
go out to the Fort and ascertain [the] exact condition of
things. He went and found Gen Gillmore whom he supposed to be in command and enquired what was the state
of affairs at the Fort Gillmore replied he did not know—
he was not in charge of the defences in that quarter and
had no orders Fry replied The Secretary understands that
you are in command at this part of the line—Gillmore pro-

duced his orders which simply assigned him to command
of 23d. Corps. 'About 800 are here,' said he, 'this is my
whole command.' Secy. sent for Gen. Augur on this report
from Fry and sharply reprimanded him for negligence.
Had enemy known the real state of things, he could easily
have entered Washington at that point. Bid goodbye to
Mr. and Mrs. Stanton. Harrington accompanied me to
Tgr. Off. at 10.30 Clark (S.M.) [, William G.] Woodside
Paym[aste]r. B & O R R and R. W. Tayler 1st Comptroller with me—Woodside had been out with engine half
a mile beyond Bladenburgh [sic] this morning—found en-
emys pickets there and returned. Going over the river
passed a number of transports going up to Washtn. heavily
laden with troops—probably 5000 Infy. & 400 Cavalry—
Passed Fort Lookout in the night—met Norfolk boat in
Bay and put Woodside on board for Baltimore. He took
for me letter to Harrington asking him to have portfolio
and bonds &c in it lodged in First National Bank. I had
carelessly left it in my library and coupon bonds might be
easily stolen.

July 14, Thursday. Sent another letter to Harrington,
[of] same tenor, by Capt. of Tiger who returned from
Maryville—obliged to go in open boat from Tiger to
Maryville abt. 3 miles—Tiger drew too much water to
get nearer. Steamer Baltimore, which had passed us coming up the bay, lay out as we passed; but soon came up
to the landing bringing Senator Sumner, Gen. Franklin
Adml. Porter,[5] F. P. Blair Sr.[6] and Mrs Montgomery
Blair and others. Old Blair came to me, but I did not talk
much with him—perhaps was too rude—Franklin told
me about his capturing [?] Gillmore and his escape. Sumner full as usual of interesting talk. Jay Cooke met me at

Depot and leaving Clark to look after baggage, rode out with him to Chelten Hills—went to supper at Wm G. Moorheads.

July 15, Friday. To New York—Clark and Jay Cooke with me—Clark having charge of State Dept. foreign Mailbags—on arrival went to Sub Treasury—found Fessenden—He has made not an arrangement [?] yet for loan —thinks banks will agree on terms.

July 16, Saturday. Breakfast with Jay Cooke—then to Astor House and with Cisco and Fessenden to Subtreasury —Cisco thinks banks will not agree on terms—told me Morgan had called—and he had charged him with false representations about his Clerks—in using document representing them as nearly all democrats when he knew that among the most prominent so represented especially Mr. [George F.] Dunning Supt of Mint and Dr. Toucey never belonged to that party—Called at Bank of Commerce and saw Mr. Stevens and Mr. Vail. dined at Astor House with Katie and Nettie—left in evening for Newport.

July 17, Sunday. At Newport attended Dr. Mercer's [7] church—very pleasant and a very good sermon. . . .

July 22, Friday. Went to Boston with Howe [8]—met Pierce at depot—rode to Howe's fathers—beautiful place.

July 23, Saturday. Many callers.

July 24, Sunday. Went with Mr. and Mrs Endicott [9] to Beverly to church—stopped at Mrs Rantouls [10] and accompanied her to Church—home with her—Saw Mrs Eastman—pleasant talk and a walk on the little piece of land across the road and between it and the lea—not an acre scarcely—which she calls her farm.

July 25, Monday. Passed the day at Mr. Endicotts— started in rain for Lynn to keep promise to Dana [11] to meet

him there and go to Nahant—recd note from him that
Mrs. D—— had been obliged to leave it—and concluded
not to go—Very heavy rain.

July 26, Tuesday. Went to Boston with Mr. Endicott
and stopped at Revere House. Howe, Dana, Pierce and
others called—rode to Milton with Pierce and walked
over the pretty place which he has lately bought.

July 27, Wednesday. To Lynn. Alley [12] met me at Depot
and had me to dinner where I met Gov. Kent [13] and others
—visited manufactories—amazing applications of machinery—since war begun new inventions save ¾th. of human
labor. Called at Mrs Lander's but did not find her at
home—In Evening many called—lawyers, ministers, man-
ufacturers—among them my old friend Gen Schouler.[14]

July 28, Thursday. Mr. and Mrs Alley took me to
Cherry Hill—took up my friend . . . R. P. Waters, between Salem and Cherry Hill—walked over farm—Alley
told me that general opinion of our friends was that I had
erred in resigning. . . .

July 31, Sunday. Passed day at Mr. Havens [15]—Sumner
dined. . . .

Aug. 2, Tuesday. Called at Beverly with Mrs Haven
on Mrs R—— & Mrs E—— returned to West Branch
and took cars for Lynn—young Warren, *en route* to New
York, accompanying me—Hooper and Dana met me at
Lynn and took me to Nahant—Agassiz,[16] Thomas H
Perkins,[17] Amos A. Lawrence [18] and others met me at dinner and we had a pleasant time—After dinner we all
played croquet with Mr. Danas young daughters—Very
merry—Agassiz in particular entered into the sport with
great zest.

Aug. 3, Wednesday. Hooper and I went to dine with

A. A. Lawrence, who has a pretty place on a most roman-
tic situation—the house almost overhanging the sea—
Recd. letter from Mellen at Wash[ington]. enclosing one
to him from Carson [19] at Cincinnati, saying that there
would be opposition to my nomination for Congress in
First District but that it could be overcome by active ex-
ertion—Wrote Telegram to Mellen 'Unanimous nomination would command acceptance but cannot compete and
must not be regarded as competitor.' No telegraph from
Nahant.

Aug. 4, Thursday. Left Nahant with Hooper for Boston—sent telegram to Mellen—Met Pierce at depot—
Forbes [20] joined me and Hooper and off for New Bedford
—saw Eliot there and asked him to accompany us but he
could not—embarked on Azalea Mr. Forbes' yacht at
1.30 P.M. Gen Barlow [21] and Col. Russell on board—
reached Naushon at 6.30. . . .

Aug. 5, Friday. Explored Island—about 7 miles long
and 1 or ½ wide—beautiful and picturesque—wonder-
fully so—the only deer in Massachusetts are found on it—
saw one—drove Mrs Forbes, a most charming lady, home
—played 'tactics' with Hooper and Chess with George S.
Hale [22] who also [was] a guest—occupied the Gov's
Room.

Aug. 6, Saturday. Went a fishing and caught nothing—
went deer hunting and Forbes shot buck. I was twice
posted and watching vigilantly but not a deer ventured to
show himself where I was!

Aug. 7, Sunday. Went to Cotuit in the Azalea with Mr.
Hooper and Mr. Forbes—Mr. Hooper's Summer residence is at Cotuit and we found there Mrs Hooper [23] the
widow of his son and spent the day quietly.

Aug. 8, Monday. Left Cotuit with Messrs. F. & H. and Col. Godman [24] for Nantucket and reached that famous island about 1 PM—welcomed by a crowd of ragged boys one of whom found out who I was and made me at once an object of marked attention . . . —in the Evg attended a fair where I took a chance in a raffle by way of giving the good folks a little money. After fair went to Sanford's where we had a cordial welcome, a nice supper, and agreeable gentlemen.

Aug. 9, Tuesday. Visited Museum—Macy [?] gave me history of Nantucket—walk with him—found man taking down house to be sent to main land—this is now a common thing in Nantucket—the house I saw going down was sold for $600 and it would cost . . . $700 to take it to Main land and put it up again—it was a good rigid double house—before leaving went to the home and shop of Miss Coffin, a nice, plump, (not to say fat), pleasant old maid where I bought some shells and specimens of moss—about noon we took leave of the island and returned to Cotuit—I forgot to note that I called on Miss Emily Shaw and saw her father and sisters. . . .

Aug. 13, Saturday. Letters to Katie and others,—at 8.30 left Boston for Hartford, via. Worcester—at 11 met Mr. Noyes [25] at depot—dined at Hotel—Mr. Howard, Mr. Day, and others called; they seem to be not satisfied with Lincoln or prospects; to Litchfield with Mr. Noyes; arrived 8.30 or 9 P.M.; changed dress; pleasant tea with Mrs. Noyes and Miss Emily.

Aug. 14, Sunday. Church morning service; preacher plain but sensible; seventy years old—evening walk to Prospect Hill Dr. Beechers [26] house, N.W. Cor. Prospect and North St.—read part of his biography.

Aug. 15, Monday. Election held today to adopt or reject proposed amendment of Constitution, allowing soldiers to vote;—Several gentlemen called— . . . evng. serenade and short speech—war just and necessary—justice to the colored man indispensable [*sic*]—ballots as well as bullets— . . . gave Miss Noyes the mosses I brought from Nantucket—agreeable and interesting ride round the Lake with Mr. Noyes.

Aug. 16, Tuesday. Breakfast at Mr. Noyes', whose guest I was— . . . very pleasant—afterwards read Beecher's Book and wrote letters—evng. a ride to the lake—a row on it and water lilies—some calls in the evng—Tallmadge house occupied by Mr. Noyes, old mansion belonged to Col. Tallmadge [27]—of revolutionary army—grandfather of Mrs. Noyes.

Aug. 17, Wednesday. Rose very early—Mr. Noyes and I to station in Wagon at 6.30 left station abt. 7.20—at Hartford abt. 9.30—Mr. Howard at Depot who took us to his house—raining—but a number of prominent gentlemen called . . . nice lunch and agreeable talk—reached Boston abt. 6 and drove to Mr. Hooper's—found them just at dinner— . . . we joined them.

Aug. 18, Thursday. Fessenden at Breakfast—insists on my going to Europe—I promised to come to Washn. in about two weeks—called on Pierce who went with me to make some purchases. called at Merchant's Bank—met Peter Harvey,[28] old friend of Webster, now strong in opposition and Mr. Amory Davis, Prest. Suffolk Bank; Mr. Haven, Mr. Davis and another talking with Fessenden; after he went out talked some time with Mr. Haven—recd. from Harrington letter and Statement of Public Debt,—returned to house with Hooper and Fessenden and talked

for a time—Fessenden expressed at breakfast his astonish-
ment at the immense work of organization which I had
done—took dinner at Union Club ... —Home to Hooper's
abt. 11 and to bed.

Aug. 19, Friday. Mr. Noyes went to N. Y. and wrote
by him to Opdyke and Ford [29]—he promised to write me
result of meeting—I have little or no faith in it—letter
from Jay Cooke with Chronicle article—what does it
mean? he asks—I ask—all ask—wrote him briefly— ...
to Merchants Bank where cashed check $200, (on J.
C[ooke] & Co. Phila.) Hooper with me—Wanted Hair
Restoration and he proposed to call at his barbers which
we did—took cars to Beverly—Mr. Haven in seat with
me ... to Mrs. R——s. pleasant hour with her & Mrs.
E.—— Waters came after tea—to Cherry Hill with him
—cool and pleasant night. ...

Aug. 22, Monday. Rain—writing letters and reading
morning—walked alone—rain returning and a little wet—
dinner—to Beverly in gig—saw Mrs. E. and pleasant talk
—got my letters which I forget and left yesterday—returned to C. Hill.

Aug. 23, Tuesday. Rode with Waters to Danvers—
called at Putnams where Gen. Israel P.[30] was born—

Maria P. Putnam, a pretty young girl of about 18 apparently, with a modest mixture of pride and sorrow
showed me her brother's wooden sword, which had more
interest for me than the native room of the old wolf-hunt-
er. '*He* used to sleep in that room' she said 'and when
the President first called for troops to save Washington
and put down the rebellion he wanted to go so much. This
was just after Fort Sumter was taken; but he was too
young only about sixteen. Afterwards he would go and sit

out doors in the summer nights and by the moonlight he
carved this wooden sword.' And she handed it to me. It
was a rude imitation; but on one side of the blade there
was this New England boy's thought 'Not to be drawn
without right' and, on the other side, this 'Not to be
sheathed without honor'; and then [']Victory or Death!
Death to Traitors.' 'Sometime afterwards' she told me
'when Gov. Andrew said the President wanted more men
he couldn't be kept back. He said he must go to defend
the Constitution and the old Flag and he went. He was
wounded in one of the terrible battles before Richmond
in July 1862 and was taken prisoner and died in Libby
Prison.['] Brief record and sad! And, of how many true!
The memorials of the old wolf hunter, hung round the
chamber or carefully preserved in drawers; the old rude
pictures; the worn wood engraving, so curiously colored
of Wolfes Death at Quebec; the memorials from Pomfret
and the wolfs cave—the Inkstand and sand box—all faded
away—There was nothing in the low ceiled chamber,
with its old beams almost touching your head, except the
memory of the brave boy who died in Libby a prisoner
that his country might live and live free forever. . . .

Aug. 24, Wednesday. At home all the morning—reading, writing &c.—Whittier [31] spent the day—much pleasant talk—Evening took him to Beverly and to horse car—
called at Castle R—— saw R. S. R.[32] and Mrs. E.—She
is agreeable as always—fixed halter for me when I came
away fearing danger from Arab horse!

Aug. 25, Thursday. W. P. Phillips [33] called; soon after
he left, Dr. Schmidt from Washn. with message to write
letter advising support of Lincoln with assurance of
French mission[;] this from Johnston [Andrew Johnson?]

and Corwin with apparent sanction of President—told him I could do nothing now. . . .

Aug. 26, Friday. . . . Wrote E. P. Powell,[34] Adrian, Mich. can't decide abt. lecturing at present—will some time next month—letter fr. Tho. Brown abt. Quick silver mine &c. wrote part of financial letter to Fessenden—rode with Mr. Waters—went to Beverly and spent Evng. with Mrs. R. and E.

Aug. 27, Saturday. Rose very early—unwell and after going down returned to bed—up again—breakfast and finished letter to Fessenden—goodbye to all the kind folks— . . . to Boston just in time to miss Concord train— went to Revere House.—sent note to Mr. Pierce and rewrote letter to Fessenden—met Mr. —— of N.Y. who told me that Mrs. W. G. Morehead [Moorhead] and her family were in the House—overseer Southron and flunkey northerners at dinner—met . . . J. R. Gilmore [35] of Cinti.—G. presented his two boys—bid them stand by freedom—Pierce came . . . —Cars to Concord. . . .

Aug. 28, Sunday. To church with family—new edifice since I was here last and very pretty but some inconveniences and too dark—Minister from N.Y. preached a very good Sermon—reading and talk rest of day except short nap. Evening . . . —talk not very profitable—retired to Chamber and read First Epistle of John and to bed.

Aug. 29, Monday. Called at Gov. Gilmore's, who was out—saw Mrs. G.—to Hopkinton with Eliza [36]—Aunt Ellen very glad to see me—now 89—sight failed and quite lame but still clear in mind and faith—visited Mother's Grave plucked a young locust growing upon it and transcribed inscription[:] Mrs. Jannette Chase, relict of Hon.

Ithmr. Chase, aged 54, died apr.—1832 : And now Lord what is our hope—Truly our hope is even in thee—Returned to Concord. Evening—several called— . . . Pierce came from Boston—advised friendly conference between Union Men and Governor G.[37] about differences between them.

Aug. 30, Tuesday. Gov. G——called and took me to ride—talked abt. differences with Leg[islature]. Gov. censured Chandler and Rollins—thought Lincoln and Stanton had behaved badly—Soldiers coming home will vote for McClellan—left with Pierce on cars for White Mountains—dined at Plymouth—Stage to Profile House arrived abt. ½ past 7. . . .

Aug. 31, Wednesday. Report that McClellan is nominated at Chicago—left Profile at 8—outside seat—grand prospects—. . . . I tired of this and got inside at last. . . .

Sept. 1, Thursday. Left at 8 for North Conway. Pierce and I outside—Notch scenery magnificent—arrived at C. 1.30—took off flannels and dressed for dinner—after dinner Miss Haven came and spoke to me—introduced Mr. P. to her—she, me to several, among others to Mrs. Caldwell. . . . —P. and I with Miss H and Mrs. C. drove to Echo Lake, Diana's Bath and Cathedral—a delightful drive[;] evng. same party to Juggler and ventriloquist—first ridiculous latter amusing—

Sept. 2, Friday. left North Conway at 6 after very early breakfast—Mrs. C. and Miss H. up and with us at breakfast. Bishop Duggan,[38] of Detroit was asked to take a buggy which was to go back to Centre Harbor which he did and asked me to take a seat with him—I drove the horse and we had [a] very pleasant ride—he seemed to favor McClellan—asked me about Pendleton—we

reached Centre Harbor abt. 12.30 dined—met Stover and
wife—Stover spoke to me. I rather cold not liking him.
Camp meeting party on board . . . —P. int[roduced] me to
Mr. Guild,[39] Unitarian Minister, who was formerly of
Marietta—at Alton Bay took cars for Boston—arrived a
little after 8—to Revere House—Sumner and Hooper
called—Sumner spoke of meeting at New York—recd letter from Fessenden and a copy of one sent him—also
from Thayer and Schmidt and call from Stevens—very
embarrassing.

Sept. 3, Saturday. Pierce to Breakfast—gave him $30
my part of expenses over abt. $5 paid direct—present
him my sleeve buttons. Called at Hoopers—Dana called
and Howe—Pierce with me to the Depot—left 11.10.
Sprague met me at Depot in Providence . . . at Kings-
ton station at 1.24 found Katie and Nettie waiting for
me—dusty ride to Narragansett—delightful place— . . .
a house full—a merry game of croquet— . . . dinner at 7.

Sept. 4, Sunday. To church at Wakefield—good sermon—afternoon went to rocks—grand roll of the ocean.

Sept. 5, Monday. Govr. and I to Providence. Easterly
storm which began in night—continued with intermission
all day—quite chilly—afternoon went to rocks—Nettie
and I to Indian rock—dash of waves magnificent.

Sept. 6, Tuesday. All the folks went to Providence—I
bought the tickets for 8. . . . Went to Mrs. Sprague's—
then with Mrs. S. and Katie to Centennial [of Brown
University]—gentleman took charge of ladies and put
me in procession—Mr. Bancroft,[40] my co-walker—in-
t[roduc]ed me to Prof. Goldwin Smith [41] and Mr. Stanley
a young Englishman—saw . . . many other leading men
in procession—in church sat next to Prof. Smith—asked

what most struck him—expected him to say absence of indications of war—but he did not—forget what he did say—I said what I thought—he said England did not exhibit more such indications in time of Crimean War—but that not a civil war. Dr. Sears [42] delivered an address which was plain and rather dry but quite good—after address dinner—John Henry Clifford [43] presided—excellent opening address—very clever poems by Judge Thomas and Mr. Thurber [44]—good speech by Goldwin Smith—I called on to respond and well recd—obliged to leave the table after which Gen. Burnside and Geo. Wm. Curtis [45] spoke—Evng. some young folks at Mrs. Sprague's. Pierce among them—

Sept. 7, Wednesday. With Gov. S. . . . to commencement some very good pieces . . . home to dinner—late 3 instead of 2—. . . .

Back to tea—after with Gov. S. to President Sears' reception—introduced to many and rather lionized—escaped soon and long talk with Gov. S. abt. Mills, business &c. . . . .

Sept. 8, Thursday. Went out with Katie to make some purchases bought only a couple of books and staid at Gov.'s Office till hour for starting—then returned to Pier. . . .

Sept. 9, Friday. . . . Gov. S— . . . and Katie had misunderstanding that evening.

Sept. 10, Saturday. Talk with Katie—walk with S[prague]. to next farm on Narrow River—then back to house—grand rollers croquet— . . . Clambake—very nice—back to house—supper—afterwards to Point Judith and visit to Light House.

Sept. 11, Sunday. Rain—all staid at home—I read testament and Misanthrope.[46]

Sept. 12, Monday. Spent morning in writing to Mr. French—(but did not send letter) and packing—Went to Providence in 3 P.M. train— . . . went on boat Election for New York—sat forward till passed Point Judith.

Sept. 13, Tuesday. Jar of boat kept me waking every few minutes—up at 6—shaved and dressed—reached New York—10 min past 7.—talk with gentleman who thought Lincoln very wise—if more radical would have offended conservatives—if more conservative the radicals —will this be judgment of history? called at Bk. of Commerce—talked with Stevens and Vail abt. sales of 5.20s by Barings—they thought best to make power to sell at limit—I approved. Stevens congratulated me on Freedom from official responsibilities—met Mr. Duer and others— all kind—some more than kind—Barney dined with us —Mr. H—— and also Orton called and Stevens, Jr.— talked with him—advised to disconnect himself from new convention project—left for Washn. Frank Moore [47] aboard who said future volumes of Rebellion Record would contain more finance.

Sept. 14, Wednesday. Arrived at Washn. Marshall and Cassie [48] in house—quite out of order—repairing &c. Mr. Harrington called—went to Treasy. Dept. reiterated advice to Fessenden to organize Agency System in Europe —or facilitate sales there—danger from fluctuations of exchange[;] examined rules cotton trade—called on Mr. McCulloch—both he and Fessenden advised taking part in Campaign—F. calling at Presidents talked with him— he wished me to call—McC. said he wd. call—Gov. S.

and K. determined to return to R.I. and went at ½ p. 6.
Stanton and several others called.

Sept. 15, Thursday. Called at War Dept.—also on
Prest.—he recd. me quite cordially—Stanton as kind as
always—at Dept. talked with Harrington and Risley abt.
Cotton Trade—advised against interference beyond lines
—let military control there—dined with Fessenden. . . .

Sept. 16, Friday. At Dept. and sundry matters—Cooke
told me he had invited Forney [49] to dine with me tomorrow—Wetmore called asking me to speak with Gov.
Andrew at flagraising tomorrow—declined to speak—but
promised to be present— . . . Went to War Dept. and
rode with Stanton to Soldiers Home—called on Mrs.
Stanton nice children—took tea with the family—we
spent evening[.] Surg. Gen Barnes [50] there and Mrs B. with
him—called at Prest's. Corwin and C. J. Wright [51] there
—they went after some talk—talk with President indifferent but cordial—home from War Dept.

Sept. 17, Saturday. Tried to give some time to speech
at Cin[cinnat]i—but poor success.[52]

I have seen the President twice since I have been here.
Both times third persons were present, and there was
nothing like private conversation. His manner was cordial and so were his words; and I hear of nothing but
good-will from him. But he is not at all demonstrative,
either in speech or manner. I feel that I do not know him,
and I found no action on what he says or does. . . . It
is my conviction that the cause I love and the general
interests of the country will be best promoted by his reëlection, and I have resolved to join my efforts to those
of almost the whole body of my friends in securing it. . . .
I have been told that the President said he and I could

not get along together in the Cabinet. Doubtless there was a difference of temperament, and on some points, of judgment. I may have been too earnest and eager, while I thought him not earnest enough and too slow. On some occasions, indeed, I found that it was so. But I never desired any thing else than his complete success, and never indulged a personal feeling incompatible with absolute fidelity to his Administration. To assure that success I labored incessantly in the Treasury Department, with what results the world knows. When I found that the use of my name in connection with the presidency would interfere with my usefulness in that department, I seized the opportunity offered by the expression, by a majority of the Union members of the [Ohio] Legislature, of a preference for Mr. Lincoln, to ask that no further consideration should be given to my name. After that, I advised all friends who consulted me, in reference to the action of the Baltimore Convention, to give him their support. But it would be uncandid not to say that I felt wronged and hurt by the circumstances which preceded and attended my resignation, and that I was far from satisfied with the indications that Mr. Lincoln sympathized more with those who assailed and disparaged than with those who asserted and maintained the views held by me in common with the great majority of the supporters of his Administration. I think even now there would never have been any difficulty about our getting along together, could he have understood my sentiments just as they were, and if he had allowed me to understand his freely and unreservedly. . . .

Sept. 18, Sunday. Church—Dr. Nadal[53] on Sunday observance—excellent, though as I thought defective in proof that 4th commandment applies to Christian Sunday—dined alone—read Spencer and other books—Evng Mr. Goodloe [54] and others called—G—— favors compensation to rebel slave-holders for slaves as peace measure—Young man from Chronicle Office abt. speeches at flag-raising yesterday—promised substance of mine and furnished it.

Sept. 19, Monday. Rose earlier than usual—read Testa[men]t &c—. . . . Forney . . . is thoroughly frightened abt. Pa. and N. York.—thinks Lincoln's chances very bad— . . . dined with Fessenden . . . Serenade and speech which took well. . . .

Sept. 20, Tuesday. . . . Saw Stanton at Fessenden's—called at his Dept. [and?] to his house—good-bye—talked with McCulloch who promised to see President and to breakfast with me to-morrow morning—Recd. telegram from Gov. S. that Katie and Nettie will join me at Eutaw House Wednesday Evening or Thursday Morning. telegraphed Jay Cooke to stop them in Phila. While at Treasury Department heard shouting of Clerks—enquired cause and was told Sheridan had captured Early and 2500 of his men [55]—called at Mrs. Goldsborough's [56] —heard Mrs. G—— read beautiful letter from Mr. Wirt, while 100 guns were being fired in honor of Sheridan's victory. Dined with Fessenden and bid him goodbye.

Sept. 21, Wednesday. Left Washington for Cincinnati intending to speak there.

Sept. 24, Saturday. Spoke at mass meeting in Market Space—most cordially received—rode down to Burnet House on Engine with Flat Iron boys.

Sept. 28, Wednesday. By rail to [one word illegible]—spoke in Market ground—attentive audience.

Sept. 29, Thursday. Back to Cincinnati—late—but L Hommedieu [57] sent special car to Hamilton, found Stanton there—both spoke.

Oct. 1, Saturday. To New Albany by way of St Louis —great crowd—heavy rain—Gov. Lane [58] spoke admirably—I, also, but not so admirably.

Oct. 3, Monday. Spoke at Louisville at City Hall—a large and attentive audience—spoke very plainly—Many callers Judge Henry Pirtle, [59] Gen Schofield, [60] James Speed G. D. Prentice [61] and others.

Oct. 6, Thursday. Went to Chillicothe and spoke there though quite unwell.

Oct. 7, Friday. Spoke at Jackson to large audience— Col. Thomas [62] of Phila there— . . . and others—all went off well—felt nearly well.

Oct. 8, Saturday. Spoke at MacArthur and returned same evng to Chillicothe. . . .

Oct. 10, Monday. Returned to Cincinnati. Many callers. . . .

Oct. 11, Tuesday. Election—voted for Republican State Ticket.

Oct. 13, Wednesday. [63] Spoke in Covington Ky—reminded audience of my speech there in 1860.

Oct. 14, 15, 16 Th. to Sun inclusive remained in Cincinnati.

Oct. 17, Monday.—To Toledo to attend Sister Helen's silver wedding—very pleasant and all quite happy. Attempts to force me out but I stuck to car.

Oct. 18, Tuesday. Returned to Cin.

Oct. 19 & 20, Wednesday & Thursday. In Cincinnati.

Oct. 21, Friday. Cars to Lexington—crowded—day be-

fore cars stopped and robbed by guerillas—Monty. Blair
on them but escaping.

Oct. 22, Saturday. Spoke in Lexington—Wade spoke
also at same meeting.

Oct. 23, Sunday. Went to Dr. Breckinridges [64] near
Lexington—(not quite sure of these exact dates).

Oct. 24, Monday. Returned to Cincinnati and left next
night for Phila.

Oct. 26, Wednesday. Reached Phila and cordially recd.
—next night (27th) addressed great meetings—Gen Cameron with me at one—Mr. J. H. Orne [65] very cordial.

Oct. 28, Friday. Went with MacVeigh [66] to West Chester and spoke to a very much interested audience—left
immediately afterward in carriage with McVeigh [sic]
and another gentleman to intercept car on Central Railroad for Pittsburgh.

Oct. 29, Saturday. Took cars a little after midnight and
reached Cleveland by way of Pittsburgh in the evening.

Oct. 30, Sunday. Attended Church at Cleveland with
my friends the Parsons who [are] exceedingly anxious
that I may be Chief Justice.

Oct. 31, Monday. Spoke at Cleveland, and took boat at
one for Detroit.

Nov. 1, Tuesday. Spoke at Detroit—Lyman Tremain [67]
there and spoke also.

Nov. 2, Wednesday. Spoke at Holly—with Wm A
Howard.[68]

Nov. 3, Thursday. Spoke at Adrian—Directors car—
collision upon returning to Detroit (this yesterday).

Nov. 4, Friday. Spoke at Chicago—Gen. Farnsworth [69]
there and spoke also—both most kindly recd. took cars
immediately after closing for St Louis.

Nov. 5, Saturday. Spoke at St Louis—to a great and attentive and enthusiastic audience—unfortunate division here between the friends of the regular Union nominee and Mr. Knox.[70]

Nov. 6, Sunday. To Church with Mr. Blow [71] in morning—met Gratz Brown and others—after Church to Carondelet with Blow to dinner.

Nov. 7, Monday. Cars early for Cin[cinnati]—met on return persons who had just been captured by the rebels in the War—reached Cincinnati in evng.

Nov. 8, Tuesday. Pres[identia]l election—voted for Lincoln and Johnson. . . .

Nov. 26, Saturday. . . . got letters—among them a telegram from McCulloch to come to Washington—he wants me to make some explanations or assurances in order to secure appointment of Chief Justice, I suppose—Ans[were]d. Can't come—Wrote Fessenden. . . .

8

The Death of Lincoln

[APRIL 1–MAY 1, 1865]

ON DECEMBER 6, 1864, Lincoln named Chase Chief Justice of the United States, and the Senate unanimously confirmed the nomination. When he learned the news, Chase at once wrote the President: "I cannot sleep before I thank [you] for this mark of your confidence, and especially for the manner in which the nomination was made. I shall never forget either and trust that you will never repent either. Be assured that I prize your confidence and good will more than nomination or office." On December 13th he was sworn in as sixth Chief Justice of the United States.

"Of Mr. Chase's ability and of his soundness on the general issues of the war there is, of course, no question," Lincoln had said when debating the nomination. "I have only one doubt about his appointment. He is a man of unbounded ambition, and has been working all his life to become President. That he can never be; and I fear that if I make him chief-justice he will simply become more restless and uneasy and neglect the place in his strife and intrigue to make himself President. If I were sure that he would go on to the bench and give up his aspirations and do nothing but make himself a great judge, I would not hesitate a moment."

Chase's backers helped remove the President's doubts, but if the President hoped the new Chief Justice would confine his interests to the cases before the Court, he was to be disappointed. Chase was used to active politics, and he had strong opinions on the controversial subjects then agitating the public mind. He had never before been on the bench and he found its isolation uncongenial and its duties often trivial. "Working from morning till midnight," he described his new life, "and no result, except that John Smith owned this parcel of land or other property instead of Jacob Robinson; I caring nothing, and nobody caring much more, about the matter."

Legal hairsplitting seemed all the more tedious to Chase during his first months as Chief Justice because of his concern over the serious issues raised by the approaching end of the war. By Christmas, 1864, Sherman's army had split the Confederacy, sweeping across Georgia and seizing Savannah, and then it turned north through the Carolinas. After cleaning the Confederates out of the Shenandoah Valley, Sheridan joined Grant for the final campaign around Richmond. Victory was in sight.

"We are all jubilant here," the Chief Justice wrote during these victories; "but some of the thoughtful ones are much alarmed about the likelihood of reconstruction without adequate guarantees against future evils." In spite of Congressional opposition, President Lincoln pushed ahead with his lenient program for peace, which permitted the seceded states to set up governments whenever ten per cent of the 1860 voters would swear renewed loyalty to the Union. In Louisiana and Arkansas, under military sponsorship, provisional governments were actually established, and other states were not far behind. None of the new Southern constitutions provided for Negro suffrage, and none imposed severe disqualifications upon ex-Confederate leaders. Chase watched these developments with growing uneasiness. "I fear our good President is so anxious for the restoration of the Union," he told his correspondents, "that he will not care sufficiently about the basis of representation. In my judgment, there is none sound except absolute justice for all, and ample security for justice in law and suffrage." In letters to Lincoln himself he pushed his plan to give the Negro the vote. "I most respectfully but most earnestly commend these matters to your attention," he admonished the President. "God gives you a great place and a great opportunity. May He guide you in the use of them."

∽ ∽ ∽

April 1, 1865, Saturday. Went to Baltimore hoping to meet some members of the bar and get a little acquainted with them before opening court, for first time as Presiding Justice. I had sent word of my coming to Mr. [William] Price the District Attorney; but he went to Annapolis without informing the bar and so nobody knew of my coming and I saw nobody.

April 2, Sunday. Remained in my room all day—read Testament and an article in the Companion to the British Almanac on the subject of the Sun and its supply. The theory was that innumerable asteroids are continually revolving round the sun in diminishing orbits until at length they fall into it and thus supply its fires. It was quite plausibly argued. Can it be so?

Towards evening Gen Barlow and Mr. Hopkins came in and passed a few minutes Gen. B—— had recently returned from Europe and seemed entirely recovered of his wounds at Cold Harbor. He was under orders to join Hancock [1] in the Shenandoah Valley, but had appealed to the War Dept. to allow him to go to Grant, and expected an answer today.

April 3, Monday. Judge Giles [2] and Mr. Price, the District Attorney called and accompanied me to the Court Room. Judge G—— had kindly prepared a note of what was proper to be said on opening the Court, and I gladly availed myself of it. There was nothing to be done except call the docket which was done and we adjourned. I walked with Judge G—— to his residence on Franklin Street where I was made acquainted with Mrs G—— and a young lady visiting them. The Judge seems very intelligent and very considerate and kind: and Mrs G—— seems to be an agreeable, well informed lady. She used to know my uncle Bishop Chase [3] very well. From Judge G——'s I went to Swanns, my old friend of lang syne, now Governor elect of the Free State of Maryland. I found no one at home but his daughter Jenny—Virginia I suppose—a sweet girl of 17 or 18 perhaps. After a few minutes of pleasant talk with her I returned to my hotel. In the afternoon and evening quite a number of gentlemen called. The news of Grants victories and capture of Richmond came.

April 4, Tuesday. Called docket to see what cases were ready—marked some for trial. Gen. Este [4] called and we went over to Washington together, and, with my daughters, drove through the city to see the illumination in honor of Grants victories—it was superb.

April 5, Wednesday. Returned to Baltimore leaving Este behind—called the trial docket in Court—found no case ready.

April 7, Friday. Dined at Dr. Fuller's—The guests were Ex Secretary Kennedy,[5] Gov. Elect Swann, Dr. Buckler, a practising physician; no ladies except Mrs Fuller and a niece of the Doctor. The dinner was good—no wine— and the talk pleasant. After dinner, in the parlor, only Messrs Swann, Kennedy, Dr. Fuller and myself being present, I expressed in the course of conversation my opinion that the only solid foundation of social order and political prosperity was universal suffrage. Gov. Swann said nothing; Mr. Kennedy intimated dissent; Dr. Fuller qualified assent. I said I thought that the nation was bound to secure the right of voting to the loyal blacks of the rebel states, upon reorganization, not only as a measure of simple justice; but also on grounds of domestic and foreign policy. To deny to those who had been loyal to the country—and eminently loyal—a right to a voice in the affairs of the country they had helped to save would be condemned by all impartial men; while the securing to them of the ballot would save us from much discord, violence and disorder, unfriendly or rather pernicious to regular industry; and would, in possible foreign complications, avert the danger of divisions in our own population. Dr. Fuller spoke of his own relations to Slavery. He said 'Formerly I felt bound to sustain the burden of the institution, but was never easy under it. My slaves were my continual anxiety. How could I die and leave them? To what? To whom? I thank God for emancipation—it has taken a great burden off my mind. My friends tell me "You have lost a hundred and fifty thousand dollars!"

I tell them Say rather that I have had one hundred and fifty thousand weights of iron taken from my conscience.' I was very glad to hear this; and hoped for more progress not only in the mind of the good Doctor, but in those of the other gentlemen.

April 8, Saturday. Nothing of material interest today. Went to Washington in the afternoon train.

April 9, Sunday. Attended the Methodist Church—Dr. Nadal preached as usual.

April 10, Monday. Returned to Baltimore and attended Court—In the evening dined with Judge Giles—Among the guests were Mr. Kennedy, Mr. A.S. Ridgely,[6] a young lawyer of good abilities, but too much inclined to potables; Mr. Price, now District Attorney, quite an old gentleman, over sixty, and a very kind and worthy though not very efficient man; Mr. [William] Schley, about as old as Mr. Price, very able, and very agreeable and courteous. Many anecdotes were related of prominent members of the bar of Maryland and particularly of Chief Justice Taney and his habit of inveterate smoking.

April 11, Tuesday. Ordinary business at Court—dined in the evening, (at 6 P.M.) with Henry Winter Davis— A different set of guests—mostly the radicals, such as Stockbridge[7] and Sterling[8] prominent lawyers—Bond, Judge of the Criminal Court, a thorough able and earnest man—Mr. Ridgely and others of the Conservative side— I took Mrs Davis to table and talked a good deal with her. Wrote letter to Prest. Lincoln.[9]

April 12, Wednesday. Read in American President Lincoln's Speech at the White House on Reconstruction [10] in which he referred to my dissatisfaction with the exceptions in his proclamation—began a letter to him—glad that he at length openly avows his wish that the very intelligent and those who have been soldiers, among the loyal blacks, should be allowed to vote but sorry that he is not yet ready for universal or at least equal suffrage—attended Court—Dined in Evening with Mr. Albert—a mixed company, Gov. Swann, Admiral Farragut, Jerome Bonaparte,[11] General Morris,[12] the brilliant Davis, Gen. Foster, Mayor Chapman,[13] Judge Bond, Mr. Stockbridge, Mr. Sterling and others—finished letter to President.[14]

April 13, Thursday. Copied and mailed letter to President—home by Evening train—Katie and Nettie went out to see illumination—tired and declined to go.

April 14, Friday. At home morning—afternoon rode out with Nettie intending to have myself left at President['s] and talk with him about universal suffrage in reorganization—felt reluctant to call lest my talk might annoy him and do harm rather than good—home a little after dusk having postponed my intended call—retired to bed about ten—sometime after a servant came up and said a gentleman, who said the President had been shot, wanted to see me. I directed that he should be shown to my room. He came in, an employé in the Treasury Department, and said he had just come from the theatre—the President had been shot in his box by a man who leaped from the box upon the stage and escaped by the rear—He could give no particulars and I hoped he might be mistaken—but soon after Mr. Mellen, Mr. [C. M.] Walker the Fifth Auditor and Mr. Plantz came in and confirmed what I had been told and added that Secretary Seward had also been assassinated, and that guards were being placed around the houses of all the prominent officials, under the apprehension that the plot had a wide range. My first impulse was to rise immediately and go to the President, whom I could not yet believe to have been fatally wounded; but reflecting that I could not possibly be of any service and should probably be in the way of those who could, I resolved to wait for morning and further intelligence. In a little while the guard came— for it was supposed that I was one of the destined victims —and their heavy tramp-tramp was heard under my window all night. Mr. Mellen slept in the house. It was a night of horrors.

April 15, Saturday. Up with the light—a heavy rain was falling, and the sky was black. Walked up with Mr. Mellen to Mr. Sewards crossing the street (13th I believe) on which is Fords Theatre and, opposite, the house to which the President had been conveyed—was informed at that point that the President was already dead—continued on to Mr. Sewards—found guards before the house and in the street denying access, but the officer allowed me and Mr. Mellen to pass—was admitted to lower hall of the house—learning from assistant surgeon that Mr. Seward had partially recovered his senses and though in a very critical [condition] might live—but that Mr. Frederick Seward's case was hopeless [15]—his skull having been penetrated to the brain by what seemed to be a blow from the hammer of a pistol—returned home full of horror and sorrow—all day long rumors flew—[John Wilkes] Booth was the assassin—he had shot the President and had made his way to Sewards instantly after—but this could not be—the deed on Mr. Seward was by a different man—every body had something to repeat or some question to ask. Soon after leaving Mr. Sewards I went to see the Vice President and found him at his hotel,

calm apparently but very grave. Soon after Secretary
McCulloch and Atto. Gen. Speed came in—they said
they were on their way to my house to ask my attendance
for administering the oath of office as President to the
Vice President—Some consultation followed as to time
and place and it was agreed that it should be in the parlor where we then were and at 10 oclock. I then went
with the Atto General to his office to look into the precedents in the cases of Vice Presidents Tyler and Fillmore
—and to examine the Constitution and laws. On our way
the topic was the late President. Mr. Speed said he had
never seen him in better spirits than on yesterday. He
met the Cabinet very cheerfully and talked with them
fully on the subject of reorganization. 'He never seemed
so near our views' said Mr. Speed. 'Before the meeting
of the Cabinet he had showed me your letter from Baltimore, which, I must say, was a very clear and compact
statement of the case. At the meeting he said he thought
had made a mistake at Richmond in sanctioning the as-
sembling of the Virginia Legislature [16] and had perhaps
been too fast in his desires for early reconstruction. The
matter was referred to Mr. Stanton to draw up a pro-
gramme for North Carolina.' All Mr. Speed said deep-
ened my sorrow for the country's great loss. After exam-
ining the precedents and the Constitution we returned
to the Hotel where, at the entrance, I encountered old
Mr. Blair and his son Montgomery. I had determined I
would bury resentments, and greeted both kindly. We entered the room together—the parlor of the hotel,—where
were assembled, some twelve or fourteen gentlemen, Mr.
McCulloch, Secy. of the Treasury, Mr. Speed the Atto
Gen, the Messrs Blair, Mr. Hale [17] and others. I admin-

istered the oath, which the Vice President solemnly repeated after me. He was now the successor of Mr. Lincoln. I said to him May God guide support and bless you in your arduous duties. The others came forward and tendered their sad congratulations. He asked me if he ought to say anything to those present. I answered that I thought it wd. be better to make a brief announcement to the people in the public prints He asked me to prepare something and I left the room for that purpose. Returning with it an hour or so later I found that the new President had gone to a room at the Treasury Department to meet the Cabinet. In the evening I saw a report of what he had said after I had left the room.

April 16, Sunday. At Church—Dr. Nadal preached— Bishop Simpson [18] was in the pulpit but took no part in the exercises—Called at Gov. Sewards—a little apparent improvement and but a little. Wrote Judge Giles, Gen Ashley and Gov. Andrew.

April 17, Monday. Gov. Sprague came this morning. Every body seems overwhelmed—The Governor and I went to the Kirkwood to call on Prest. Johnson. He was just leaving to go to a meeting of Heads of Departments at the Treasury.

April 18, Tuesday. Called on President at Kirkwood and had a long talk with him—he seems thoroughly in earnest and much of the same mind with myself.

April 19, Wednesday. Called on Gov. Brough [19] and other friends at Willards—they were out and I left cards.

April 20, Thursday. Called at Treasy Dept. and saw McCulloch and Prest. Johnson. On the street heard rumors of an officer with news from Sherman of Johnston's surrender.[20]

April 21, Friday. Governor Brough called—asked him to breakfast with me on Monday and he agreed—talk about the news from Sherman and Grant's leaving at 2 this morning. Brough said he had predicted it in talk with Stanton—thinks it doubtful if Union Party will carry Ohio at next election—should be more democratic and more liberal to democrats. does not expect himself to be candidate for reelection.

April 22, Saturday. Called at Willards—met Rosecrans, Campbell [21] and others—invited them to breakfast Monday—went to see McCulloch—talked to him about Denisons removal—said Prest. Lincoln made a special point of it.

April 24, Monday. Worked on opinions on cases argued at Baltimore—letter from Jay Cooke—result of investment a net profit of 1232.63—wrote him—At breakfast were Gov. Brough, H. D. Cooke,[22] Gen. Butler, Gen. Rosecrans, H. D. Cooke [*sic*], W. P. Mellen, L. D. Campbell, Whitelaw Reid, Mr. Wetmore our State Agent, and Col Mussy. It seemed to go off well. Wrote Mrs Eastman.

April 25, Tuesday. Went to Balt[imor]e and read opinions—left cards at Dr. Fullers and Mr. Bonapartes—called on Dr. Collins—returned to Washington in the afternoon. Write Flanders [23] and Denison at New Orleans.

April 26, Wednesday. Took a ride with Nettie in the Evening—in the morning called on McCulloch, Speed, and Prest. Johnson.

April 27, Thursday. Recd. a letter from Col. Key about Semmes case [24] and sent petition to the President with note commending Col. K. to his esteem and consideration.

April 28, Friday. Wrote Col. Key—made some arrangements for starting South [25]—and fixed the day for Monday.

April 29, Saturday. Wrote a note to Stanton asking for such a general letter as he might think best to enable me to get on conveniently and see all I could see on my southern journey and recd. one from him well adapted to the purpose. Wrote a note to Prest. Johnson saying that Johnstons surrender put a new face on affairs and suggesting further conference [?] before going south, and received a request that I would come up to his room. Went taking with me the rough draft of an address in which I had embodied the substance of what I thought ought to be now said to the People on the subject of the reorganization of the rebel States preparatory to their resumption of loyal relations to the Union. . . . In this address I incorporated a distinct recognition of the loyal colored men as citizens, entitled to the right of suffrage. I read it to Mr. Johnston [*sic*] and at his request a part of it more than once. He said I agree to all you say, but I dont see how I can issue such a document now. I am new and untried and cannot venture what I please. I said Mr. President If you will just put forth not this, but some simple declaration that the colored people are free and are citizens and therefore entitled to vote in reorganization and to be protected in that right you will have on your side all the young brain and heart of the country and you will have, of course, all those who feel bound to sneeze when the President takes snuff—no small number—and you will be irresistible. Besides this your declaration will be reprinted in every language under heaven civilized and uncivilized, and it will excite the admiration of all men and the gratitude of all good men, and give you a name and fame equal to that acquired by the Proclamation of Emancipation. Much more was said and much on both sides. I almost hoped the Presidents reluctance was conquered and that the new and crowning proclamation wd be issued securing equal and universal suffrage in reorganization. Wrote to Mr. Hastings and Mr. Schuckers [26] at Albany [?] expressing my regret that I cannot attend graduation of Law Class; and to W.G. Deshler,[27] Columbus, enclosing subscription to Sherman Fund and some words of what I thought just praise and defence. Recd. a letter from Gov. Sprague—somewhat harsh on Sherman.

April 30, Sunday. Wrote Gov. Sprague anxious about Katies cough. Wrote a parting note to the President . . . enclosing the Bible on which he was sworn into office with passage marked which was pressed by his lips.

May 1, Monday. Wrote Tilton Sorry I cannot come to Meeting of Cong. Ministers—sent copies of my two letters to Prest. Lincoln—gave briefly my views of the situation—and bid goodbye. Recd. letters from President and Secy. Welles in furtherance of my journey.

Notes

INTRODUCTION

[Notes for pages 1 to 45]

[1] Frederic William Maitland, *The Life and Letters of Leslie Stephen* (London: Duckworth & Co., 1906), p. 120.

[2] Carl Schurz, *The Reminiscences of Carl Schurz* (New York: The McClure Company, 1907), II, 34.

[3] Ben: Perley Poore, *Perley's Reminiscences of Sixty Years in the National Metropolis* (Philadelphia: Hubbard Brothers, 1886), I, 461.

[4] Schurz, *op. cit.*, II, 34.

[5] Henry Villard, *Memoirs of Henry Villard, Journalist and Financier, 1835–1900* (Boston: Houghton Mifflin Company, 1904), I, 171.

[6] George Wilson Pierson, *Tocqueville and Beaumont in America* (New York: Oxford University Press, 1938), p. 557.

[7] Charles Richard Williams, ed., *Diary and Letters of Rutherford Birchard Hayes* (Columbus: Ohio Archæological and Historical Society, 1922), I, 384.

[8] Jacob W. Schuckers, *The Life and Public Services of Salmon Portland Chase* (New York: D. Appleton and Company, 1874), p. 141.

[9] Reinhard H. Luthin, "Salmon P. Chase's Political Career Before the Civil War," *Mississippi Valley Historical Review,* XXIX (1942–43), 526–7.

[10] See Chapter 5, diary entry for Aug. 30, 1863, page 179.

[11] C. Robinson to Chase, Dec. 21, 1860, Chase MSS., Lib. of Cong.

[12] Hayes to Chase, June 29, 1861, *ibid.*

[13] Hugh McCulloch, *Men and Measures of Half a Century: Sketches and Comments* (New York: Charles Scribner's Sons, 1888), p. 185.

[14] Harry J. Carman and Reinhard H. Luthin, *Lincoln and the Patronage* (New York: Columbia University Press, 1943), p. 244.

[15] Gideon Welles, *Diary of Gideon Welles, Secretary of the Navy under Lincoln and Johnson* (Boston: Houghton Mifflin Company, 1911), II, 121.

[16] A. Curtis Wilgus, "Some London Times' Comments on Secretary Chase's Financial Administration, 1861–1864," *Mississippi Valley Historical Review*, XXVI (1939–40), 398.

[17] Ishbel Ross, *Proud Kate: Portrait of an Ambitious Woman* (New York: Harper & Brothers, 1953), p. 158.

[18] Royal Cortissoz, *The Life of Whitelaw Reid* (London: Thornton Butterworth Ltd., 1921), I, 197–8.

[19] See Chapter 4, diary entry for Sept. 12, 1862, page 135.

[20] Donnal Vore Smith, *Chase and Civil War Politics* (Columbus, 1931), p. 25.

[21] MS. in Robert Todd Lincoln Collection, Lib. of Cong.

[22] Chase to Thaddeus Stevens, Jan. 9, 1861, copy, Chase Letterbooks, Lib. of Cong.

[23] Schuckers, *op. cit.*, p. 116.

[24] *Ibid.*, p. 380.

[25] Robert Bruce Warden, *An Account of the Private Life and Public Services of Salmon Portland Chase* (Cincinnati: Wilstach, Baldwin & Co., 1874), p. 371.

[26] Chase to William H. Seward, Jan. 1861, copy, Chase MSS., Lib. of Cong.

[27] Warden, *op. cit.*, p. 380.

[28] Jan. 28, 1861, R. T. Lincoln Coll., Lib. of Cong.

[29] Chase to Lincoln, Mar. 16, 1861, *ibid.*

[30] Chase to Lincoln, Mar. 29, 1861, *ibid.*

[31] Schuckers, *op. cit.*, p. 380.

[32] Albert Bushnell Hart, *Salmon Portland Chase* (Boston: Houghton, Mifflin and Company, 1899), p. 125.

[33] Chase to Lincoln, Jan. 11, 1861, R. T. Lincoln Coll., Lib. of Cong.

[34] William Ernest Smith, *The Francis Preston Blair Family in Politics* (New York: The Macmillan Company, 1933), II, 83–4.

[35] Schuckers, *op. cit.*, p. 429.

[36] *Ibid.*, pp. 419–20.

[37] *Ibid.*, p. 450.

[38] *Ibid.*, p. 445.

[39] Hart, *op. cit.*, p. 296.

[40] Thomas Harry Williams, *Lincoln and the Radicals* (Madison: University of Wisconsin Press, 1941), p. 177.

[41] Schuckers, *op. cit.*, p. 430.

[42] A. Howard Meneely, ed., "Three Manuscripts of Gideon Welles," *American Historical Review,* XXI (1925–26), 493–4.

[43] Warden, *op. cit.*, pp. 462, 385–6.

[44] *Ibid.*, p. 547.

[45] Chase to J. W. and J. B. Antram, April 8, 1861, copy, Chase MSS., Lib. of Cong.

[46] Welles, *op. cit.*, I, 124, 136; II, 58.

[47] Warden, *op. cit.*, p. 484.

[48] *Scribner's Magazine,* XLV (1909), 147.

[49] Warden, *op. cit.*, p. 586.

[50] Schuckers, *op. cit.*, p. 110.

[51] Albert G. Riddle, "The Election of Salmon P. Chase to the Senate, February 22, 1849," *The Republic,* IV (1875), 182.

[52] *Annual Report of the American Historical Association, 1902,* II, 123.

[53] Chase to Mrs. Randall Hunt of New Orleans, Nov. 20, 1860, copy, Chase Letterbooks, Lib. of Cong.

[54] Chase to Charles A. Dana, Nov. 10, 1860, *ibid.*

[55] Schuckers, *op. cit.*, p. 395.

[56] *Private and Official Correspondence of Gen. Benjamin F. Butler during the Period of the Civil War* (1917), I, 633.

[57] Warden, *op. cit.*, p. 423.

[58] Chase to Lincoln, May 16, 1862, R. T. Lincoln Coll., Lib. of Cong.

[59] Butler, *Correspondence,* etc., I, 633.

[60] *Ibid.*, II, 133–4.

[61] *Ibid.*, II, 324.

[62] Chase to the Loyal National League, April 9, 1863, printed letter, R. T. Lincoln Coll., Lib. of Cong.

[63] Warden, *op. cit.*, p. 454.

[64] *Ibid.*, p. 549.

[65] See Chapter 6, diary entry for July 1, 1864, page 226.

[66] Warden, *op. cit.*, p. 569.

[67] See Chapter 7, diary entry for Sept. 13, 1864, page 253.

[68] See Chapter 5, diary entry for Sept. 11, 1863, page 190.

[69] Hart, *op. cit.*, p. 435.

[70] Tyler Dennett, ed., *Lincoln and the Civil War in the Diaries and Letters of John Hay* (New York: Dodd, Mead & Company, 1939), p. 110; William Henry Herndon, "Analysis of the Character of Abraham Lincoln: A Lecture," *Abraham Lincoln Quarterly*, I (1941), 406–7.

[71] James Garfield Randall, *Lincoln the Liberal Statesman* (New York: Dodd, Mead & Company, 1947), p. 67.

[72] Charles R. Wilson, "The Original Chase Meeting and *The Next Presidential Election*," *Mississippi Valley Historical Review*, XXIII (1936), 61–79.

[73] Warden, *op. cit.*, p. 70.

[74] Schuckers, *op. cit.*, p. 393.

[75] Warden, *op. cit.*, p. 565.

[76] *Ibid.*

[77] Schuckers, *op. cit.*, 495.

[78] Thurlow Weed Barnes, *Memoir of Thurlow Weed* (Boston: Houghton Mifflin Company, 1884), p. 445.

[79] Chase to Isaac N. Arnold, Feb. 18, 1867, copy, Chase Letterbooks, Lib. of Cong.

[80] Warden, *op. cit.*, p. 56.

[81] Schuckers, *op. cit.*, p. 211.

[82] Margaret Leech, *Reveille in Washington, 1860–1865* (New York: Harper & Brothers, 1941), p. 317.

[83] Chase to Lincoln, May 18, 1861, R. T. Lincoln Coll., Lib. of Cong.

[84] Mary Clemmer Ames, *Ten Years in Washington. Life and Scenes in the National Capital* . . . (Hartford: A. D. Worthington & Co., 1874), p. 308.

85 Chase to Lincoln, April 18, 1861, R. T. Lincoln Coll., Lib. of Cong.

86 Chase to Lincoln, Sept. 19, 1863, *ibid.*

87 James A. Rawley, "Merchant in Politics: Edwin D. Morgan" (unpublished Ph.D. dissertation, Columbia University), p. 357.

88 Chase to Lincoln, May 11, 1863, R. T. Lincoln Coll., Lib. of Cong.

89 Dennett, *op. cit.,* pp. 110, 199.

90 McCulloch, *op. cit.,* p. 166.

91 Warden, *op. cit.,* p. 582.

92 W. E. Smith, *op. cit.,* II, 257.

93 Carman and Luthin, *op. cit.,* p. 57.

94 Sidney Ratner, *American Taxation: Its History as a Social Force in Democracy* (New York: W. W. Norton & Company, 1942), p. 68.

95 Wesley Clair Mitchell, *A History of the Greenbacks* . . . (Chicago: University of Chicago Press, 1903), p. 419.

96 Don C. Barrett, *The Greenbacks and Resumption of Specie Payments, 1862–1870* (Cambridge: Harvard University Press, 1931), p. 36.

97 Albert S. Bolles, *The Financial History of the United States, from 1861 to 1885* (New York: D. Appleton and Company, 1886), p. 116.

98 Robert T. Patterson, "Government Finance on the Eve of the Civil War," *The Journal of Economic History,* VII (1952), 35–44.

99 Fred Albert Shannon, *Economic History of the People of the United States* (New York: The Macmillan Company, 1934), p. 384.

100 Secretary of the Treasury, *Report, 1863,* p. 10.

101 Warden, *op. cit.,* motto on title-page.

102 Chase's diary, Mar. 4, 1829, manuscript, Lib. of Cong.

103 Pierson, *op. cit.,* p. 557.

104 Schuckers, *op. cit.,* p. 99.

105 Chase to T. R. Stanley, Oct. 25, 1859, copy, Chase Letterbooks, Lib. of Cong.

106 Andrew McFarland Davis, *The Origin of the National Banking System* (Washington: Government Printing Office, 1910–11), p. 31.

107 Warden, *op. cit.*, p. 305. Italics have been deleted.

108 Schuckers, *op. cit.*, p. 101.

109 "Selections from the Follett Papers," *Quarterly Publication of the Historical and Philosophical Society of Ohio*, XIII (1918), 61.

110 Secretary of the Treasury, *Report, 1861*, p. 13.

111 Secretary of the Treasury, *Report, 1863*, p. 14.

112 Schuckers, *op. cit.*, pp. 226–7.

113 Mitchell, *op. cit.*, p. 27.

114 Secretary of the Treasury, *Report, 1863*, p. 15.

115 *Ibid.*, p. 14. For a full account of Chase's relations with Cooke, see Ellis P. Oberholtzer, *Jay Cooke, Financier of the Civil War* (1907).

116 Davis Rich Dewey, *Financial History of the United States*, 10th ed. (New York: Longmans, Green & Company, 1928), p. 321.

117 Secretary of the Treasury, *Report, 1863*, p. 19.

118 Amasa Walker to Chase, Dec. 16, 1861, Chase MSS., Lib. of Cong.

119 Chase to John R. Young, June 26, 1867, copy, Chase Letter-books, Lib. of Cong.

120 James Garfield Randall, *The Civil War and Reconstruction* (Boston: D. C. Heath & Company, 1937), pp. 457–8.

121 Secretary of the Treasury, *Report, 1861*, p. 18.

122 Undated interview of Chase with Jacob W. Schuckers, Schuckers MSS., Lib. of Cong.

123 Bolles, *op. cit.*, p. 98.

124 D. V. Smith, *op. cit.*, pp. 145–6.

125 Warden, *op. cit.*, p. 570.

126 *The Nation*, XVI (May 15, 1873), 331.

---

[1] John Austin Stevens, president, and Henry F. Vail, cashier, Bank of Commerce, New York City.

[2] Hamilton Fish, of New York, Whig Congressman, 1843–45; Governor, 1849–50; Senator, 1851–57; later Secretary of State in the Grant administration.

[3] Eliphalet Case, an old friend of Chase's, formerly of Patriot, Indiana, now of Portland, Maine.

[4] Edward Haight, Congressman from New York, 1861–63; president, Bank of the Commonwealth, New York City.

[5] James Gallatin, president, National Bank, New York City.

[6] Henry Ebenezer Davies, of the New York Court of Appeals; Richard O'Gorman, a lawyer of New York City; and probably James W. Savage, another New York attorney.

[7] Michael Corcoran had been wounded and captured at First Bull Run. After a year's confinement, he was exchanged. See Chapter 3, diary entry for Aug. 19, 1862, page 115.

[8] Walter W. Smith, of the Confederate privateer *Jeff. Davis,* was convicted of piracy, October 25, 1861. Chase apparently did not know that Confederate authorities had selected Corcoran to stand as hostage for Smith.

[9] John Ellis Wool, who had served in the army since 1812, commanded the Department of Virginia, with headquarters at Fort Monroe.

[10] Benjamin Huger, of South Carolina, Confederate commander of the Department of Norfolk.

[11] Charles Ferguson Smith, commander of the District of Western Kentucky.

[12] Morris Ketchum, New York banker; Chauncy Pratt Williams, president, Albany Exchange Bank; George Simmons Coe, president, American Exchange Bank, New York City.

¹³ Benjamin Franklin Wade, Senator from Ohio, 1851–69; leader of Radical Republicans in Congress and opponent of Lincoln's reconstruction policies.

¹⁴ James Mitchell Ashley, Republican Congressman from Ohio, 1859–69; later governor of the Territory of Montana.

¹⁵ Chase was here anticipating his later famous ruling as Chief Justice: "The Constitution, in all its provisions, looks to an indestructible Union composed of indestructible States." (Texas v. White, 1869)

¹⁶ Andrew Johnson, of Tennessee; Democratic Congressman, 1843–53; governor, 1853–57; Senator, 1857–62, remaining loyal to the Union despite the secession of his state; Federal military governor of Tennessee, 1862–65; Vice-President of the United States, 1865, whose accession to the presidency is recorded in Chapter 8.

¹⁷ In October, 1861, William Tecumseh Sherman had been placed in command of Union forces in eastern Kentucky, opposing the Confederate troops of Simon Bolivar Buckner. The minor engagement at Camp Wild Cat (Rockcastle Hills) on October 21st was considered a Union victory.

¹⁸ James Speed, brother of one of Lincoln's closest friends, was a principal Unionist leader in Kentucky. In 1864 he succeeded Bates as Attorney-General.

¹⁹ William P. Mellen, supervising special agent of the Treasury Department, stationed at Cincinnati.

²⁰ Samuel Hooper, Boston importer and iron manufacturer; Republican Congressman, 1861–74; one of the strongest Congressional supporters of Chase's financial program.

²¹ Montgomery Cunningham Meigs, quartermaster-general with the rank of brigadier-general, 1861–82; John F. Lee, judge-advocate of the army with brevet rank of major.

²² Winfield Scott, brigadier-general in the War of 1812; leader of American forces in the Mexican War. A Virginian, Scott remained loyal during the Civil War and continued to serve as commander-in-chief until his age compelled his retirement in November, 1861.

²³ William Henry Aspinwall, New York merchant; promoter of railroads and of the Panama Steamship Company; an active supporter of Lincoln and later a founder of the Union League Club.

William Sprague, Rhode Island cotton manufacturer, governor, 1860–63, and Republican Senator, 1863–75, who was to marry Chase's daughter Kate in 1863. Robert B. Minturn, of Grinnell, Minturn & Company, New York shipowners and merchants.

[24] Thomas M. Key, formerly a Cincinnati attorney and judge, now aide-de-camp to McClellan. After the Antietam campaign he was stingingly rebuked by Lincoln and discharged from the army for declaring "that it would have been impolitic and injudicious to have destroyed the Rebel army."

[25] John H. Sullivan, of Bellaire, Ohio, a special agent of the Treasury Department.

[26] On October 26th Benjamin Franklin Kelly's Federal troops forced the Confederates at Romney, Virginia, to retire toward Winchester. General Joseph Eggleston Johnston then commanded the Southern forces in northern Virginia, with headquarters near Manassas.

[27] Hosmer G. Plantz, Chase's private secretary.

[28] Susan Walker of Cincinnati, a frequent correspondent and platonic admirer of Chase.

[29] Edward de Stoeckel, Russian envoy extraordinary and minister plenipotentiary to the United States, 1854–68.

[30] Richard Bickerton Pennell, second baron and first Earl Lyons, British minister to Washington, 1858–65.

[31] Charles Sumner, of Massachusetts; Free Soil and then Republican Senator, 1851–74; chairman of the Senate Committee on Foreign Relations, 1861–71.

[32] John Work Garrett, Baltimore banker; since 1858 president Baltimore and Ohio Railroad.

[33] Simon F. Barstow, of Massachusetts, was acting aide-de-camp to General Frederick West Lander, who successfully defended Hancock, Maryland, from Confederate troops under Thomas J. (Stonewall) Jackson. A close friend of Chase, Lander was wounded and died in 1862.

[34] Zachariah Chandler, Senator from Michigan, 1857–75; leader of the Radical Republicans and bitter foe of McClellan.

[35] Nathaniel Prentice Banks, Massachusetts Congressman and governor, had been made major-general of volunteers in May, 1861.

Later he was given an important command in Louisiana and led the expedition against Port Hudson and the Red River campaign.

[36] Henry Ulke, photographer, 278 Pennsylvania Avenue. Chase's photograph appeared on the one-dollar greenback.

[37] Established in December, 1861, the Joint Committee on the Conduct of the War investigated war contracts, expenditures, the competency of military officers, etc. It was dominated by Radical Republicans and was hostile to McClellan. Members not previously identified were Moses Fowler Odell, New York Congressman, 1861–65, and John Covode, Pennsylvania Congressman, 1855–63.

[38] William Pitt Fessenden, of Maine; James Fowler Simmons, of Rhode Island; John Sherman, of Ohio; Timothy Otis Howe, of Wisconsin; James Alfred Pearce, of Maryland; Thaddeus Stevens, of Pennsylvania; Justin Smith Morrill, of Vermont; Elbridge Gerry Spaulding, of New York; Erastus Corning, of New York; Valentine Baxter Horton, of Ohio; John L. N. Stratton, of New Jersey; Samuel Hooper, of Massachusetts; Horace Maynard, of Tennessee; Jesse David Bright, of Indiana; James Alexander McDougall, of California; and John Smith Phelps, of Missouri.

[39] Either William M. or Washington R. Vermilye, of Vermilye & Co., bankers, New York City.

[40] In a long oration on the *Trent* affair, Senator Sumner asserted that the British, by protesting the seizure of Mason and Slidell, had repudiated their former stand on belligerent rights and concluded: "And now, behold, this champion of belligerent rights has 'changed his hand and checked his pride.' . . . Welcome to the peaceful transfiguration!"

[41] The entry for January 12th is from *Memories of Many Men and Some Women* (1874), pp. 267–9, by Maunsell B. Field, who copied it from Chase's manuscript diaries, now lost.

[42] William Buel Franklin had commanded a division at First Bull Run. Later he was to serve in the Peninsular campaign and at Fredericksburg.

[43] Joseph Holt, of Kentucky, Postmaster-general and Secretary of War under Buchanan; after September, 1862, judge-advocate of the army, succeeding John F. Lee.

[44] Dated January 11th, Lincoln's letter to Cameron curtly pro-

posed "nominating you to the Senate, next monday, as minister to Russia." A longer, "private" letter bearing the same date gave "assurance of my undiminished confidence."—Roy P. Basler, ed., *The Collected Works of Abraham Lincoln* (New Brunswick: Rutgers University Press, 1953), V, 96–7.

[45] Benjamin Franklin Butler, Massachusetts Democratic politician, had been named major-general of volunteers in May, 1861. He was now about to command the land forces in the joint army-navy expedition against New Orleans. After a stormy career in Louisiana and later in Virginia, he resigned from the army in 1865 to embark upon an equally tumultuous political career as a leading Republican Radical during the reconstruction period and later as Greenback-Democratic governor of Massachusetts.

[46] William Pitt Fessenden, of Maine; Whig Congressman, 1841–43; Whig and Republican Senator, 1854–64, when he specialized in financial affairs; Chase's successor as Secretary of the Treasury, 1864–65; Senator, 1865–69.

[47] On August 5, 1861, Congress had authorized the issue of $50,-000,000 demand notes receivable for all public dues, bearing no interest, and payable on demand. These notes were thus like the later greenbacks except for the fact that they were not made legal tender.

[48] Samuel H. Walley, Massachusetts Congressman, 1853–55; president, Revere Bank.

[49] Hiram Barney, New York attorney; Republican leader, who raised $35,000 for Lincoln's 1860 campaign; collector of customs for the Port of New York.

[50] Rufus F. Andrews, surveyor of customs, New York City.

[51] George Opdyke, Republican mayor of New York, 1862–63; merchant and manufacturer of Federal uniforms.

[52] The President did not adopt most of Chase's suggestions. For Lincoln's message, see Basler, ed., Lincoln's *Collected Works*, V, 144–6.

[53] Richard Fuller, born at Beaufort, South Carolina; since 1847 pastor of the Seventh Baptist Church, Baltimore.

[54] William D. Bickham, later editor of the Cincinnati *Commercial* and publisher of the Dayton *Journal*.

[55] Rufus Saxton, quartermaster to T. W. Sherman's Port Royal expedition; military governor of the Department of the South, 1862–65.

[56] Mansfield French, chaplain with Saxton's forces at Beaufort.

[57] J. A. Snydam, introduced to Chase (Feb. 18, 1862) by W. H. Reynolds, Treasury agent at Hilton Head, as "a Gentleman who has rendered me valuable assistance in the Collection of Cotton, and other property from these Islands."—Chase MSS., Lib. of Cong.

[58] William Dennison, Republican governor of Ohio, 1860–62; chairman, Republican National Convention, 1864; Postmaster-general, 1864–66.

[59] The problem of Colonel Minor Milliken, 1st Ohio Cavalry, has not been identified.

[60] Luther M. Donaldson, of Miller, Donaldson & Co., bankers, Columbus.

[61] David Wilmot, Pennsylvania Congressman, 1845–51; author of Wilmot Proviso, to exclude slavery from territories acquired by Mexican War; Senator, 1861–63; judge of U.S. Court of Claims, 1863–68.

[62] Probably S. M. McKean, disbursing clerk, Treasury Department.

[63] Thomas Church Haskell Smith, formerly a Cincinnati lawyer; lieutenant-colonel, 1st Ohio Cavalry; later brigadier-general under Pope.

[64] Robert James Walker, former Senator from Mississippi, Secretary of the Treasury, and governor of Kansas Territory, was now a Washington lobbyist, associated with Frederick Perry Stanton, a former Tennessee Congressman who had served as acting governor of Kansas Territory until relieved by Walker. The Porter case (Porter et al., v. Foley) concerned the legality of land titles in Covington, Kentucky. For information on this point I am indebted to Mr. James Shenton, of Columbia University, who is preparing a biography of Walker.

[65] Gustavus Woodson Smith, New York City street commissioner, 1858–61; major-general in Confederate army during Peninsular campaign.

[66] On April 26, 1862, David Glasgow Farragut, flag officer of

the Western Gulf Squadron, demanded the surrender of New Orleans. The mayor, John T. Monroe, refused to haul down the Confederate flag and declared that his people in surrendering yielded only "the obedience which the conqueror is entitled to extort from the conquered."

[67] When Confederate troops at Fort Macon, North Carolina, surrendered on April 26th to Burnside, they were released, with their personal property, upon signing their paroles.

[68] Ebenezer Lane, judge of the Supreme Court of Ohio, 1830–45; now a lawyer and railroad president.

[69] John Wilson, land commissioner of the Illinois Central Railroad.

[1] The copies of these letters in the Division of Manuscripts, Library of Congress, are so marred by clerical abbreviations as to make difficult reading. I have spelled out all words which might be misunderstood. Schuckers includes a few paragraphs not found in the Library of Congress copies.—Jacob W. Schuckers, *The Life and Public Services of Salmon Portland Chase* (New York: D. Appleton and Company, 1874), pp. 366–74.

[2] Egbert Ludovicus Viele had served as second in command of the Port Royal expedition. After the bombardment on April 10–12, 1862, Confederate forces had evacuated Fort Pulaski, which guarded the approaches to Savannah.

[3] Louis Malesherbes Goldsborough, since September, 1861, commander of the Atlantic Blockading Squadron. In February, 1862, he had led the fleet which supported Burnside's expedition against North Carolina. Criticism of his inaction during the Peninsular campaign was to cause his retirement.

[4] James L. Lardner had been a member of the Port Royal expedition. Later he commanded the East Gulf Blockading Squadron.

[5] Edwin Augustus Stevens, railroad man and inventor, built at his own expense a small ironclad, a twin-screw steamer, and gave it to the United States.

[6] Ambrose Everett Burnside, who had distinguished himself at First Bull Run, in January, 1862, led Federal troops in the attack on Hatteras Inlet, North Carolina. Later Burnside was to command the Army of the Potomac at Fredericksburg, to lead an army in eastern Tennessee, and to serve under Grant in the Wilderness campaign.

[7] Thomas J. Cram, aide-de-camp and acting inspector-general of Wool's forces.

[8] No sketch now accompanies the letters.

[9] Joseph King Fenno Mansfield, former inspector-general of the

army, held a command under Wool. Made a major-general in July, 1862, he was killed leading the XII Corps at Antietam.

[10] Max Weber, a German-born "forty-eighter," colonel of 20th New York Infantry. Later made brigadier-general, he fought at Antietam and in the 1864 Shenandoah Valley campaigns.

[11] Charles C. Dodge, son of the New York merchant, William E. Dodge; commander of a New York sharpshooting unit.

[12] James Garfield Randall, *The Civil War and Reconstruction* (Boston: D. C. Heath & Company, 1937), pp. 292–5.

[13] Again I have spelled out the numerous abbreviations which a clerk made in copying this memorandum.

[14] James Shields, born in Ireland, had a varied political and military career. He had been an Illinois judge, commissioner of the general land office, governor of Oregon Territory, Senator from Illinois (1849–55), and Senator from Minnesota. At the beginning of the Civil War he was made brigadier-general of volunteers.

[15] On May 23rd Jackson struck Front Royal, disastrously routing the Union forces commanded by Colonel John R. Kenly, which fled toward Winchester with Jackson in pursuit.

[16] John White Geary, of Pennsylvania, served in some of the most important campaigns of the war—Cedar Mountain, Wauhatchie, Lookout Mountain, Missionary Ridge, the March to the Sea. After the war he became governor of Pennsylvania.

[17] Edward Otho Cresap Ord, brigadier-general of volunteers, 1861; major-general, May, 1862; later served under Grant in the West.

[18] Rufus King, minister to the Papal States in 1861, resigned to accept a commission as brigadier-general and to serve in the defences of Washington in 1862. He returned to the Papal States, 1863–68.

[19] Brigadier-General George Archibald McCall served in the Seven Days battles, was captured at New Market Crossroads, June 30th, and was confined for a few months in a Confederate prison.

[20] Fort Darling, on Drewry's Bluff, commanded navigation on the James River.

[21] Bottom's Bridge, across the Chickahominy River, was at approximately the left end of McClellan's line.

22 John Adams Dix, veteran of the War of 1812; Senator from New York, 1845–49; Secretary of Treasury under Buchanan; major-general in the Federal army, 1861–65. After the war Dix became minister to France, 1866–69, and governor of New York, 1873–75.

[1] The eccentric Polish nobleman, Adam Gurowski, held a minor position in the State Department. His violent hostility toward Seward, as revealed in his published *Diary,* led to his dismissal.

[2] Gabriel Garcia y Tassara, Spanish envoy extraordinary and minister plenipotentiary to the United States, 1857–67.

[3] John Snyder Carlile, of Virginia, elected as a Unionist to fill the Senate vacancy caused by the retirement of R. M. T. Hunter; served 1861–65.

[4] John J. Speed, of the Union-loving Kentucky family.

[5] Samuel Lewis Casey, elected as a Republican to fill the vacancy caused by the expulsion of Henry C. Bullitt; served 1862–63.

[6] Valentine Baxter Horton, of Ohio, Whig and then Republican Congressman, 1855–59, 1861–63.

[7] The First Legal Tender Act had provided that the legal-tender notes might, at the desire of the holders, be converted into 6 per cent bonds—called 5–20's from the fact that they were redeemable after five and payable after twenty years.

[8] For this first draft of the Emancipation Proclamation see Roy P. Basler, ed., *The Collected Works of Abraham Lincoln* (New Brunswick: Rutgers University Press, 1953), V, 336–7.

[9] The militia act of July 17, 1862, had authorized the President to issue regulations for enrolling the militia where state laws were inadequate. As a conscription act it was quite ineffectual.

[10] Ormsby MacKnight Mitchel (whose name Chase consistently misspelled), a nationally known astronomer and mathematician. As brigadier-general of volunteers he served with distinction in the Western campaigns of 1861–62 but asked to be relieved because of friction with his superior, Buell. He did not receive the Mississippi command which Chase urged, but in September, 1862, was assigned to the Department of the South, where he died a month later.

[11] Hiram Walbridge, of Ohio and New York; Democratic Congressman, 1853–55; personal friend and adviser of Lincoln.

[12] Samuel Ryan Curtis, of Iowa; Republican Congressman, 1857–61; brigadier-general commanding Union troops at Pea Ridge; commander of the Department of the Missouri, 1862–63, of the Department of Kansas, 1864–65, and of the Department of the Northwest, 1865.

[13] Green Adams, former Whig and American Congressman from Kentucky, 1847–49, 1859–61, was Sixth Auditor.

[14] William Rabé, United States Marshal for the Northern District of California, and secretary of the Republican central committee of that state. Factional rivals in the California Republican party engineered plans for his ouster.

[15] Benjamin Welch, Jr., aide-de-camp to Pope.

[16] Brigadier-General George Washington Morgan of Ohio resigned because of illness and dissatisfaction over the use of Negro troops in the Federal armies. After the war he became Democratic Congressman from Ohio.

[17] James Abram Garfield, of Ohio; president, Hiram College, 1857–61; rose from lieutenant-colonel to major-general in United States Army, 1861–63; Republican Congressman, 1863–80; President of the United States, 1881.

[18] Peter H. Watson, Assistant Secretary of War.

[19] Thomas D. Jones, by birth a New Yorker, had for some years lived in Ohio, making portrait busts of Chase, Harrison, Corwin, Clay, and others. After the war he designed the Lincoln memorial in the Ohio State House at Columbus.

[20] Cuthbert Bullitt, acting collector of customs in New Orleans and later United States marshal for Louisiana, had forwarded a copy of a letter from Thomas J. Durant, New Orleans Unionist, who complained that the presence of Federal troops disturbed the relations of loyal masters to their slaves and also objected to police and blockade regulations. Lincoln's reply (Basler, ed., Lincoln's *Collected Works*, V, 344–6) bluntly declared that the war could not be prosecuted "with elder squirts, charged with rose water."

[21] George Whitefield (1714–1770), the English revivalist.

[22] Henry Ward Beecher, influential minister of Plymouth Church,

Brooklyn; editor of the Independent, a strongly antislavery religious periodical.

[23] Coggin's Point, across the James River from Harrison's Landing, was seized by McClellan's men on August 1st.

[24] For Chase's letter to Butler, see Introduction, p. 21. To Pope, Chase wrote: "If I were in the field, I would let every man understand that no man loyal to the Union can be a slave."

[25] Don Carlos Buell, of Indiana; brigadier-general of volunteers in 1861, sent by McClellan to command the Army of the Ohio and to organize Union forces in Kentucky. Despite successes at Bowling Green and Nashville, he was regarded as slow and cautious, and his failure to win a decisive victory over Braxton Bragg in October, 1862, led to his removal.

[26] Ulysses S. Grant at this time was favorably known for his victories at Fort Henry and Fort Donelson, but Halleck thought his negligence responsible for the Confederate near-success at Shiloh (April 6–7, 1862).

[27] George H. Thomas, a Virginian who remained loyal to the Union, fought in the Shenandoah, in Tennessee, and in Kentucky in 1861; in Kentucky, Mississippi, and Tennessee, 1862–65. His greatest fame was to come later in connection with the battles of Chickamauga, Missionary Ridge, and Nashville.

[28] This word is lightly crossed through, with "and from" substituted.

[29] At the time of First Bull Run, Union General Robert Patterson had been ordered to hold in check the Confederate forces in the Shenandoah Valley while McDowell advanced upon Manassas. Patterson's failure permitted Joseph E. Johnston to join Beauregard and defeat the Federal army.

[30] Edward Ithamar Chase, born 1810.

[31] Horace Y. Beebe, of Portage County, Ohio; named assessor under the Internal Revenue Act.

[32] John R. French, member of the Ohio legislature.

[33] Isaac Smith Homans, of New York; civil engineer; editor of Hunt's Merchants Magazine.

[34] Stephen Molitor, editor of Das Volksblatt, Cincinnati.

[35] Edward Purcell, editor of the Cincinnati Catholic Telegraph.

[36] John Palmer Usher, of Indiana; Assistant Secretary of the Interior, 1861–63; Secretary of the Interior, 1863–65.

[37] Edited by John H. Harney, the Louisville *Democrat,* at first a Union organ, later became the voice of the Kentucky Peace Democrats.

[38] Above these two words, "assuming that" has been lightly penciled.

[39] William Joseph Hardee, author of the standard *Rifle and Light Infantry Tactics,* used in both armies; one of the chief Confederate generals in the West, engaged at Shiloh, Perryville, Murfreesboro, and Missionary Ridge.

[40] Sterling Price, a former Missouri governor and Congressman, had been given command of Missouri troops by the secessionist Governor Claiborne Jackson. Successful at Wilson's Creek, he was defeated in the Corinth-Iuka campaign. Later he helped repel Banks's Red River expedition, and at the end of the war he fled to Mexico.

[41] James Streshley Jackson, a former Unionist Congressman from Kentucky, served at Shiloh, Corinth, and Iuka, and was later killed at Perryville.

[42] At a public meeting held in front of the Capitol, resolutions were adopted regretting "a want of readiness and determination" on the part of Northern military leaders but commending the recent call for a draft of 300,000 men. After a speech by Lucius E. Chittenden, Register of the Treasury, Lincoln refuted "a very widespread attempt to have a quarrel between Gen. McClellan and the Secretary of War."—Basler, ed., Lincoln's *Collected Works,* V, 358–9.

[43] Probably Daniel Read, professor of philosophy at the University of Wisconsin (later president of the University of Missouri), and his son, Theodore, who was killed in the war.

[44] Charles F. Schmidt, clerk in the Fifth Auditor's office.

[45] Princess Alice Maud Mary, daughter of Queen Victoria, was married on July 1st to Prince Frederick William Louis Charles, nephew of the Grand Duke of Hesse.

[46] The abbreviations are not clear, but presumably Chase was reading Victor Hugo's *Les Misérables,* one section of which is titled "Marius."

[47] On August 14th the President told a deputation of Negro leaders: "You and we are different races. We have between us a broader difference than exists between almost any other two races. Whether it is right or wrong I need not discuss, but this physical difference is a great disadvantage to us both. . . . If this is admitted, it affords a reason at least why we should be separated." He urged colonization of free Negroes in Central America.—Basler, ed., Lincoln's *Collected Works,* V, 370–5.

[48] George S. Boutwell, former governor of Massachusetts; first United States Commissioner of Internal Revenue, 1862–63; later Republican Congressman and Secretary of the Treasury under Grant.

[49] James F. Babcock, editor of the New Haven *Palladium;* collector of the Port of New Haven.

[50] Orville Hitchcock Platt, at this time merely a state senator, was to serve from 1879 to 1905 in the United States Senate, Connecticut's leading spokesman for protectionism and "stand-pat" Republicanism.

[51] John B. Wright, of Clinton, was named assessor for the Second Internal Revenue District of Connecticut.

[52] Possibly Chase meant John B. Mix, a candidate for the collector's post.

[53] Henry Hammond, of West Killingly, was a friend of Senator Dixon. In 1864, he was nominated as United States marshal, a selection which Gideon Welles termed "eminently unfit to be made."

[54] David F. Hollister, of Bridgeport, was named collector for the Fourth Internal Revenue District of Connecticut.

[55] Alfred Avery Burnham, Republican Congressman from Connecticut, 1859–63.

[56] Mark Howard, a pro-Chase Radical Republican, the choice of the Connecticut "State" faction, was nominated collector for the First Internal Revenue District of Connecticut, but the Senate failed to confirm him because of Senator Dixon's strong opposition. The controversy led in February, 1863, to one of Chase's threats to resign.

[57] Henry Beebe Carrington, appointed adjutant-general of Ohio by Governor Chase, had reorganized the state militia and helped muster in troops at the beginning of the war. Made a brigadier-

general in 1862, he exposed the plots of the Sons of Liberty against the Lincoln administration.

[58] On July 20th Pope had issued an order threatening expulsion or death for all "disloyal male citizens" within Union lines who failed to swear allegiance to the United States government. The Confederates replied with an order declaring that Pope and his officers were "not entitled to be considered soldiers" and promising that, if captured, they would be held in close confinement, without privilege of exchange.

[59] Richard Chappell Parsons, of Cleveland, one of Chase's closest friends; consul to Rio de Janiero, 1861; Collector of Internal Revenue, 1862–66; marshal of the Supreme Court, 1866–72.

[60] Joseph B. Varnum, Jr., a New York attorney and Chase's financial agent in that city.

[61] On July 17th, because of the rapid disappearance from circulation of small coins, Congress, at Chase's request, had authorized the use of "the postage and other stamps of the United States" as currency. At first ordinary postage stamps were tried, but their small size and their stickiness made them inconvenient. To take their place, Chase had prepared a series of special stamps, in denominations of 5, 10, and 25 cents. They were about 2¾ by 3⅜ inches in size, printed on both sides, and not gummed.

[62] Christian Roselius, born in Germany, became a leader of the Louisiana bar and professor of law in the University of Louisiana. His stanch Unionism alienated Louisiana secessionists as later his conservatism and opposition to military rule antagonized the radical Free State faction during reconstruction.

[63] Dr. Thomas E. H. Cottman, a leader of the conservative Unionist faction in Louisiana who wished the restoration of the state "with its Constitution unimpaired, and with all its rights recognized," was chosen to Congress but resigned in December, 1863, before his credentials were scrutinized.

[64] Reverdy Johnson, a leading Maryland lawyer and conservative politician; Attorney-General under President Taylor, 1849–50; Senator, 1845–49, 1863–68; minister to Great Britain, 1868–69.

[65] William Winston Seaton, mayor of Washington, 1840–50; with Joseph Gales, long-time editor of the *National Intelligencer*.

[66] Austin Blair, Republican governor of Michigan, 1861–64; Congressman, 1867–73.

[67] Luther Stanley, of Birmingham, Oakland County, became assessor for the Fifth Internal Revenue District of Michigan.

[68] Charles C. Trowbridge asked Seward to intercede with the President in order to secure his appointment as Collector of Internal Revenue.

[69] William S. Mills, of Lexington, Mich.

[70] Thurlow Weed, of New York; since 1830 editor of the Albany *Evening Journal*; one of the most influential and astute politicians of his day; formerly an Anti-Mason and Whig, now a Republican and close ally of William H. Seward.

[71] Orlando Bolivar Willcox, wounded and captured at First Bull Run, later served with distinction at Antietam, Fredericksburg, Knoxville, and in the final Eastern campaigns.

[72] James Madison Cutts, father-in-law of Stephen A. Douglas; Second Comptroller of the Treasury.

[73] Adele Cutts Douglas (mentioned later as "Mrs. D." in the diary), widow of Stephen A. Douglas; famed as one of the most beautiful hostesses in Washington.

[74] Robert G. Corwin, attorney, of Dayton, Ohio.

[75] Either John Benedict Steele, of New York, or William Gaston Steele, of New Jersey.

[76] Alfred Ely, Republican Congressman from New York, 1859–63, who was captured while witnessing the battle of First Bull Run and not released by the Confederates for nearly six months.

[77] Thomas Brown, special agent for the Treasury Department on the Pacific coast.

[78] The memorandum declared that to continue McClellan in command would result in "the waste of national resources, the protraction of the war, the destruction of our armies, and the imperiling of the Union."

[79] David Dudley Field, of New York; lawyer and law reformer; a leader of the Radical wing of the Republican party in his state.

[80] Fitz-John Porter, a close friend of McClellan's, had commanded the V Corps during the Peninsular campaign. Accused of disobedi-

ence, disloyalty, and misconduct at Second Bull Run, Porter was cashiered in 1863. In 1879 a court-martial reversed the decision.

[81] Edwin Vose Sumner, who had commanded Federal troops in Kansas during the 1850's, led the II Corps on the Peninsula and was later to serve at Antietam and Fredericksburg.

[82] For this order, dated August 30, 1862, see *War of the Rebellion: Official Records* . . . ser. 1, vol. XI, p. 103.

[83] Caleb Blood Smith, the Secretary of the Interior, plays a very insignificant role in the diaries of his cabinet colleagues.

[84] Frederick W. Seward, son of William H. Seward and Assistant Secretary of State.

[85] This word has caused some controversy among historians. Warden transcribed it as "place," which would make it seem that Lincoln thought of resigning the Presidency (Robert Bruce Warden, *An Account of the Private Life and Public Services of Salmon Portland Chase* (Cincinnati: Wilstach, Baldwin & Co., 1874), p. 460). But the word—which, after all, is in a copyist's handwriting—is not clear and seems more like "plan." As J. G. Randall has pointed out, Lincoln's alleged resignation is not only out of character, but it also suffers from want of any confirmatory evidence in the other cabinet diaries (James Garfield Randall, *Lincoln the President* (New York: Dodd, Mead & Co., 1945), II, 112–3).

[86] In the Peninsular campaign McClellan had an elaborate staff, including Louis Philippe d'Orléans, Comte de Paris; Robert d'Orléans, Duc de Chartres; their uncle, the Prince de Joinville; John Jacob Astor, of the famous New York family; and Colonel Thomas T. Gantt, who served as judge-advocate.

[87] Pope's Report on Second Bull Run, dated September 3, 1862 (*Official Records*, ser. 1, vol. XII, pt. 2, pp. 12–17) charged Simon Goodell Griffin, who commanded one of Porter's brigades, with spending "the day in making ill-natured strictures upon the general commanding," accused Franklin and Porter of disobedience and dilatoriness, and reflected severely upon McClellan's failure to forward reinforcements and ammunition.

[88] The charges against McDowell included drunkenness, insubordination, carelessness of his men's welfare, etc. On September 6th

McDowell asked Lincoln for a court of inquiry (*Official Records*, ser. 1, vol. XII, pt. 1, pp. 39–40), and after a long hearing the court-martial reported the accusations groundless.

[89] James T. Worthington, of Ellinsmere, near Chillicothe, Ohio.

[90] Probably Captain Franklin Haven, Jr., of Boston, aide-de-camp to McDowell.

[91] The collector of customs at New York had the privilege of selling a labor contract to haul goods from the docks to storehouses, to unpack boxes, to sample incoming merchandise, etc. On May 11, 1861, the unexpired portion of the labor contract was assigned by Collector Hiram Barney to his own firm, Barney, Parsons, and Butler. Barney admitted that if the government did the work itself, it could annually save $37,000. For a study of these problems, see William J. Hartman, "Politics and Patronage: The New York Custom House, 1852–1902" (unpublished Ph.D. dissertation, Columbia University).

[92] Colonel Ebenezer B. Andrews of the 36th Ohio Infantry.

[93] George Crook was named brigadier-general of volunteers, to date from August, 1862. Later he served at Antietam and Chickamauga and with Sheridan in the 1864 Shenandoah Valley campaigns.

[94] James Samuel Wadsworth, of New York; brigadier-general of volunteers; gubernatorial candidate of the anti-Seward New York Republicans, 1862. Defeated by Horatio Seymour, the Democratic candidate, Wadsworth returned to the army and was killed in the Wilderness.

[95] Jesse Lee Reno, who had served with Burnside in North Carolina and at Second Bull Run, was shortly to be killed at South Mountain.

[96] Since February, 1862, Chase had used a system of temporary loans, by which he received "on deposit in the sub-Treasury the funds of individuals or corporations at a rate of interest not exceeding five per cent. per annum; the depositors retaining the privilege of withdrawing their funds at any time—on ten days' notice—after thirty days." The funds thus secured became "one of the most important supports of the Treasury" (Jacob W. Schuckers, *The Life and Public Services of Salmon Portland Chase* (New York:

D. Appleton and Company, 1874), pp. 269–70). Chase was now trying to reduce the interest rate.

[97] Cassius Marcellus Clay, Kentucky abolitionist and Republican
politician; minister to Russia, 1861–62. Replaced by Simon Cameron, Clay was made a major-general, but in 1863 he returned to
his diplomatic post in Russia.

[98] Erasmus Darwin Keyes commanded the IV Corps, which was
left on the Peninsula after McClellan's withdrawal from Harrison's
Landing.

[99] John James Peck had served in the Peninsular campaign. Made
a major-general in July, 1862, he later commanded at Suffolk.

[100] David Emanuel Twiggs, commanding the Federal troops in
Texas, surrendered all forces and stores to the Confederates in February, 1861. Dismissed from the United States service, he became a
major-general in the Confederate army.

[101] The Knights of the Golden Circle, at first a secret order re-
cruited in the South to promote proslavery policies and to forward
the annexation of Mexico, became during the Civil War an order
of Northern Peace Democrats strongly opposing Lincoln.

[102] John Buchanan Floyd, of Virginia, Secretary of War under
President Buchanan; Howell Cobb, of Georgia, Secretary of the
Treasury; Jefferson Davis, Senator from Mississippi, who became
President of the Confederate States; John Cabell Breckinridge, Vice-
President of the United States, 1857–61.

[103] Benito Pablo Juarez, President of Mexico, 1861–72.

[104] James Murray Mason, of Virginia, one of the Confederate envoys aboard the *Trent*; Charles James Faulkner, of Virginia, minister to France, 1859–61.

[105] Abram Hyatt, of Sing Sing, nominated as assessor of internal
revenue.

[106] Isaiah Rogers, prominent architect; engineer in charge of the
Treasury Department's bureau of construction.

[107] Francis Preston Blair, Jr., brother of the Postmaster-general,
had been instrumental in saving Missouri for the Union. He was
later to win a military reputation in the Western campaigns, and
as Congressman was to blast Chase's administration of the Treasury.

[108] Henry Van Rensselaer, son of the last patroon of New York;

Whig Congressman; chief-of-staff to Winfield Scott; assigned to Department of the Rappahannock, 1862; transferred to Department of Ohio, 1862–64.

[109] George S. Denison, acting surveyor of customs at New Orleans, wrote Chase, August 26, 1862, that Federal troops had been evacuated from Baton Rouge and that General Butler had formed a "free Colored Reg't" which was "intelligent, energetic and industrious."

[110] William Stuart, Secretary of the British Legation at Washington.

[111] Ralson Skinner, Chase's brother-in-law.

[112] James Alexander Hamilton, son of Alexander Hamilton, had for many years been active in New York politics, first as a Democrat, later as an anti-Seward Republican. Early in the war he urged emancipation, and he frequently advised Chase on financial matters.

[113] At the end of August the governors of the New England states had met at Providence to take concerted action with regard to securing credit in the draft quota of each state for men who had enlisted in the navy.

[114] Radical Republicans objected to Seward's refusal, in his diplomatic dispatches, to declare the war a crusade for emancipation. To Charles Francis Adams, United States minister to Great Britain, Seward had written on April 10, 1861: "Only an imperial or despotic government could subjugate thoroughly disaffected and insurrectionary members of the State." He added that President Lincoln, therefore, was attempting to avoid war and to wait till "returning reflection" brought the Southern states back into the Union—a view not greatly different from Chase's at that time.

[115] Thomas L. Smith, First Auditor, Treasury Department.

[116] James Birney, eldest son of James G. Birney, the antislavery agitator, was lieutenant-governor of Michigan in 1861 and later judge of the eighteenth judicial circuit. His brother, David Bell Birney, commanded a brigade in the division of Philip Kearny, who was killed at Chantilly, September 1, 1862. D. B. Birney did not become a major-general until May, 1863.

[117] Thomas Leiper Kane, organizer of the Pennsylvania "Bucktails," had been named brigadier-general on September 7, 1862.

[118] The New York committee, composed of Hamilton, John E.

Williams, McKnight, and J. A. Stevens, demanded a change in the cabinet. According to Hamilton's *Reminiscences* (pp. 529–33), Lincoln said: "You, gentlemen, to hang Mr. Seward, would destroy this Government."

[119] David Taylor, Republican leader of Bryan County, Ohio; major and paymaster in the United States Army.

[1] Chase referred to the encounter between Joseph Hooker's division of Pope's army and R. S. Ewell's division of Jackson's corps at Bristow Station (Kettle Run), August 27, 1862.

[2] Daniel Butterfield, wounded at Gaines's Mill, had joined Pope at Second Bull Run. In November, 1862, he commanded the V Corps, and at Fredericksburg he served as chief-of-staff to Hooker.

[3] Major Dwight Bannister, paymaster with McDowell's forces and later in the Department of the South.

[4] Col. John A. Wright, on Governor Curtain's staff.

[5] Andrew Gregg Curtin, Republican war governor of Pennsylvania, 1861–67; minister to Russia, 1869–72; Democratic Congressman, 1881–87.

[6] In July, 1862, Congress had passed a confiscation act, directing the President to seize the property of those who participated in the rebellion and declaring free the slaves of persons convicted of treason or rebellion.

[7] For this memorandum, titled "Notes on the Union of the Armies of the Potomac and the Army of Virginia," see Jacob W. Schuckers, *The Life and Public Services of Salmon Portland Chase* (New York: D. Appleton and Company, 1874), pp. 445–50.

[8] John Milton Brannan, who directed operations on the St. Johns River and at Pocotaglio, South Carolina, in October, 1862, later was transferred to the Army of the Cumberland.

[9] Curtis Field Burnham, of Richmond, Kentucky; firmly Unionist chairman of his state legislature's committee on Federal relations.

[10] George F. O'Harra, a cotton buyer and speculator of Columbus, Ohio.

[11] Probaby J. W. S. Cummings, clerk in the post-office, Philadelphia.

[12] Pitt Cooke, brother of Jay Cooke and partner in Jay Cooke & Co.

[13] Gustavus Vasa Fox, advocate of ironclad naval vessels, was Assistant Secretary of the Navy throughout the war.

[14] James Island guarded the southern approaches to Charleston Harbor.

[15] Brigadier-General George Washington Cullum, of Halleck's staff; later superintendent of the Military Academy and compiler of military historical records. He referred to the September 6–16 campaign in which W. W. Loring's Confederate troops drove the Federal forces of Colonel J. A. J. Lightburn down the Kanawha River and captured Charleston, West Virginia.

[16] S. Morton Clark, disbursing agent and chief of the first division of the National Currency Bureau in the Treasury Department.

[17] Robert C. Schenck, of Ohio; Whig Congressman, 1843–51; minister to Brazil, 1851–53; brigadier-general of volunteers in Virginia and West Virginia, 1861–62; major-general in command in Maryland, 1862–63; Congressman, 1863–70; minister to Great Britain, 1870–76.

[18] Chase's skepticism about these figures and the earlier estimates of Halleck was warranted. Lee had about 55,000 men.

[19] Rev. B. Peyton Brown, pastor of Waugh Chapel, Washington.

[20] Brigadier-General Julius White withdrew from Martinsburg to Harpers Ferry, where his troops were surrendered along with those of Dixon S. Miles, who arranged the apparently unnecessary capitulation. Miles was killed by a burst of shell just after the surrender. White, after release from Confederate prison, was tried by a Union court-martial, which found him not responsible for Miles's course.

[21] Emile Saisset, "Recherches Nouvelles sur l'Ame et sur la Vie," *Revue des Deux Mondes*, XL (Aug. 15, 1862), 957–87.

[22] Ogden Hoffman, William H. Sharp, and C. W. Rand were named, respectively, judge, district-attorney, and marshal of the United States district court for the Northern District of California. Timothy Guy Phelps was a California Republican Congressman, 1861–63. Palmer, Cook & Company was the influential banking house of San Francisco.

[23] M. J. Franklin, optician, 244 Pennsylvania Avenue.

[24] John Sherman, of Ohio, Republican Congressman, 1855–61; Senator, 1861–77, 1881–97; Secretary of the Treasury, 1877–81; Secretary of State, 1897–98.

[25] Oran Follett, an old friend of Chase's; editor of the *Ohio State Journal,* Columbus.

[26] Horace Greeley, influential editor of the New York *Tribune,* 1841–72; prominent antislavery leader and Republican organizer; leader of anti-Seward, Radical wing of New York Republican party.

[27] Thomas Dawes Eliot, of New Bedford, Massachusetts; Republican Congressman, 1859–69.

[28] Samson Mason, a member of the Ohio legislature, was concerned about his son, Colonel Rodney Mason, of the 71st Ohio Infantry, captured by J. H. Morgan at Clarksville, Tennessee, without a show of resistance. Mason was cashiered by order of the President, but subsequently the order was revoked and he was honorably discharged.

[29] Probably William B. Lloyd, of Cleveland, colonel of Ohio cavalry.

[30] John Sanford Mason, of the 4th Ohio Infantry, became a brigadier-general in November, 1862.

[31] James C. Wetmore, Ohio state military agent at Washington.

[32] George Stoneman, who had served under McClellan in the Peninsular campaign, in November, 1862, took command of the III Corps as major-general. Hooker later gave him command of the cavalry of the Army of the Potomac.

[33] George A. Benedict, of Fairbanks, Benedict & Co., printers, Cleveland.

[34] Charles Pettit McIlvaine, Episcopal bishop of Ohio; unofficial ambassador to Great Britain in the early stages of the war.

[35] Daniel W. Tolford, clergyman of Dayton, Ohio, was made hospital chaplain.

[36] Either Chase or his copyist was in error, for according to Welles's *Diary,* the reference was to Commander John P. Bankhead of South Carolina.—Gideon Welles, *Diary of Gideon Welles, Secretary of the Navy under Lincoln and Johnson* (Boston: Houghton Mifflin Company, 1911), I, 130.

[37] James Longstreet, one of Lee's most trusted lieutenants, who fought at both battles of Bull Run, in the Peninsular campaign at Antietam, Fredericksburg, Chickamauga, and the Wilderness.

[38] Edwin Dennison Morgan, of New York; chairman, Republican National Committee, 1856–64; governor, 1859–62; Senator, 1863–69.

[39] Franz Sigel, a German "forty-eighter," had fought at Pea Ridge and Second Bull Run. In September, 1862, his troops were transferred to the Army of the Potomac as the XI Corps.

[40] Carl Schurz, another influential German-American, after serving as minister to Spain, 1861–62, was named brigadier-general and fought at Second Bull Run. Later he was to see action at Chancellorsville and Gettysburg and in 1863 to be made major-general. After the war he became a Senator from Missouri (1869–75) and Secretary of the Interior (1877–81).

[41] George Hoadly, formerly a law student of Chase's in Cincinnati; judge of the superior court of Cincinnati; governor of Ohio, 1883–85.

[42] Robert Dale Owen, son of the British reformer, Robert Owen; Democratic Congressman from Indiana, 1843–47; minister to the Kingdom of the Two Sicilies, 1854–58. A strong abolitionist, he was now commissioned by the governor of Indiana to buy arms in Europe. His letter to Lincoln, dated September 17, 1863, urged: "Extirpate the blighting curse . . . that has smitten at last with desolation a land to whom God has granted everything but wisdom."

[43] Halleck's telegram actually read: "I have not seen the order as published, but will write to you in the morning. You will retain the command of everything in this vicinity not temporarily belonging to Pope's army in the field. I beg of you to assist me in this crisis with your ability and experience. I am utterly tired out."

[44] Dr. S. W. Forsha, maker of a balm in which Chase had great faith.

[45] Artemus Ward, the pseudonym of Charles Farrar Browne. The "High-Handed Outrage at Utica" appeared in *Artemus Ward: His Book* (1862), pp. 24–5.

[46] This sentence has been added to the diary in another handwriting.

[47] See Roy P. Basler, ed., *The Collected Works of Abraham Lincoln* (New Brunswick: Rutgers University Press, 1953), V, 433–36, for the changes suggested by the cabinet.

[48] Edwards Pierrepont, judge of the superior court of the city of New York, 1857–60, who helped organize the War Democrats in support of Lincoln; attorney-general, 1875–76; minister to Great Britain, 1876–77.

[50] Major Donn Piatt, of the 13th Ohio Infantry, made his reputation after the war as editor of the *Capital.*

[51] Possibly George Peabody Este, a Toledo lawyer and colonel of the 14th Ohio Infantry.

[52] General Joseph Hooker, who had received a foot wound at Antietam, was in the Hospital for the Insane because Washington hospitals were overcrowded. Dr. C. H. Nichols was superintendent of the hospital.

[53] The last eight words have been added to the diary in another handwriting.

[54] John Cook Rives, since 1833 publisher of the *Congressional Globe.*

[55] William Dwight, of Massachusetts, lieutenant-colonel of the 70th New York Infantry, was later made a brigadier-general.

[56] Probably J. J. R. Pease, of Janesville, for whom Welles in 1865 was still seeking an appointment.

[57] Charles Gibson, Missouri Whig and Unionist leader, solicitor of the United States Court of Claims, 1861–64, broke with the President and supported McClellan in 1864.

[58] Hamilton Rowan Gamble, made governor of Missouri after the flight of secessionist officials in June, 1861, was an opponent of Missouri Radical Republicans and a supporter of gradual, compensated emancipation.

[59] Benjamin Farrar, Assistant Treasurer of the United States at St. Louis, and Franklin A. Dick, provost-marshal of Missouri under General Curtis, were leaders of the anti-Gamble faction of Missouri Republicans.

[60] Eli Thayer, Massachusetts educator and Congressman; originator of the Emigrant Aid Company, to subsidize Northern emigration to Kansas in the 1850's; advocate of military colonization in Florida.

[61] Major Henshaw B. Walley, son of banker Samuel H. Walley, of Boston.

[62] John Ross, the Cherokee chief, at the outset of the war tried to keep his tribe neutral, but in October, 1861, they signed a treaty of alliance with the Confederacy. It was repudiated in 1863.

[63] William F. Clark, collector for the Twentieth Internal Revenue District of Pennsylvania.

[64] William David Lewis, Philadelphia merchant; collector of customs, 1849–53; president, Philadelphia Academy of Fine Arts.

[65] Garfield was a minister of the Disciples of Christ.

[66] On January 10, 1862, Garfield's troops defeated Confederate forces under Humphrey Marshall, a Kentucky Whig and Knownothing Congressman turned general, and they entered Prestonburg the next day.

[67] Chase seems to have made an understandable error as to the titles of the British visitors. Spencer Compton (Cavendish), Marquis of Hartington and later Duke of Devonshire, and his brother, Lord Edward Cavendish, then stationed with his regiment in Canada, were touring the United States. Lincoln, Lord Hartington thought, was "a very well-meaning sort of a man, but . . . about as fit for his position as a fire shovel." The British nobleman's record of the dinner did not mention Chase.—Bernard Holland, *The Life of Spencer Compton, Eighth Duke of Devonshire*, I, 40–45.

[68] John Gordon Kennedy, attaché at the British embassy.

[69] Edward Everett, of Massachusetts; Congressman, 1825–35; governor, 1836–40; minister to Great Britain, 1841–45; president, Harvard College, 1846–49; Secretary of State, 1852–53; Senator, 1853–54.

[70] James Monroe, formerly of Oberlin and a member of the Ohio legislature, now a resident of New York.

[71] After their conference at Altoona, the Northern governors came to Washington. Those named were: Richard Yates, of Illinois; Nathaniel S. Berry, of New Hampshire; Samuel J. Kirkwood, of Iowa; Edward Saloman, of Wisconsin; John A. Andrew, of Massachusetts; Augustus W. Bradford, of Maryland; William Sprague, of Rhode Island; David Tod, of Ohio; Austin Blair, of Michigan; Francis H. Pierpont, of Virginia.

[72] John Alexander McClernand, Democratic Congressman from Illinois, 1843–51, 1859–61; brigadier-general in the West, 1861–64. He was authorized by the President to raise an army in the Northwest for the opening of the Mississippi River, but differences with Grant led to his removal from command.

[73] The New York *Herald,* September 25, 1862, reported the Altoona conference as "A Second Hartford Convention."

[74] Jacob D. Cox, of Ohio, briefly commanded the IX Corps after Reno's death. Later he served in West Virginia, in the Atlanta campaign, and at Nashville. After the war he had a distinguished career as governor of Ohio, Secretary of the Interior, Congressman, and president of the University of Cincinnati.

[75] Lieutenant-Colonel Melvin Clarke, of the 36th Ohio Infantry.

[76] George Bliss, private secretary to Governor Morgan of New York, and paymaster of that state.

[77] Rev. Smith Pyne, of St. John's Church, Washington.

[78] Columbian College later became George Washington University.

[79] William Selby Harney had commanded the Department of the West (St. Louis) at the outbreak of the war. F. P. Blair, Jr., who thought him too timid in dealing with the secessionists, urged his removal.

[80] Major-General William Nelson, of Kentucky, commanded the Federal forces at Louisville, preparing for an attack by Braxton Bragg's advancing army. Hot-tempered and intemperate, Nelson publicly reprimanded Brigadier-General Jefferson C. Davis, who shot him.

[81] Gideon Johnson Pillow, of Tennessee; law partner of James K. Polk; master-mind behind the nomination of Franklin Pierce; quarrelsome commander in the Mexican War; Confederate brigadier-general at Fort Donelson.

[82] Pierre Gustave Toutant Beauregard, of Louisiana; commander of Confederate forces at Fort Sumter and First Bull Run; second in command, under A. S. Johnston, at Shiloh.

[83] B. F. Butler wrote, on July 21, 1862, that he would "assure safe conduct, open market, and prompt shipment of all cotton and sugar

sent to New Orleans, and the owner, were he Slidell himself, should have the pay for his cotton. . . ."

84 When W. T. Sherman reached Memphis, he had "ordered . . . that gold, silver, and Treasury notes, were contraband of war, and should not go into the interior, where all were hostile" and "required cotton to be paid for . . . by an obligation to pay at the end of the war, or by a deposit of the price in the hands of a trustee, viz., the United States Quartermaster." But on August 11, 1862, he was obliged to announce: "In pursuance of orders from the Headquarters of the Army at Washington all restrictions on the sale of cotton and prohibition of the payment of gold therefor are hereby annulled. Every facility possible will be afforded for getting cotton to market." The directive was issued "By order of Maj. Gen. U.S. Grant," who, nevertheless, deplored the action.

85 William Davis Gallagher, Ohio editor and poet, whose anthology included some of Chase's own verses; special collector of customs and commercial agent in the Upper Mississippi Valley; later surveyor of the customs at Louisville.

86 John Austin Stevens, Jr., son of the New York banker; secretary, New York Chamber of Commerce; one of the founders of the Loyal National League and the Loyal Publications Society.

87 Andrew Jackson Hamilton, Texas Unionist who fled to Mexico at the beginning of the war, was later named brigadier-general and provisional governor of his state.

88 Oliver Perry Morton, Republican war governor of Indiana, 1861–67; Senator, 1867–77. The fall elections went strongly against the Republicans. In Indiana George Washington Julian and Schuyler Colfax were reëlected, but John P. C. Shanks was defeated.

89 Kenner Garrard, later brevet major-general, served at Gettysburg, in the Atlanta campaign, and at Nashville.

90 John G. Foster, who had participated in Burnside's Cape Hatteras expedition, was made commander of the Department of North Carolina. Later he fought at Knoxville and commanded the Department of the Ohio.

91 Colonel Simon H. Mix, of the 3rd New York Cavalry.

92 John Cochrane, of New York; Congressman, 1857–61; brigadier-general of volunteers, 1862–63; adviser of McClellan; chairman

in 1864 of the Independent Republican National Convention at Cleveland which opposed Lincoln and nominated Frémont.

[93] Elisha Whittlesey, Ohio Congressman, 1823–38; Sixth Auditor of the Treasury, 1841–43; First Comptroller, 1847–57, a post to which Chase reappointed him in 1861.

[94] Major-General Alexander D. McCook commanded the left wing of Buell's army in the battle of Perryville, October 8, 1862, against the forces of Braxton Bragg. Though the Confederates claimed a victory, they withdrew to Harrodsburg.

[95] Colonel Anson Stager, chief of the military telegraph service, stationed at Cleveland.

[96] Charles G. Halpine, author of the "Miles O'Reilly" sketches and a member of General Hunter's staff.

[97] Edgar Cowan, Republican Senator from Pennsylvania, 1861–67.

[98] With 1800 picked men, Confederate General "Jeb" Stuart made a raid around McClellan's army, entered Chambersburg, and destroyed property valued at $250,000.

[99] Edgar Needham, Louisville marble dealer; in November, 1862, assessor of the Third Internal Revenue District of Kentucky.

[100] John Jay, grandson of Chief Justice John Jay; New York lawyer, author, abolitionist; minister to Austria, 1869–74.

[101] George Wilkes, sensational New York journalist; founder of the *National Police Gazette* and *Wilkes's Spirit of the Times*.

---

¹ The 1863 *United States Official Register* lists Thomas M. Smith as chief clerk in the Fifth Auditor's Office.

² Hanson A. Risley, supervising special agent, Treasury Department.

³ In March, 1863, Congress authorized the issue of short-term Treasury notes, bearing 5 per cent interest, legal tender for face value, not intended to circulate as currency but to be held by investors.

⁴ John Brooks Henderson, of Missouri, appointed to fill the Senate vacancy caused by the expulsion of Trusten Polk; served 1862–69.

⁵ Lemuel Jackson Bowden, of Virginia, Republican Senator, 1863–64.

⁶ Lucius H. Chandler presented his credentials as member-elect to the 38th Congress from the Second District of Virginia but was denied a seat.

⁷ Joseph Eggleston Segar, another Virginia Unionist, had presented his credentials as member-elect to the 37th Congress but was denied a seat; was subsequently reëlected and permitted to serve, 1862–63; but was again denied his seat when he presented his credentials to the 38th Congress.

⁸ Samuel Shellabarger, of Ohio; Republican Congressman, 1861–63, defeated in the Democratic sweep of 1862; reëlected, 1865–69; minister to Portugal, 1869; again Congressman, 1871–73; member of United States Civil Service Commission, 1874–75.

⁹ Philemon Bliss, of Ohio; Republican Congressman, 1855–59; chief justice of the Supreme Court of Dakota Territory, 1861–68; associate justice, Supreme Court of Missouri, 1868–72.

¹⁰ John A. Bingham, of Ohio; Republican Congressman, 1855–63, defeated in the Democratic victories of 1862; reëlected, 1865–73; a leading Radical.

[11] William Lawrence, of Ohio; judge of the Court of Common Pleas, 1857–64; Republican Congressman, 1865–71, 1873–77. He was offered the Florida judgeship in 1863 but declined it.

[12] William Marvin, judge of the United States Court for the Southern District of Florida, resigned in 1863 because of ill health. In 1865 President Johnson appointed him provisional governor of Florida.

[13] William Starke Rosecrans, of Ohio, had in November, 1862, replaced Buell as commander of the Army of the Ohio. After the fierce battle at Murfreesboro in late December his army did not advance for six months. It was not until September 9th that he finally maneuvered his way into Chattanooga.

[14] George Washington Wright, one of the founders of the San Francisco banking house of Palmer, Cook & Co.; Congressman, 1850–51.

[14a] Probably Stuart Gwynn, who had a contract to supply the Treasury Department with paper and presses for the manufacture of fractional currency. S. M. Clark was superintendent of the National Currency Bureau.

[15] Samuel M. Breckinridge, of St. Louis; judge of the Circuit Court, 1859–63; a stanch Unionist who had helped keep Missouri loyal in 1861.

[16] D. G. Barnitz, supervising special agent, Treasury Department.

[17] Both Chase and his Congressional critics were seriously disturbed about the amount of the commission paid Jay Cooke for his promotion of the 5–20 bond issue.

[18] Robert Huston Milroy, commander of the VIII Corps during Lee's Pennsylvania invasion of 1863, had been driven back with such disastrous losses that he was subjected to a military investigation, which exonerated him.

[19] John S. Whittaker, appointed in 1862 judge of the second district court of the parish of Orleans; later a leading Louisiana Radical Republican.

[20] Major B. Rush Plumley, a former Frémont aide, accompanied Banks to New Orleans and was named to a commission "to regulate the enrollment, recruiting, employment, and education of persons of color" in the Department of the Gulf.

[21] John F. McJilton, editor of the *Patriot* and surveyor of customs, Baltimore; John F. Meredith, appraiser-general of customs, Baltimore.

[22] Thomas Swann, president, Baltimore and Ohio Railroad, 1847–53; mayor of Baltimore, 1856–60; governor of Maryland, 1864–69; Democratic Congressman, 1869–79.

[23] Henry Winter Davis, of Maryland; Whig, Know-nothing, and Republican Congressman, 1855–61, 1863–65. A leader of the Radical Republicans, he was an author of the Wade-Davis bill concerning reconstruction.

[24] Alphonso Taft, of Cincinnati; lawyer, traction magnate; judge of Ohio Superior Court, 1865–72; Secretary of War and Attorney-General under Grant; later minister to Austria-Hungary and to Russia.

[25] James W. Parker, of Parker's Express Company, St. Louis.

[26] William McKee, joint proprietor, with G. W. Fishback, of the *Missouri Democrat*.

[27] Theodore Tilton, close friend of Henry Ward Beecher; editor of the influential religious periodical, the *Independent*, 1862–71; articulate Radical Republican; whose reputation was later besmirched in the Beecher-Tilton scandal.

[28] Henry M. Turner, pastor, Israel Methodist Church, Washington.

[29] Benjamin Sherwood Hedrick, who had been driven from his professorship at the University of North Carolina for declaring his willingness to vote for Frémont in 1856, was a patent examiner.

[30] Hugh Lenox Bond, judge of the Baltimore criminal court, 1860–68; judge of the United States Circuit Court, 1870–93.

[31] Edward Y. Goldsborough, United States marshal at Baltimore.

[32] Joseph J. Stewart, appointed collector for the Second Internal Revenue District of Maryland to replace James J. Ridgeley.

[33] David Heaton, special agent of the Treasury Department, at Newbern, North Carolina.

[34] Lyman D. Stickney, United States commissioner and special agent of the Treasury Department in Florida.

[35] Morris Island guarded Charleston Harbor on the south.

[36] Quincy Adams Gillmore, who had commanded the expedition

against Fort Pulaski and had served in Kentucky and West Virginia, now commanded the X Corps in the Department of the South and was engaged in an attempt to capture Charleston.

[37] Samuel Galloway, secretary of state of Ohio, 1844–50; Republican Congressman, 1855–57; now judge-advocate at Camp Chase.

[38] For Lincoln's letter, see Roy P. Basler, ed., *The Collected Works of Abraham Lincoln* (New Brunswick: Rutgers University Press, 1953), VI, 440.

[39] Sullivan's Island guarded Charleston Harbor on the north.

[40] Fort Moultrie, on the south shore of Sullivan's Island, and Cummings Point, on the northern end of Morris Island, occupied the two capes at the entrance of Charleston Harbor.

[41] Perhaps David Reese, 377 Sixth Avenue, West, Washington.

[42] James M. Edmunds, of Michigan, commissioner of the general land office, who was very active in soliciting contributions for the Republican campaign funds.

[43] Probably Joseph C. Brand, clerk, Treasury Department.

[44] Private James ("Scottie") Gray, of the 50th Ohio Infantry, who distinguished himself at Port Republic and Cedar Mountain.

[45] John Cadwalader, judge of the United States District Court for Eastern Pennsylvania; Wilson McCandless, judge of the United States District Court for Western Pennsylvania. Both had been appointed by Buchanan.

[46] Leslie Stephen, English man of letters and editor of the *Dictionary of National Biography*. For his comments on the meeting, see Introduction, p. 1.

[47] Joseph Gillespie, of Edwardsville, Illinois; a close personal friend of Lincoln's; now circuit judge of the Twenty-fourth Judicial District.

[48] *U.S. Statutes at Large*, XII, 37 Cong., 3 sess., chap. lxxxi, pp. 755–8.

[49] On September 15th Lincoln issued a proclamation suspending the writ of habeas corpus.—Basler, ed., Lincoln's *Collected Works*, VI, 451–2.

[50] Maunsell Bradhurst Field, deputy Assistant Treasurer of the United States at New York, 1861–63; Assistant Secretary of the

Treasury, 1863–65. Chase's attempt to appoint Field Assistant Treasurer of the United States at New York, to succeed John J. Cisco, was to lead to the Secretary's resignation in 1864.

[51] James E. Yeatman, member of the Western Sanitary Commission; law commissioner at St. Louis; in 1865 a strong candidate for head of the Freedmen's Bureau.

[52] Probably D. M. Leatherman, of Tennessee, who came to Washington "about some property claimed by a woman in or near Memphis, under a deed from her husband who is in the rebel service." —Basler, ed., Lincoln's *Collected Works*, VI, 431.

[53] Philip D. Moore, of Olympia, succeeded Hugh A. Goldsborough, brother of the naval officer and Northwestern explorer, as Collector of Internal Revenue for Washington Territory.

[54] Dr. John Allyn had contracted with Victor Smith, collector of customs and special agent of the Treasury in the Puget Sound District, to provide lodgings and medical attention to seamen in the marine hospital at Port Townsend, and he accused Smith of embezzling public funds. Smith, an eccentric Cincinnati newspaperman, abolitionist, and spiritualist, was trying to remove the customs house from Port Townsend to Port Angelos. Local residents strongly protested, and Dr. Anson G. Henry, an intimate friend of Lincoln's, now surveyor-general for Washington Territory, brought their complaints to Washington. Without consulting Chase, Lincoln ordered Smith removed, and, in a stiffly worded letter (see Introduction, p. 30), Chase threatened to resign.

[55] Edward Lillie Pierce, Massachusetts Republican and friend (later biographer) of Charles Sumner, had studied law in Chase's Cincinnati office. He was sent by the Secretary to Port Royal to supervise the raising of cotton by the freedmen. In 1864, Pierce became Collector of Internal Revenue in Massachusetts.

[56] James Miller McKim, Pennsylvania abolitionist; founder of Philadelphia Port Royal Relief Committee; one of the originators of the *Nation*.

[57] Judge Ransom Balcolm, of Binghamton, New York.

[58] Major Grotius R. Giddings, who had commanded the 14th United States Regulars at Gettysburg, now led a brigade of Sykes's Corps.

[59] Guido Ilges, captain of one of Giddings's companies.

[60] William Augustus Newell, of New Jersey; Whig Congressman, 1847–51; governor, 1857–60; Republican Congressman, 1865–67.

[61] Edwin Hansom Webster, Republican Congressman from Maryland, 1859–65; colonel, 7th Maryland Infantry.

[62] For Lincoln's letter, dated September 2, 1863, see Basler, ed., Lincoln's *Collected Works*, VI, 428–9.

[63] Henry Eugene Davies, son of Judge H. E. Davies, and colonel of the 2d New York Cavalry, was brevetted brigadier-general in September, 1863.

[64] Straughn seems not to have secured the job he wanted, but in October he was appointed to hear claims by alleged owners of slaves enlisted in the army from Maryland and the Eastern Shore.

[65] Probably an error for George W. Russum, of Denton, Caroline County, assessor for the First Internal Revenue District of Maryland.

[66] Charles Anderson Dana, after working for Horace Greeley's *Tribune*, became a special commissioner from the War Department at Grant's headquarters. After the fall of Vicksburg, he was made Assistant Secretary of War. Of the Union disaster on September 20th he wired: "Chickamauga is as fatal a name in our history as Bull Run."

[67] The entry for September 21st and the first four sentences of the following entry have been added from Chase's "Miscellaneous Journal."

[68] Major-General Gordon Granger had earlier distinguished himself at Wilson's Creek and Island No. 10.

[69] Mrs. Charles Ludlow Jones, Chase's sister-in-law, wired concerning Lieutenant Israel Ludlow, of the 5th United States Artillery.

[70] In July, 1864, Charles A. Coolidge was listed as a lieutenant, 7th United States Infantry.

[71] William Prescott Smith, master of transportation for the Baltimore and Ohio Railroad.

[72] Johns Hopkins, wealthy Baltimore merchant, railroad man, and philanthropist; later founder of the Johns Hopkins University and the Johns Hopkins Hospital.

[73] William Birney, son of the abolitionist leader, James G. Birney,

and chief mustering and recruiting officer for Negro troops in Maryland.

[74] Samuel A. Duncan, a tutor at Dartmouth College in 1858, now colonel of the 4th United States Colored Infantry.

[75] Joshua Vansant & Son, hatters and hat and fur dealers, Baltimore.

[76] Charles D. Drake, of St. Louis, led a delegation of Radical Republicans who demanded immediate emancipation and drastic disfranchisement of secessionist sympathizers. To Drake's appeal for the removal of General Schofield, Lincoln replied: "I hold whoever commands in Missouri, or elsewhere, responsible to me, and not to either radicals or conservatives" (Basler, ed., Lincoln's *Collected Works*, VI, 499–504). After the war Drake became Senator from Missouri, 1867–70, and chief justice of the United States Court of Claims, 1870–85.

[77] The remaining entries in this chapter have been added from Chase's "Miscellaneous Journal."

[78] Henry Charles De Ahna wrote the President his version of these events on January 31, 1864: "As Your Excellency probably recollects, it was brought to the knowledge of the Government several months ago, that through a singular mistake in a name, I found myself approached by an agent of the Rebel government and an offer of $50,000 was made to me, if I would undertake to enter into a negotiation with Col. Percy Wyndham and by offering him in the name of the Rebel Government the sum of 100,000 Dollars, would succeed in persuading the said Percy Wyndham to allow himself to be taken prisoner with his whole Cavalry Brigade." De Ahna told his story to V. Hogan, "who was then well known as Secretary Chase's Detective," and he also had an interview with Chase himself, but he claimed that Chase failed properly to investigate the matter.—R. T. Lincoln Coll., Lib. of Cong.

[79] Judah Philip Benjamin, formerly Attorney-General and Secretary of War in the Confederate government, was now Davis's Secretary of State.

[80] Charles D'Arnaud served as a spy for Frémont in 1861, traveling behind the Confederate lines and making sketches of Forts Henry and Donelson.

[81] Sir Percy Wyndham, English-born colonel of the 1st New Jersey Cavalry, serving in the Shenandoah Valley.

[82] Dr. Aaron Van Camp, Washington dentist, who had been arrested in December, 1861, and for a time committed to Old Capitol Prison as a Confederate spy.

[83] Daniel Edgar Sickles, New York Democratic Congressman, 1857–61, had served in the Peninsular campaign, at Chancellorsville, and at Gettysburg, where he lost a leg. After the war he became minister to Spain and was reëlected to Congress.

[84] David Kellogg Cartter, of Ohio; Congressman, 1849–53; minister to Bolivia, 1861–62; chief justice of the Supreme Court of the District of Columbia, 1863–87.

[1] William Orton, collector for the Sixth Internal Revenue District of New York.

[2] Probably James W. Taylor, special agent of the Treasury Department in the Pacific Northwest.

[3] John Conness, Republican Senator from California, 1863–69.

[4] *U.S. Statutes at Large*, XIII, 38 Cong., 1 sess., chap. ccv, pp. 343–4.

[5] George Washington Julian, of Indiana; Free Soil and Republican Congressman, 1849–51, 1861–71; surveyor-general of New Mexico, 1885–89.

[6] On June 20th Chase invited Denning Duer, New York banker, to accept Cisco's post. When he refused, it was offered to John A. Stewart of New York.

[7] William Elder, statistician, Treasury Department.

[8] Dudley Sanford Gregory, of New York; Whig Congressman, 1847–49; director of sixteen railroad companies.

[9] Richard Milford Blatchford, New York City lawyer; close friend of Seward and one of the committee of three appointed by Lincoln in 1861 to disburse funds for the purchase of arms and supplies; minister to the Papal States, 1862–63.

[10] Freeman Clarke of New York; Republican Congressman, 1863–65, 1871–75; Comptroller of the currency, 1865–67.

[11] Chase's letter transmitting M. B. Field's nomination, together with much other correspondence on the subject, is in the R. T. Lincoln Collection, Lib. of Cong.

[12] On June 29th Chase sent a strongly worded letter to Thaddeus Stevens, chairman of the House Ways and Means Committee, demanding a supplementary tax law.—Copy, *ibid*.

[13] Representative F. P. Blair, Jr., of Missouri, charged that Wil-

liam Sprague, Rhode Island Senator, cotton manufacturer, and son-in-law of Chase, had received special privileges from the Treasury Department which would permit his cotton firm to make a profit of two million dollars. On July 4, 1864, Sprague formally denied the charges, attributed them to the Blairs' hostility to Chase, and declared that he "had no favors or advantages which all others have not had."—*Cong. Globe,* 38 Cong., 1 sess., IV, 3543.

[14] *U.S. Statutes at Large,* XIII, 38 Cong., 1 sess., Resolution No. 49, p. 411.

[15] For Lincoln's two letters to Chase of this date, see Roy P. Basler, ed., *The Collected Works of Abraham Lincoln* (New Brunswick: Rutgers University Press, 1953), VII, 412–4.

[16] Lot Myrick Morrill, governor of Maine, 1858–60; Senator, 1861–76; Secretary of the Treasury under Grant and Hayes.

[17] "An Act . . . concerning Commercial Intercourse between loyal and insurrectionary States, and to provide for the Collection of captured and abandoned Property, and the Prevention of Frauds in States declared in Insurrection," approved July 2, 1864.—*U.S. Statutes at Large,* XIII, 38 Cong., 1 sess., chap. ccxxv, pp. 375–8.

[18] The Loan Act of June 30, 1864, authorized a loan of $400,000,-000, and the issue of bonds redeemable after five and within thirty years, with interest rate not to exceed 6 per cent; but in place of half of these bonds, the Secretary could issue three-year Treasury notes bearing 7.30 per cent interest.

[19] Probably Elihu Benjamin Washburne, of Illinois; Republican Congressman, 1853–69; Secretary of State and minister to France under the Grant administration.

[20] Edward A. Rollins, whose regular position was that of cashier, Internal Revenue Division.

[21] "I have telegraphed Mr. Cisco begging him to withdraw his resignation. . . . If he declines . . . I must repeat that, in my judgment, the public interests require the appointment of Mr. Field. One of the gentlemen named by Senator Morgan is over seventy and the other, I think, over sixty years old, and neither has any practical knowledge of the duties of the office."—Chase to Lincoln, June 28, 1864, R. T. Lincoln Coll., Lib. of Cong.

[22] Garrett Davis, of Kentucky; Whig Congressman, 1839–47;

elected to the Senate to fill the place created by the expulsion of
John C. Breckinridge; served, 1861–72.

²³ The act establishing a Bureau of Freedmen, Refugees and
Abandoned Lands was not adopted until March, 1865.

²⁴ No record of Elijah Sills' appointment has been discovered.
Atkinson was replaced as Third Auditor by John Wilson of Illinois.

²⁵ John T. Hogeboom, a Chase supporter, appointed general ap-
praiser in the New York Customs House.

²⁶ The two letters here mentioned are in the R. T. Lincoln Collection, Lib. of Cong.

²⁷ On July 2nd the gold act was repealed.

²⁸ Justin Smith Morrill, of Vermont, Republican Congressman,
1855–67; author of the tariff act of 1861 and of the land-grant bill.

²⁹ Lincoln wrote: "Your resignation . . . is accepted. Of all I have
said in commendation of your ability and fidelity, I have nothing
to unsay; and yet you and I have reached a point of mutual embarrassment in our official relation which it seems can not be overcome, or longer sustained, consistently with the public service."—
Basler, ed., Lincoln's *Collected Works,* VII, 419.

³⁰ David Tod, coal and iron magnate; Republican governor of
Ohio, 1862–64.

³¹ William G. Moorhead, of Philadelphia; brother-in-law and
partner of Jay Cooke; president, Philadelphia and Erie Railroad.

³² Thomas Williams, of Pittsburgh; Republican Congressman,
1863–69.

³³ Thomas M. Howe, Pittsburgh financier interested in steel, cop-
per, and cotton manufacturing.

³⁴ Rufus Paine Spalding, associate judge of the Ohio Supreme
Court, 1849–52; Congressman, 1863–69.

³⁵ Sponsored by B. F. Wade and H. W. Davis, the reconstruction
act passed by Congress on July 2nd provided for the reorganization
of the seceded states only after a majority of the white male citizens
had taken an oath of allegiance and had drawn up a constitution
acceptable to the President and to Congress.

³⁶ James Moore Wayne, of Georgia; appointed to the Supreme
Court by Andrew Jackson; a firm Unionist throughout the war.

³⁷ The word "perform" has been inserted above "administer."

[38] James Frazier Jaquess, a Methodist clergyman; colonel of the 73rd Illinois Infantry. Garfield's story undoubtedly referred to Jaquess's 1863–64 attempts, with J. R. Gilmore, to bring about peace by personal negotiations at Richmond.

[39] Samuel Clarke Pomeroy, of Kansas; Republican Senator, 1861–73; leading Congressional supporter of Chase.

[40] Jesse Olds Norton, of Illinois; Republican Congressman, 1853–57, 1863–65.

[41] On June 19th, off the port of Cherbourg, the U.S.S. *Kearsarge* sank the Confederate raider, *Alabama*.

[42] Thomas Ewing, veteran of Ohio politics; Secretary of the Treasury under Harrison; Secretary of the Interior under Taylor; appointed, but not confirmed, Secretary of War by Johnson.

[43] Hezekiah Hosmer, former editor of the Toledo *Blade*; secretary of the House committee on territories, 1861–64.

[44] Whitelaw Reid, war correspondent of the Cincinnati *Gazette*; later succeeded Greeley as editor of the New York *Tribune*.

[45] George Hunt Pendleton, of Cincinnati; Democratic Congressman, 1857–65; Democratic vice-presidential nominee, 1864; Senator, 1879–85.

[1] John Cabell Breckinridge, of Kentucky; Democratic Congressman, 1851–55; Vice-President of the United States, 1857–61; now major-general in the Confederate army.

[2] Major-General John Brown Gordon, of Georgia; later Senator, 1873–80, 1891–97; governor, 1886–90.

[3] Christopher Columbus Augur commanded the XXII Corps, Department of Washington.

[4] Major William H. Fry ordinarily commanded the 16th Pennsylvania Cavalry, but in this emergency he led a provisional cavalry regiment.

[5] David Dixon Porter led the mortar flotilla in the expedition against New Orleans and commanded the naval forces in the Vicksburg and Red River campaigns. In 1865, he became superintendent of the Naval Academy.

[6] Francis Preston Blair, Senior, father of both General F. P. Blair, Jr., and Attorney-General Montgomery Blair, was one of the most powerful supporters of Lincoln's reëlection and of his reconstruction policies.

[7] Alexander G. Mercer, pastor, All Saints Chapel, Newport.

[8] Probably Estes Howe, of Boston; treasurer, Union Railroad Company and Cambridge Gaslight and Railroad Company; Massachusetts Republican leader.

[9] William Endicott, Jr., Boston drygoods merchant.

[10] Jane Elizabeth (Woodbury) Rantoul, widow of the Massachusetts Democratic Senator and opponent of capital punishment.

[11] Richard Henry Dana, II, author of *Two Years before the Mast*; United States District Attorney for Massachusets, 1861–66.

[12] John Bassett Alley, Massachusetts Republican Congressman, 1859–67.

[13] Edward Kent, twice governor of Maine; justice of the Maine Supreme Judicial Court, 1859–73.

[14] William Schouler, editor of the Boston *Atlas and Daily Bee* and adjutant-general of Massachusetts, whom Chase had known in Ohio in the 1850's.

[15] Franklin Haven, of Boston; president, Merchants National Bank.

[16] Jean Louis Rodolphe Agassiz, one of the world's outstanding geologists, pioneer student of glaciers and fossil remains; professor at Harvard.

[17] Thomas H. Perkins, of Head & Perkins, stockbrokers, Boston.

[18] Amos Adams Lawrence, Massachusetts merchant; textile manufacturer; supporter of Eli Thayer's Emigrant Aid Company; founder of Lawrence University, Appleton, Wisconsin.

[19] Enoch T. Carson, surveyor of customs, Cincinnati.

[20] John Murray Forbes, Boston merchant and railroad builder; aide of Governor John A. Andrew; unofficial ambassador to Great Britain in 1863 in a vain attempt to purchase the Laird Rams, being built for the Confederacy. Forbes had his summer home on the island of Naushon, off the southern coast of Massachusetts.

[21] Francis Channing Barlow, after a brilliant military career that had included the Peninsular campaign, Antietam, Chancellorsville, Gettysburg, and the Wilderness, had been wounded. After the war he was secretary of state and attorney-general of New York.

[22] George Silsbee Hale, Boston attorney.

[23] Alice (Mason) Hooper, widow of the Congressman's son, was shortly to marry Senator Charles Sumner.

[24] Colonel James H. Godman, of the 4th Ohio Infantry.

[25] William Curtis Noyes, New York attorney and law reformer; member of the Radical, anti-Seward wing of the New York Republican party, strongly supporting emancipation and favoring Chase's nomination.

[26] Lyman Beecher, the distinguished Presbyterian clergyman and father of Henry Ward Beecher and Harriet Beecher Stowe, had preached at Litchfield before he moved to Cincinnati, where he became president of Lane Theological Seminary.

[27] Benjamin Tallmadge, lieutenant-colonel in the American Revolution; Connecticut Congressman, 1801–1817.

[28] Peter Harvey, Boston merchant, railroad man, and banker; trusted friend of Webster and author of *Reminiscences and Anecdotes of Daniel Webster* (1878).

[29] Probably George F. Fort, governor of New Jersey, 1851–54, and later judge of the Court of Errors and Appeals.

[30] Israel Putnam, veteran of the French and Indian War, while living at Pomfret, Connecticut, learned the news of the battle at Lexington and left his plow in the field to join the Revolutionary army. Stories of his youth, such as his capture of a wolf in its den, were a part of American legendary history.

[31] John Greenleaf Whittier, the Massachusetts Quaker poet and antislavery leader.

[32] Robert Samuel Rantoul, son of Senator Rantoul; mayor of Salem.

[33] Williard P. Phillips, of Salem.

[34] Edward Payson Powell, Congregational pastor at Adrian, Michigan, who later preached at Chattanooga and Chicago and wrote many books on religious subjects.

[35] James Robert Gilmore, associate of Jaquess in his efforts to negotiate peace between Richmond and Washington.

[36] Eliza Chase Whipple, Chase's niece.

[37] Joseph Albree Gilmore, New Hampshire railroad man, had been elected governor in 1863, but he was on bad terms with the state Republican party, led by his son-in-law, William Eaton Chandler (later to achieve fame as a Republican policy-maker and Secretary of the Navy under President Arthur), and by Edward Henry Rollins, Republican Congressman, 1861–73 (Senator, 1877–83). Chandler and Rollins had forced through the New Hampshire Republican convention early in 1864 a resolution urging Lincoln's reëlection. As speaker of the House, Chandler opposed Governor Gilmore's demand for a bond issue and a new militia act, and in August the Republican legislators refused to receive the governor's veto of a bill which permitted soldiers to vote.

[38] James Duggan, born in Ireland and ordained at St. Louis, was made coadjutor archbishop in 1857 with title Bishop of Antigone.

He was nominated Archbishop of Chicago, but his health was failing and he was obliged to travel abroad.

[39] Edward Chipman Guild, Unitarian minister who had his first charge at Marietta, later preached at Canton, Massachusetts, Ithaca, Baltimore, Waltham, and Brunswick, Maine.

[40] George Bancroft, the noted historian, diplomat, author of the *History of the United States from the Discovery of the American Continent.*

[41] Goldwin Smith, professor of history at Oxford University, follower of Cobden and Bright, and a supporter of the North during the Civil War, was making a three-month visit in the United States. He received an LL.D. degree from Brown University.

[42] Barnas Sears, Baptist theologian and preacher; president of Brown University since 1855.

[43] John Henry Clifford, a Brown alumnus; governor of Massachusetts, 1853; president of the state senate in the 1860's.

[44] F. B. Thomas, of Worcester; Charles Thurber, of New York. John Hay, Lincoln's private secretary, also read a poem.

[45] George William Curtis, author of *Nile Notes of a Howadji* and *Prue and I;* editor of *Harper's Weekly.*

[46] Presumably Molière's "Le misanthrope."

[47] Frank Moore, editor of the *Rebellion Record,* a compilation of contemporary records of the war which ultimately reached eleven volumes plus a supplement.

[48] Cassie Vaudry, Chase's housekeeper.

[49] John Wien Forney, editor of the Philadelphia *Press* and the Washington *Chronicle;* secretary of the Senate, 1861–68.

[50] Joseph K. Barnes, since August 1864 surgeon-general of the United States Army.

[51] Colonel Crafts J. Wright, of the 13th Missouri Infantry.

[52] The remainder of the entry for September 17th is from Jacob W. Schuckers, *The Life and Public Services of Salmon Portland Chase* (New York: D. Appleton and Company, 1874), pp. 511–2.

[53] Rev. Bernard H. Nadal, pastor, Wesley Chapel.

[54] Daniel Reaves Goodloe, North Carolina antislavery leader; since 1844 a resident of Washington; contributor to the *Chronicle,* 1863–65.

[55] On October 19th Sheridan's forces had routed the Confederates at Cedar Creek, but they did not capture Jubal A. Early.

[56] Elizabeth Gamble (Wirt) Goldsborough, wife of Louis M. Goldsborough, had been a friend of Chase's ever since he studied law with her father, William Wirt.

[57] S. S. L'Hommedieu, president of the Cincinnati, Hamilton & Dayton and the Dayton & Michigan Railroads.

[58] James Henry Lane, Democratic Congressman from Indiana, 1853–55, had moved to Kansas, where he was made Republican Senator, 1861–66. He was one of the earliest supporters of Lincoln's reëlection.

[59] Henry Pirtle, Kentucky circuit judge, 1826–33; after 1862 chancellor of the Louisville chancery court.

[60] John McAllister Schofield had commanded Federal troops in faction-ridden Missouri during much of the war. Later he led the Army of the Ohio under Sherman and fought in the battles of Franklin and Nashville.

[61] George Dennison Prentice, founder and editor of the Louisville *Journal*, one of the most influential papers in the West.

[62] William B. Thomas, collector of customs at Philadelphia; colonel, 192d Pennsylvania Infantry.

[63] Chase was a bit confused here as to dates. October 12, 1864, fell on Wednesday.

[64] Robert Jefferson Breckinridge, of the famous Kentucky family; teacher, college president, and superintendent of public instruction; temporary chairman of the Republican National Convention at Baltimore in 1864.

[65] J. H. Orne, Philadelphia merchant and Republican politician.

[66] Isaac Wayne MacVeagh, district attorney of Chester County, Pennsylvania, 1859–64; major of Pennsylvania militia; chairman of Republican state committee in 1863; Attorney-General under Garfield.

[67] Lyman Tremain, unsuccessful Republican candidate for Lieutenant-Governor of New York, 1862; Congressman, 1873–75.

[68] William Alanson Howard, Michigan Republican Congressman, 1855–59; postmaster of Detroit, 1861–66.

[69] John Franklin Farnsworth, Illinois antislavery leader, Repub-

lican Congressman, 1857–61; served in the Peninsular and Antietam campaigns, and returned to Congress, 1863–73.

[70] Samuel Knox, St. Louis Republican lawyer, in 1862 had opposed F. P. Blair, Jr., for Congress, and, though Blair was declared elected, later succeeded in getting him unseated and served himself from June, 1864, till March, 1865.

[71] Henry T. Blow, Missouri merchant, mine-owner, and manufacturer; minister to Venezuela, 1861–62; Republican Congressman, 1863–67.

[1] Winfield Scott Hancock, veteran of the Peninsular campaign, Fredericksburg, Chancellorsville, Gettysburg, and the Wilderness, had been recalled to Washington to recruit a veterans corps, and in February, 1865, relieved Sheridan in the Shenandoah Valley.

[2] William F. Giles, judge of the United States District Court, Baltimore.

[3] Philander Chase, Episcopal bishop and founder of Kenyon and Jubilee Colleges.

[4] Probably Major William M. Este, in charge of the Freedmen's Bureau of the Middle Department of the Army, Baltimore.

[5] John Pendleton Kennedy, of Baltimore; author of *Swallow Barn* and *Memoirs of . . . William Wirt*; Whig Congressman, 1841–45; Secretary of Navy under Fillmore.

[6] Andrew Sterrett Ridgeley, attorney and United States commissioner at Baltimore.

[7] Henry Stockbridge, Baltimore lawyer; a leading advocate of emancipation in Maryland.

[8] Possibly Thomas J. Sterling, Baltimore conveyancer and accountant.

[9] Chase's long letter to the President (R. T. Lincoln Coll., Lib. of Cong.) concerned reconstruction: "The easiest and safest way seems to me to be the enrollment of the loyal citizens, without regard to complexion, and encouragement and support to them in the reorganization of State Governments under constitutions securing suffrage to all citizens. . . ."

[10] Lincoln's speech, the last he ever made, defended the provisional government of Louisiana which had been established under the terms of his amnesty proclamation of December 8, 1863. To critics of his reconstruction program he observed: "This plan was, in advance, submitted to the then Cabinet, and distinctly approved

by every member of it. One of them [i.e., Chase] suggested that I should . . . apply the Emancipation Proclamation to the theretofore excepted parts of Virginia and Louisiana; that I should drop the suggestion about apprenticeship for freed-people, and that I should omit the protest against my own power, in regard to the admission of members to Congress; but even he approved every part and parcel of the plan. . . ."—Roy P. Basler, ed., *The Collected Works of Abraham Lincoln* (New Brunswick: Rutgers University Press, 1953), VIII, 402.

[11] Jerome Napoleon Bonaparte, son of the King of Westphalia and Elizabeth Patterson; one of the richest men in Baltimore.

[12] William Walton Morris, commander of the Middle Department and the VIII Corps.

[13] John Lee Chapman, mayor of Baltimore.

[14] In his long letter, dated Baltimore, April 12, 1865 (R. T. Lincoln Coll., Lib. of Cong.) Chase claimed he had made another reservation to Lincoln's reconstruction plan—"an objection to the restriction of participation in reorganization to persons having the qualifications of voters under the laws of their several states just before rebellion. Ever since questions of reconstruction have been talked about, it has been my opinion that the colored loyalists ought to be allowed to participate in it. . . ."

[15] Frederick Seward recovered and lived till 1915.

[16] On April 6th Lincoln ordered General Godfrey Weitzel to permit "the gentlemen who have acted as the Legislature of Virginia, in support of the rebellion" to assemble so that they could withdraw Virginia troops from the support of the Confederacy. After his return to Washington from his Richmond visit, Lincoln withdrew the offer.

[17] John P. Hale, of New Hampshire; Senator, 1847–53, 1855–65; Free Soil candidate for President, 1852; minister to Spain 1865–69.

[18] Matthew Simpson, bishop of the Methodist Episcopal Church since 1852; one of the most influential clergymen in the country.

[19] John Brough, Ohio railroad man, War Democrat, and Union governor, 1864–65.

[20] On April 18th the last major Confederate army, under Joseph E. Johnston, surrendered to Sherman. The terms of capitulation,

which aroused much concern among Radicals in Washington, were in harmony with Lincoln's ideas and included political reconstruction. Stanton ordered the agreement set aside, and Grant was sent to confer with Sherman.

[21] Louis D. Campbell, of Ohio; Congressman, 1847–59, 1871–73; colonel, 69th Ohio Infantry, 1861–62; minister to Mexico, 1866–67.

[22] Henry David Cooke, brother of Jay Cooke and an intimate of Chase's, was in charge of the Washington office of Jay Cooke & Co. during the war.

[23] Benjamin Franklin Flanders, Unionist Congressman from Louisiana, 1862–63; special agent, Treasury Department, 1863–66; military governor of Louisiana, 1867.

[24] Chase may have been concerned about Admiral Raphael W. Semmes, commander of the Confederate raiders, the *Sumter* and the *Alabama,* who was jailed from December, 1865, to April, 1866, on a charge of treason.

[25] Chase was about to commence a fact-finding tour through the defeated Southern states, paying especial attention to the plight of the freedmen and to the prospects for reconstruction.

[26] Jacob W. Schuckers, formerly a clerk in the Treasury Department and later private secretary of the Chief Justice; author of the authorized biography of Chase published in 1874.

[27] William Green Deshler, of the National Exchange Bank, Columbus, Ohio. By contributing to a gift for W. T. Sherman, Ohio citizens were expressing their continued faith in the general, who had come under severe censure because of his leniency toward Joseph E. Johnston.

Index

DATE DUE

DATE DUE			
JAN 2 7 '64			
DEC 5 '68			
GAYLORD			PRINTED IN U.S.A